THE TEENAGE ZONE

THE
TEENAGE
ZONE

JOHN SOUTER

Tyndale House Publishers, Inc.   Wheaton, Illinois

Unless otherwise noted, Scripture quotations are from the *New American Standard Bible,* copyright © 1960, 1962, 1963, 1968, 1971, 1972,
1973, 1975, 1977 by The Lockman Foundation. Used by permission.

The Amplified Bible, Old Testament copyright © 1958, 1987 by The Zon-
dervan Corporation. The Amplified New Testament copyright © 1958,
1987 by The Lockman Foundation. Used by permission.

Library of Congress Cataloging-in-Publication Data

Souter, John C.
   The teenage zone / John Souter.
      p. cm.
   Includes bibliographical references.
   ISBN 0-8423-1289-7 (soft cover) :
     2. Parent and teenager—United States. 2. Parenting—Religious
aspects—Christianity. I. Title.
HQ799.15.S68   1994
649′.125—dc20   93-35794

Printed in the United States of America

99 98 97 96 95 94
 8   7   6   5   4   3   2   1

To Rebecca and Julie, who helped teach me everything I know about raising teenagers.

CONTENTS

....

INTRODUCTION:
WHAT THIS BOOK
CAN DO FOR YOU

If you are the parent of a brand-new teenager—a junior higher—you may suddenly be wondering, *What's happened to my kid?* One parent claimed that ever since his boy turned twelve he's been begging the kid to run away from home.

Let's face it: When our children reach junior high, everything changes. We find ourselves struggling with ineffective methods of discipline. We can't seem to even come close to curbing the rising rebellion that is fermenting in the back bedrooms of our homes. After many years of apparent success in the "parent business," we are caught off guard and feel unprepared by this rush of puberty.

You probably picked up this book out of desperation because you have entered this teenage "tribulation period." Perhaps you are desperately hoping for some kind of "rapture" that might whisk your kids out of this incomprehensible phase. Although I can't promise you that God will miraculously reach down and touch your teenagers and make them "normal" again, I have good news for you: There *is* hope!

Now don't expect any foolproof cure-all guaranteed to

solve all your teenager's problems. Effective parenting is a trial-and-error process; it takes prayer and a willingness for parents to examine themselves and deal with their own weaknesses. As we journey down this road together, your family can become a unified team—perhaps for the first time in its history. Your household can be transformed from a combat zone to an enclave where love and peace reside.

This book is a survival kit, a parental toolbox full of ideas to help you "fix" the things that are breaking down. I will place particular emphasis on what's happening with the family in this country as well as what is happening in the typical household. In doing this, I lean on the Scriptures, knowing that no one knows better how to guide us through this parenting minefield than the God who made our teenagers.

To get the most out of this book, you should read the information in the order in which it has been written. In the first few chapters, you'll find clarification of some of the basic principles we all need to grasp if we are going to be successful parents. So do yourself a favor and fight the temptation to skip ahead to the chapters that seem to promise the quick fix—there is no such thing, especially if you haven't prepared yourself for the work by reading the foundational material!

So, are you ready? Buckle your seat belt, and *let's go for it!*

1

THE TEENAGE ZONE

"If it was going to be easy to raise kids, it never would have started with something called labor." ~Anonymous

NARRATOR: Enter Roger Davidson, a typical businessman—overworked, underpaid. What Mr. Davidson doesn't know is that he has entered a whole new dimension, where his very sanity will be challenged.

"The juvenile crime spree continues. . . ."

Mr. Davidson flicked his car radio to another station; he didn't feel like being depressed. It had been a long week—a long year, for that matter—but for once he had refused to work overtime. He'd even left his briefcase in his office.

"The forecast for the weekend: snow level down to two thousand feet."

Roger frowned. *The last time I took the kids to play in the snow was—two years ago.* He suddenly felt guilty. *Why have I let my job keep me so busy?*

Twenty minutes later, he walked into his house and called, "Hon, I'm home." Thirteen-year-old Brad flashed past the entryway, followed by another boy whose bizarre haircut resembled that of a Raggedy Andy doll. The two seventh graders carried Cokes and nacho-crested plates. Brad offered a slight acknowledgment of his father's presence with a halfhearted wave from his elbow before both boys disappeared down the hallway.

"Oh, hi, dear," said his wife as she came from the master bedroom. "You're home early."

"Karen, who's that kid with Brad?"

"You mean Chris? He's Brad's new friend from school."

"What's he like?" he said, suddenly worried that his son might be influenced by this odd-looking boy.

"I don't know. I never really see him except for when they come out for food," Karen answered, kissing him.

As they moved toward the kitchen, six-year-old Jason spotted his father and came running. "Daddy!" He jumped into Roger's arms.

"Hey buddy, you still my pal?"

"You bet, *pal!*"

Roger sat down on the couch with the newspaper as Jason turned back to the television set. For a moment he watched his son watch the characters on the screen as they chased and clobbered one another.

"Karen, I've been thinking. What do you think about driving up to McGrady Hill tomorrow so the kids can play in the snow?"

"That's a great idea, Daddy!" cried Jason from the floor.

"Well, . . . I don't know, honey. It might be a job getting the kids up for it."

Up for it? You must be kidding! he thought. *Jason's certainly ready, and there are only two more to go.* Karen's indifference surprised him. She used to be so glad whenever he expressed a willingness to do something with the children. "We haven't driven to the snow for at least two years. I thought it might be time."

"OK," she said, peering into a pan. "Why don't you check on road conditions?"

"Good idea."

Roger picked up the receiver and was about to dial when he heard a boy's voice.

"Hello? Who is this?"

"*Da-aad,*" protested his fourteen-year-old daughter, Jamie. "I'm on the phone."

He waited for a moment, hoping to hear the boy's voice again, but neither of them spoke.

"Oh? . . . Well, I need to make a call," he said, then placed the receiver back in its cradle. He glanced at his wife. "Jamie is talking to a boy. You know who he is?"

"No," his wife responded. "I didn't hear the telephone ring. She probably called him."

"She called *him?* When I was a kid, a girl would never *think* about calling a boy. Who *is* that guy?"

Karen sighed. "It could be Denny, or maybe even Daryl. Sometimes Jim calls, too."

Denny, Daryl, or Jim? When did Jamie get interested in boys? He thought back to the way he had been in junior high, and a shiver crawled up his spine. Karen's voice broke into his thoughts. "You want to call the kids?"

When Roger stepped into the hallway, the throbbing sounds of rock music pulsated from Brad's room. He knocked loudly but heard no answer, so he popped the door open—and was instantly assaulted by the music. Brad sat playing a Nintendo game, while his friend had his face in a heavy metal magazine.

"Dinner's ready!" Roger shouted.

Brad acknowledged him with an elbow, but Chris didn't even look up. Roger frowned before moving on down the hallway toward his daughter's room.

"Jamie, dinner's ready."

Her lips seemed glued to the telephone.

"Can you believe that Sylvia—" She broke off and glanced up at him. "Sure, Dad." Then she resumed her phone conversation, barely missing a beat. "How could she? But Jim said Daryl told him it was true."

As Roger closed her door, Jason streaked out of his bedroom wearing mittens and a snowsuit that no longer fit.

"Dad, I'm ready for snow!"

Roger laughed. "Later, pal. Now it's time for dinner."

They both went into the dining room, where Karen sat waiting.

"Do Brad and Jamie always come to the dinner table so late?"

"Usually," she said. "Ever since you started working so much overtime, it's been difficult getting everyone together at the table."

After a few moments Brad and Jamie reluctantly joined them at the table.

"Mom, I'm really not very hungry," said Brad. Roger frowned at the boy.

"*Mom!* This spaghetti has *meat* in it!" complained Jamie, as if Karen had put fried ants in the sauce.

"Oh, I'm sorry," said Karen. "I forgot to make a separate sauce for you."

"Since when did you stop eating meat?" Roger asked.

Jamie shook her head. "Dad, I haven't eaten red meat for a year. It's bad for my complexion. Every time I eat it I break out."

"Mom, I'm *really* not hungry," said Brad. "Besides, Chris is in my room all by himself."

"I'm sure that . . . that Chris fellow can entertain himself," Roger said, trying to keep his voice calm.

His two teenagers proceeded to fall into silence, pushing their food around on their plates. The atmosphere in the room was so thick with tension that Roger was tempted to lift his knife and try to cut through it. Maybe the snow trip would cheer everyone up.

"What do you guys think about driving up to McGrady Hill tomorrow?" he asked, forcing himself to sound enthusiastic.

"Yeah! Let's go to the snow!" yelped Jason.

"But *Da-aad,* I'm baby-sitting *all day* tomorrow for

Mrs. Krause," complained Jamie. "I really need the
money."

"And I'm spending Saturday night at Chris's house,"
Brad chimed in. "He wants me to hear this great new CD."

Karen looked at her husband with one of those I-told-
you-so expressions. Roger Davidson gazed around the
table and wondered what had happened to his family.

NARRATOR: Somewhere between childhood and the real
world is a land beyond the logic of grown-ups. In that
country, adults are tolerated but not wanted. One's ticket
for admission must include puberty, pimples, or peach
fuzz. For the first time in his life, Roger Davidson has discovered that his family has entered *The Teenage Zone*. But
he hasn't seen *anything* yet.

The Coming Tribulation

If you have children, sooner or later you too will enter the
teenage zone. You may shrug your shoulders and think,
*Hey now, how bad can it get? After all, we're a close fam-
ily. There will never be a generation gap at our house.* In
the words of one much wiser than I: "Therefore let him
who thinks he stands take heed lest he fall" (1 Corinthians
10:12).

When we first have children, most of us discover that
the majority of the problems we encounter can be worked
out if we're patient and teach our children correctly. As we
become comfortable with parenting, we develop a certain
sense of confidence in ourselves. Then, overnight, the rules
change. Our kids mutate. Then they mutiny. And we discover that parenting isn't quite so easy after all. For the
first time in our lives we are forced to admit that we don't
have all the answers.

If you have children, make no mistake about it, a storm

is blowing your way. Sooner or later most families encounter a full-scale adolescent hurricane. The first waves generally hit during the junior high years, when it seems your children have sudden attacks of insanity. Fortunately, most kids eventually recover their sanity at the other end of the teenage zone. The big question is: Will we, by the time our children finally return to the human race, have lost our minds in the process?

Exactly when this seven-year teenage tribulation period known as adolescence will hit your household is not much of a mystery. Give or take a few months (maybe even a year), it will overtake you when your child enters junior high school. The mysterious period of time called adolescence is the season between puberty and maturity, when teenagers age seven years—and their parents age seventy-five years. It's a time when the only thing stronger than a mother's love is a daughter's stubbornness, when a boy stops quoting Dad and starts criticizing him.

If you have a son, here are several signs that indicate he has passed into this zone. To begin with, he'll probably drive anything with wheels that runs on gas—except the lawn mower. His first smoke will make him sick, and his first love will make everyone else sick. He'll be the kid who can't imagine that someday he'll be as old-fashioned as his father.

And what are some of the signs that your daughter is becoming a teenager? She'll probably be the one who discovers a whole new glamorous personality that can be scrubbed off with soap and water. When she has reached junior high, she'll determine that hard work takes all the fun out of earning money. And, for the first time since birth, she'll begin to complain she has nothing to wear.

Obviously, those are just a few of the many signs to watch for. When you see these things, get ready—not only for what your children are about to go through, but for what you are about to face. Because, though I hate to be the bearer of bad news, you should realize that the task of raising adolescents will be more difficult for parents today than it was for any previous generation. The environment in which our kids are being raised is much different from what we or our parents experienced when growing up—and it is an environment that is increasingly hostile toward our goals as parents.

It is often difficult for us to realize just how fast our society is changing because we usually measure things from day to day. But there is no denying that we no longer live in the "Leave It to Beaver" generation. As depressing as the following facts and statistics may be, you need to know the kind of world your teen is facing. So take a deep breath, and read on.

For starters, look at what's happening to the family unit. The divorce rate in America continues to skyrocket. Today alone, thirty-three hundred marriages will break up, and 28 percent of the households in America are run by a single parent.[1] We have 2 million latchkey kids who have to fend for themselves while their parents are working. Only 7 percent of American families are made up of a dad who works and a mom who stays home with the children.

Then there are the schools. Despite the fact that America spends more on education than any other country, our illiteracy rate is higher than that of any other industrialized nation. In 1986, Dan Rather broadcast over CBS the alarming contrast between school discipline problems in the 1940s and the 1980s. The biggest problems in the forties? Excessive talking, making noise, gum chewing, running in the halls, cutting in lines, breaking the dress code, and littering. By the eighties the problems had changed to

....

[1]"Clinton presidency inherits plethora of riches, problems," *Redding Record Searchlight,* January 17, 1993.

alcohol and drug abuse, pregnancy, suicide, rape, robbery, and assault. According to the Gallup poll, the lack of discipline in schools has been rated the number-one problem every year since 1969. It is estimated that 135,000 guns are transported to junior and senior high schools each day, and that one in twenty students carries some kind of weapon. Each day, forty students are shot or killed in or on their way to or from school.[2]

If you think those figures are scary, you'd better sit down—because the most unsettling figures of all are those concerning teens and sex. So much has happened so fast in this country. Back in 1960, 53 percent of America's teenagers had never kissed or been kissed by a boyfriend or girlfriend, 57 percent had never "made out," and 92 percent were still virgins.[3] But by 1990, 20 percent of teens had lost their virginity before their *thirteenth birthday*; 19 percent of American teenagers had been with more than four sexual partners by the time they reached graduation; 75 percent had become sexually active by the time they were eighteen.[4]

Teens are reaping the consequences of premarital sex. Each day 2,795 students get pregnant, 1,100 have abortions, and 1,200 give birth out of wedlock.[5] Sexually transmitted diseases are of epidemic proportions, too. AIDS infection among high-school students went up an alarming 700 percent in the last two years alone, and half of all teenagers will contract a sexually transmitted disease by the time they graduate from high school. Sexual crimes are also taking their toll on children: One girl in three will

....

[2]"Children in Crisis" in *Fortune,* August 10, 1992, pp. 40–41.

[3]*Encyclopedia of 7,700 Illustrations: Signs of the Times,* by Paul Lee Tan (Rockville, Md.: Assurance Press, n.d., n.p.).

[4]Information from "Struggling to Save Our Kids" in *Fortune,* August 10, 1992, pp. 34–36; and the video *America's Godly Heritage,* by David Barton (Aledo, Tex.: Wallbuilders).

[5]Ibid.

have been sexually abused by the time she reaches eighteen, as will one boy in five.[6]

As you can see, your teens are confronted with many more dangers than you were when you entered junior high. As parents, we are facing some serious problems!

Why This Deterioration?

Why has there been such an erosion of moral values in our country? I believe that you can blame the erosion of our nation on two major causes (and of course, many minor ones): Most important, the reinterpretation of our U.S. Constitution by our own Supreme Court, and the manipulation of the public by the media/entertainment industry.

The effects of Supreme Court decisions

Most of us have been taught that the majority of the founding fathers of our country were deists, meaning that while they advocated natural religion and emphasized morality, they believed that the Creator simply made the world, then left it to its own devices. In reality, the vast majority of the signers of the Constitution were committed Christians. One of their primary goals was to provide an opportunity for the expression of their Christian beliefs under a government that did not promote any one particular denomination.

For years all of the decisions of the Supreme Court consistently upheld Christianity as the predominant way of life in this country. For example, in 1811 the Supreme Court upheld the conviction of a man who had publicly slandered the Bible. In 1844 the Court disagreed with a public school whose leadership had decided to teach morality without relying on the Bible. In 1853 a group petitioned Congress to separate church and state, but after a year of

....
[6]Ibid.

study our Congress made it plain that there could be no separation of church and state because the country was founded upon Christian principles.

Now, however, in light of the shift in our country's beliefs, it would seem incongruous to consider the United States a "Christian" nation. So what happened? In 1947, the Supreme Court deviated from almost two hundred years of precedent and proclaimed for the first time that there should be a wall between church and state, a wall that must be kept high and impregnable. As a result of that decision, most people today think that the Constitution demands this very separation, when in reality the document suggests no such thing.

This decision was followed in 1962 by the Court claiming that it was unconstitutional to pray in a public school. In 1963 Bible reading was outlawed in our school system, and abortion on demand was ushered into our land. In 1965 the Court took away the right of a student to bow his head and pray audibly over his food. In 1980 the Court banned the posting of the Ten Commandments because, in the words of the court, "Someone might actually obey them." (Ironically, these very commandments are inscribed on the wall behind the justices.) In one generation's time, our jurists turned this nation in a completely different direction. No longer do we as a nation travel up the road toward God. Instead, we have taken a detour and are traveling in the opposite direction.

Why is this so important for parents to understand? Because as you send your teenager to public school, it is almost inevitable that he will pick up, at least in part, the values, morality, and violence of the society that is attempting to teach him. From his teachers to his peers, the vast majority of the educational experience he is receiving is diametrically opposed to what Christian parents want him to receive. Furthermore, you can count on this input to greatly complicate your task as a parent. Just at the time when your child becomes open to listening to outside voices, he may be thrust into an educational system that is no longer working on your behalf.

Still, we need to keep in mind that God holds us, the parents, responsible for how our kids turn out. If we don't do some serious work, the educational system here in America may well turn our offspring further away from our values and our God.

The media/entertainment industry

I believe the second biggest cause of change in our society has been the manipulation of our morality and our beliefs through the media/entertainment industry. After the regulation of the motion pictures was lifted, the standards for decency continued to change as filmmakers kept pushing the limits of what is considered acceptable. And television has become increasingly more manipulative of public opinion. Today any political candidate recognizes that public opinion can be dramatically altered with an effective media campaign.

Although the world of pornography has existed for a long time, it has in the last few years come out of the closet and grown into a multibillion-dollar industry. Adult bookstores and magazines have proliferated like rats in a vacant field, spewing out glossy full-color photographs and videos that graphically depict every imaginable sex act. Never before has any society had the opportunity to corrupt itself so quickly and so completely. We can't stick our heads in the sand and say that all this won't impact our family— our children—in tremendous ways. With the advent of videotape, pornographic movies have moved from downtown theaters and into neighborhood video stores. Many statistics would show that very few young men have *not* viewed an X-rated video. That means that there is a great chance of your teenagers coming into contact with such materials and being affected by them.

Films and videos are substitute realities that tend to mesmerize the human brain. Few things impact our minds more than the images brought to us by these tools. Some feel that once these visions enter our heads, they are never removed; they stay in the subconscious, ready to be brought back like the memories from life itself. So when we view a movie or TV program with a message that undermines our values and beliefs (and how many don't have such messages?), that message will remain with us many years.

As an example, consider the impact of Saturday-morning TV on our children. Secular researchers have performed over three thousand studies during the last two decades, and for many, the evidence is unmistakably clear: violence portrayed on television influences the attitudes and behavior of children who watch it. Believe it or not, there is *five times more violence* on children's programming than on what adults watch (26.4 violent acts per hour on children's programming as compared to 5 violent acts per hour of prime-time viewing). If your elementary-aged child watches an average of only two to four hours of television a day, he will have witnessed eight thousand murders and one hundred thousand other acts of TV violence by the time he is ready for junior high.[7]

There Are Answers

So why have I inundated you with all this depressing information? Why did you need to see this unpleasant picture of our society? Because it is important that we realistically examine the situation we face as parents of children enter-

....
[7]"Kids absorb violence," *San Francisco Chronicle*, April 29, 1992.

ing the teenage zone. I don't want anyone misled by the notion that this job is going to be easy. Thanks to the disintegration of our society, the task of parenting gets harder every day.

We live in enemy-held territory. Almost all of the books, magazines, TV programs, videos, and movies thrown at our children are designed to divert them from the truths found in the Bible. This includes school textbooks, many library books, and even such things as museum displays. The entire secular educational system and your son's or daughter's peers are more than likely moving away from God, not toward him. Don't live in a fantasy world, believing that the system is really working for you. If you do, you may well wake up and find you've lost the war. It is imperative that you do not let anyone have a greater impact on your kids than you do. If that happens, the chances are great that you will lose them. Until you recognize that you are in a war for the hearts and souls of your own children, you will be at the mercy of your enemy.

No wonder our kids begin to march to a different drummer once they enter the teenage years. They're constantly being seduced by some new Pied Piper. If you haven't recognized this struggle because you've been so involved in your adult world, you may one day discover you feel like a stranger in your own home as your teens suddenly begin to challenge everything you hold sacred.

This book will concentrate on what you can do to survive this crazy time in your family's life. Although I will give you lots of practical suggestions and solutions, I will concentrate more on helping you develop the proper understanding—from God's point of view—of what to do with those squirmy junior high kids.

My prayer is that God will empower you to read this entire book, because I believe that there are life-changing spiritual messages in each chapter. So let's work together to get you "on top" of the parenting task that lies ahead.

SUMMARY OF KEY POINTS

1. Most children change dramatically when they reach adolescence.
2. Parents often are caught unprepared when puberty strikes their teenagers and throws their house into an uproar.
3. Teenage rebellion tends to grow if parents don't deal with it wisely.
4. The degeneration in our society is hindering us in our job as parents.
5. The decisions of our own Supreme Court have dramatically turned our nation—and especially its educational system—away from God and biblical morality.
6. Assume that the public school system is working against you, not for you as a parent.
7. The media (movies, television, radio, videos, magazines, etc.) will highly influence your children away from your values if you let it.

2

IS THERE A FAMILY IN THE HOUSE?

"A family is a place where principles are hammered and honed on the anvil of everyday living." ~Charles Swindoll

....

Sally, why aren't you ready for church?"

The teen glanced up from the Sunday comics still dressed in her bathrobe. "Oh, Dad, do I have to go to church? It's *so-o-o* boring."

"Young lady, as long as you live in this house, you will go to church."

"Well, I didn't ask to be born into this family," Sally complained. "Why couldn't I have been born in a family like Mary Ralston's? At least *her* parents are cool." So saying, the girl stalked off down the hallway.

You may already have heard words like these from your teen. And you're confused because it wasn't all that long ago that your kids were so docile and loving! They're barely even teenagers, and already you feel the trickle of rebellion leaking through the dam of parental authority— and that trickle is threatening to burst into a full-force flood.

What does it mean to be a parent, anyway? No one gave you a parenting manual at the hospital, and sometimes it seems that you're in this way over your head. Someone once called parents "family shock absorbers," and you probably feel like you're taking more than your fair share of shocks lately.

If parenthood rates as a generally thankless task, raising

a houseful of adolescents must rank somewhere way below zero on the gratitude scale. Why don't your teenagers at least try to understand what you're attempting to do or even show a little appreciation for all your efforts? It seems that most teenagers stop seeking parental approval and begin to woo the outside world in what is a not-so-subtle attempt to replace their elders. Suddenly you feel as though your entire family may be at risk.

What Is a Family?

The family has been defined as a group of related people who are most likely to stay together if they play together. Some see the family as a domestic drama in which parents only get supporting roles; others see it as a social unit where the father provides, the mother decides, and the teens override.

When your kids reach adolescence (and even before), it's often difficult to locate the "real family" in the house because all seem to be living by their own self-driven agendas. Most families just happen. Although both husband and wife probably wanted kids, parents panic when it suddenly dawns on them that the little bundles come without instructions. The result is leadership by default.

Everyone's goal within the family unit seems to be to keep himself or herself happy while contributing little to unity within the house. I remember my father saying to me, "Son, for once in your life, why don't you do something *for the family!*" That statement brought on a twinge of guilt—for all of a nanosecond. But, of course, I quickly discarded the emotion because it conflicted with the general procedure at our house. Besides, didn't I take out the trash and mow the lawn? Even if they did pay me for those tasks, I felt that I was already doing my bit in the interest of preserving domestic tranquility.

Like most other adolescents, I treated the family as my hangout between visits to school. I seldom performed any unnecessary chores (trying to keep such work on the "favor" basis), preferring to save my energy for my own diversions. I was never motivated to contribute toward making our family a better place to live because I had determined it wasn't *my* family—it belonged to my parents. My motto back then could be summed up as It's Every Man for Himself.

Does all this sound familiar? Actually, *your* kids called to talk to me when I was doing the research for this book. (Just kidding.) It's my guess that your house is probably run a lot like the one you grew up in, and your kids are probably acting similar to the way you did in your parents' home. This generally means that everyone is doing his or her own thing.

This lack of direction and leadership may not seem so bad because everyone seems to survive, *until* the kids reach their teenage years and things start to break loose. As the teenagers begin to rebel, statements start coming out of their mouths that offer a great deal of insight into what is happening, such as: "I didn't ask to be born into this family." "You only had me to do the dishes so you wouldn't have to do them!" "You don't care about me at all! You only want to look good in front of your friends." "You don't *really* care about my feelings!" Let me interpret what these adolescent words mean. Odds are that what your teenager really is saying is: "I give up on this family because no one here really cares about me. My parents are in their own worlds, so I'm going to be just like them. I'm going to think only about myself and go through the motions of being part of this family until the day comes when I can finally get out of here."

A teenager will give up on his parents if he feels they are too busy in their own world to help him shape his. This may be communicated by the lack of effort parents put into the family—in other words, they spend more time at work, the club, or wherever than they do at home with the family. If a teen decides his parents don't really care, then why should he? Once he views the family as not being *his,* he concludes that it is a bad investment to contribute anything to it. He then decides to bide his time waiting for the day when he can get out on his own.

You might wonder how any kid could feel this way. Can't he remember all the years he's been fed and clothed? And what about all the vacations he's been taken on and the things he has been given? *How ungrateful!* True. In view of what he has received, any kid who rebels for some silly reason is ungrateful, to say the least. But the reason teens see things as being "so unfair" is not because their parents haven't given them things, but because the parents have failed to communicate what their true values are, what really matters most to them.

When parents fail to provide adequate direction or leadership, teens receive the message that they are not a vital part of the family. And if the parents' limited communication consists mainly of criticism, they've only confirmed that message, and teens begin to feel like they are just passing through. As their resentment grows, they find every excuse they can to spend time with someone else. This problem often is compounded in "blended families," where the children from several marriages come together. (In a later chapter we will deal with problems particular to this situation.)

When the loyalties of family members are divided in several different directions, it becomes increasingly difficult for parents to create a home where everyone feels he or she is working together toward some meaningful purpose. Today few families seem to have any goals or sense of direction. Too often the family of the 1990s can be defined as a group of people who live together in the same building, but who continue to have less and less in common.

How Did We Become So Scattered?

Why is this division of loyalties happening to so many modern families? Even Christian families are not exempt from this lack of direction. What happened to us?

When the United States was founded, it is estimated that 95 percent of the people lived off the land. On the farm, work was hard and physical. Everyone participated and benefited from shared labor. Likewise, if the crops didn't come in or were destroyed by the weather, everyone participated in the consequences. Either way, there was a sense of unity. Schools were not a necessity; they were a luxury. The church provided most of the family's socialization among people of like mind and beliefs. The crime rate was low, divorces were rare, and few teenagers rebelled.

But during the twentieth century, our society changed radically. We changed from an agrarian society to one that now has less than 2 percent of our population working on the farm. As the majority of people shifted into the city, all sorts of new influences began to assault the integrity of the family. As we discussed in chapter 1, the media and our public school system have become powerful tools in shaping our minds and behavior. And, as our life-styles changed, so did our values.

One example of that is the increasing trend in our nation away from both the traditional family and marriage. One woman told me, in reference to her live-in boyfriend, "I would never marry him. He's just not stable enough for me." Yet, remarkably, that woman lived with the man and had three children by him. You can bet that her family life was a little scattered. In the hit teenage movie *Wayne's World,* Garth questioned if Wayne's interest in Cassandra might lead to marriage. Wayne responded by saying, "Don't you know that in some countries marriage is the penalty for shoplifting?" Though audiences found that quip funny, it is an all-too-realistic reflection of our society's attitude. Sadly, statistics prove that millions today seriously believe that marriage isn't a very good idea.

"Now, don't get me wrong," said a caller to a southern California radio show on which I was a guest author. "I just don't believe in marriage anymore. I've been married twice, but I think it's best for a guy and a girl to have their own lives. My girlfriend and I both have separate apartments, and I think our relationship works better that way." Like so many others, that man had given up on the institution because he had twice failed at it. Now he prefers a relationship without any permanent commitment. But what happens if he and his girlfriend have children? What kind of life will they have?

When people reject marriage, for whatever reason, it's like throwing out the bathwater without first checking to see if there's a baby in it. As a result we see the traditional family unit breaking up in this country. New terms have entered our vocabulary. Now we have unmarried parents, single-parent families, joint-custody parents, blended families, foster parents, group home families, and gay parents.

First Things First

With our society self-destructing around us, what can we do to keep our families together? Obviously, we can't all pack up the teenagers and return to the farm, but we can return to the One who has all the answers. After all, if you're trying to build a house, it makes sense to consult the blueprints put together by the architect, doesn't it?

Before you can solve any problems with your teenager, it is important to take a careful look at yourself. What's your personal direction? Are you moving toward God or away from him? If you have not answered this most basic of questions, you will have a very tough time leading your teenagers in a godly direction. This is a bedrock problem. We must find out what we're building our house on because we don't want to wake up one day and discover our foundation is built on sand (see Matthew 7:24-27).

A few years ago, a couple who lived near us were having marital difficulties. One afternoon the husband came down to my home office and said, "John, I understand you're a pastor. I wonder if you could counsel me about my problems with my wife and kids."

"Sure," I said. "I'd love to. But first, tell me whether you want an aspirin or a cure."

"What do you mean?"

"Well," I said, "I can give you help on the 'aspirin level'—you know, some suggestions to solve the immediate difficulties you're facing. Or, we can discuss the ultimate cure to your problems—your need for forgiveness from a holy God. Although aspirins do work, they only deal with symptoms, not with what's causing the pain."

My neighbor wanted to hear about the cure, so we discussed what it meant to become a Christian. That day he allowed the Lord to come into his life, and the direction of his whole family changed as a result of his getting in touch with the One who made him.

When I use the term *Christian*, I'm not referring to whether or not someone goes to church. A lot of people attend church, but that no more guarantees that they are Christians than walking into a garage would turn them into cars. I'm not even referring to someone who believes in Christianity. In the Bible, James tells us that even the demons believe, but that they also shudder because they're still under the judgment of God.

The Bible says that we have broken God's laws. We

have put many other gods before us; we've taken the Lord's name in vain; we've been disrespectful to our parents; we've hated, lusted, stolen, lied, and coveted. We all have turned away from God's righteousness, and the result has been that we are now under the curse of sin. We have been living self-centered lives, and God says that such behavior deserves "the fires of hell."

The bleakness of our condition is revealed by the fact that most of us don't really think we've done anything all that bad. We compare ourselves to murderers and other violent criminals and convince ourselves that everything is OK. But God doesn't grade on a curve. Jesus says in the Bible that if we have been angry with someone in our hearts, we are as guilty as if we had murdered that person (Matthew 5:22). He also says we are guilty of adultery if we've ever lusted after someone (Matthew 5:28)—and who hasn't done so?

Jesus tells us that God's standard is perfection (Matthew 5:48), but we all know that's a standard so far out of our reach that we have no hope of achieving it—at least, not apart from God's mercy. To show you just how bad our condition is, realize that God had to send his Son to die in our place. Had there been any other way of washing away our sins, I'm sure God would have done it. But our sin demands death (Romans 6:23), and so Jesus took our place on that cross; he suffered what we'll have to suffer if we don't turn from our sins.

The only remedy for our condition is what Jesus Christ did on the cross, but before we can truly get Christ into our lives, we have to agree with God that our spiritual condition is hopeless. We'll never be good enough. We're lost. We're doomed to hell unless we fall on our faces before God. Even if you've been attending a church, you may never have heard this message before. The Western world has come up with a sanitized message of Good News that offers salvation to people who don't really understand that they are lost. But God tells us, "Do not be deceived, God is not mocked; for whatever a man sows, this he will also reap. For the one who sows to his own flesh shall from the flesh reap corruption" (Galatians 6:7-8). The Bible also states that "if you are living according to the flesh, you must die; but if by the Spirit you are putting to death the deeds of the body, you will live" (Romans 8:13).

What about you? God wants your heart to be broken over your sin. He wants you to understand how great your trespasses have been against his holiness. If you will fall before him, he will save you from the wrath to come. Jesus said, "Unless you repent, you will all likewise perish" (Luke 13:3). God hates sin, but he's not willing "for any to perish but for all to come to repentance" (2 Peter 3:9).

Agree with God that you are a sinner, ask for his forgiveness, and allow Jesus to come in and take control of your heart and your life. Do it *right now*, because today is the day of salvation. Set this book aside and give yourself to him in prayer. Tell him that you want to turn from your sin and ask him to give you the power to do so. Invite Jesus Christ to come into your heart and take residence there. Do it right now. Don't settle for an aspirin; get a cure.[1]

If you have turned away from a self-centered life-style and invited Jesus into your life, then you are on the road toward a long-term solution to present and future problems with your teens. Sure, there will be potholes in the road ahead, but at least you're moving in the right direction. With Christ, you have excellent resources to do this parenting job right. I don't think any person in his or her right mind would want to take on the job of being a par-

....

[1]If you are still undecided about responding to the Lord, I would encourage you to skip ahead and read chapter 14, which discusses how to become a Christian in much greater detail.

ent—let alone being the parent of a teenager—without God's help and assistance. If both you and your spouse are committed to Jesus Christ and are determined to let him be in control of your lives, your marriage, and the way you respond to the kids, your chances of success will have gone up dramatically.

God Has a Better Idea

What is God's way of running the family? It's important to recognize that your marriage and its health are major keys to having a successful family. Marriage is the primary building block for creating a godly family, and if it is struggling, everything else will suffer.

The Bible recognizes marriage as three things: a covenant of two people (one of each sex), legal and/or community recognition of the union, and a sexual consummation of the oneness between husband and wife. It is important here to stress that the Bible refers to marriage as a covenant, not a contract (see Malachi 2:14; Proverbs 2:17). Contracts are designed for people who don't really trust one another so that when one party does not fulfill the agreement, the other will have justification for legal action. A covenant, on the other hand, is entered into in the presence of God. Because marriage was God's idea, he promised to bless the participants in that covenant; but he also promised to take away his blessing and deal harshly with those who broke the covenant (see especially Malachi 2:10-17).

If you are in a blended family because of one or more divorces, it becomes even more important for you to reaffirm that you and your present spouse have a lifetime commitment to each other. That commitment probably needs to be verbally renewed every time a domestic crisis takes place. Don't ever talk divorce; always talk about the lifetime covenant you've made with each other. God will bless everyone in your family because of that ongoing commitment. The healthier your marriage becomes, the easier it will be for the two of you to work together as a team.

We know God invented marriage, but don't forget that in doing so he also created the first family. Ephesians 3:14-15 claims that every family derives its name (i.e., its origin) from the Father. God proclaimed that the family would be the result of two married people uniting sexually to become parents. This is what the world is now referring to as the biological family (which is becoming increasingly rare these days). The biological family is set up as our pattern—even if you no longer have such a family unit, pattern your blended family, as far as is possible, upon God's original example.

God's version of marriage and the family includes a definite structure with a specific plan of order. If members of your family do not know what their position is supposed to be, they will contribute to the disunity of your family. Because our society has come to have such a struggle in the area of authority, it is highly likely that your family has also been caught up in accepting many of our secular society's beliefs. So let's begin by examining the family chain of command, from the bottom up.

Children are to obey

It is God's will that children obey their parents. (*Yeah! Preach it, brother!*) Unfortunately, many of our kids seem somehow to have missed the message. Could it be that we have failed to teach it to them properly?

I'm reminded of two children who attended the preschool department a few years ago. The teacher noticed the girl holding an upside-down Bible while pretending to read.

"Lemme have that book. You can't read," mumbled a preschool boy.

"Yes *I can,*" proclaimed the girl.

"OK, what does it say?" challenged the boy.

The girl sat up straight and began to "read." "It *says:* 'Be ye kind, one to your mother.' "

Now where did she find *that* verse? First Hezekiah? Or maybe it came from her mother? It seems our children often get the wrong message from us—perhaps because we're broadcasting contradictory signals to them.

The foundational passage that established order in the family is Genesis 2:24. That verse tells us that when two people wed, they are to leave their parents and cleave (or bond) to each other. This leaving and cleaving is extremely important for the health of the new family (and the parents left behind). Spouses who run to their parents at the first sign of marital difficulty generally escalate their problems. If a grown child is coddled, someone isn't obeying the Lord. Parents who do not properly prepare their children to leave home may have a secret desire to retain control over them; the "help" they offer may be designed to make the new family dependent upon them.

This often happens if the child was at the center of his or her parents' marriage relationship. God designed the major focus of a family to be on the bonding between husband and wife. And any two people who build their lives around their children will erode the cleaving process between husband and wife that forms the foundation for the happiest families.

If the children are placed at the center of a family, the parents will usually fail to discipline effectively; children who are not taught to obey soon learn how to manipulate their parents by threatening to become disruptive at key moments. Such child-dominated families seethe with domestic disturbances and produce spoiled adults. How can you avoid having a child-centered family? Train your children that their role is to obey. Anything less than that will place them on center stage.

Another way children can become the focus of a relationship is when a couple stops cleaving—stops building their love relationship. If the husband withdraws into his work or some other activity like sports, the wife will often throw herself into her children in an attempt to obtain from them what she can't seem to acquire from her husband. Both parents unintentionally send the message to their kids that they are more important than the other spouse and create an atmosphere perfect for increased disobedience.

The wife's position

The wife is the keystone of the family. Your role is critical in helping everyone else maintain their own positions in God's plan of order. Let me suggest three foundational things that you should be doing. First, understand that your husband must be the first priority and focus in your marriage relationship. Second, love and respect your husband, teaching your children to do the same. And third, be as consistent as you can in helping your children learn how to obey.

A key word the Bible uses, in Ephesians 5 (NIV, TLB), to differentiate a wife's role from that of her children is *submission*. To many women in our self-destructing society *submission* is an obscene word; they're upset because they misunderstand what that term implies, thinking that a woman is instructed to become a servant, a doormat, or even a slave. Actually, if you look carefully at the passage, you'll see that we are all told to be in submission to one another (verse 21). So the husband has a responsibility to be sensitive to his wife as well.

But we must not make light of the order found in this and other Bible passages. God definitely places a woman under a man's authority. Now this doesn't mean a woman loses her own identity, her opinions, or her free will, but she voluntarily agrees to defer to her husband so that they can work together as a team. In every working relationship someone needs to have the final decision-making power, and God appointed the husband to fill this position so that the family could function smoothly.

Now, obviously, you can be the most dutiful wife in the world and still have major turmoil in your home if your husband does not fulfill his appointed role as the family's leader. (We'll address fathers in the next chapter.) If he acts like the lord of the manor, refusing to do anything more than grunt, your family will definitely have problems. But *your* goal should be to work on the fulfillment of the role God gave to you. And if your husband is not a believer (or is just disobedient to the Word), 1 Peter 3:1-6 provides some suggestions as to how God might use you to bring him to the Lord.

In Genesis 2:18 the wife is specifically called a "helper." It is important for a wife to see herself working with her husband to establish the policies of the family, helping him implement them. Even if you don't understand (or agree) with the order that God set up in the family, you are wise if you work on performing your role and assisting the other family members to execute their jobs as well. As you perform your role, just as it is defined in the Bible, God will bless your family and make the task of raising your teenagers much, much easier.

SUMMARY OF KEY POINTS

1. Most families have no real leadership or direction.
2. Many teenagers don't feel that their family is *theirs* because their parents have not effectively involved them in the family's decision-making process.

3. Teenagers often resent their parents because all they receive is criticism.
4. The family unit is being broken down by the urbanization that has taken place in this country.
5. With the rejection of marriage by much of our society, the integrity of the family has suffered tremendously.
6. Being a true Christian is foundational to having a truly successful Christian family.
7. The Bible presents marriage as a lifetime covenant, not just a contract that can be broken at will.
8. When God invented marriage, he invented the family. Successful families are usually based upon the plan of order God set up.
9. Children (which includes teenagers) are commanded to obey their parents.
10. Children should not be at the center of a family. God set the marriage union up as the central focus of each family.
11. A wife is the keystone in any marriage, holding it together.
12. When a woman fully understands God's desire for her to be in submission to her husband, she will recognize that it is of paramount importance to the success of her family.

3

FOLLOW THE LEADER

"Authentic men aren't afraid to show affection, release their feelings, hug their children, cry when they're sad, admit it when they're wrong, and ask for help when they need it." ~ *Charles Swindoll*

············

If you are a father, I wouldn't be surprised if this chapter is the first one you've read. Perhaps your wife has insisted, and so here you are, stuck making an attempt to at least *look* like you're reading. Well, don't feel alone. A few years ago, my wife would have stuck a book like this under my nose. Most men like the idea of having kids, but it is the rare dad who spends much time thinking about what he's supposed to do as a father.

Almost any red-blooded man can become a father. Because the position requires no education, no test-taking, and no licenses, they let anyone into this club. And because the little woman usually does most of the work, a father can loaf around like a male lion. Occasionally most of us will roar or snarl a little to remind everyone who's in charge, but other than that, we're convinced that there really isn't all that much to this job.

But being an effective father is much more difficult than it appears. Because it seems so easy, we are lulled into thinking this job is a piece of cake. And we certainly don't need anyone to tell us how to run our families because, after all, we know what we're doing. What's there to know anyway? The English poet Ben Jonson quipped, "He that is taught only by himself has a fool for a master." All too often we fathers fool ourselves into believing that if we bring home the paycheck and don't beat the wife or the kids, everything will probably turn out just fine.

And you're right, everything *could* turn out just fine with your kids. If you are a passive father, caught up in your own world, your kids *may* end up just fine. Yep, you *could* get lucky. But then again, with the way things are going in the world today, I wouldn't count on it. Having your kids turn out decent is getting harder and harder to pull off.

Vacation from the Family

If you're anything like I used to be, you are probably not convinced that your role in the family is all that important. You go to work, take up space at the dinner table, do the yard work on the weekends, and maybe—if your wife is lucky—go to an occasional PTA meeting. But you never really think about your impact on your kids, feeling sure that it's all no big deal. Besides, you've got enough problems of your own worrying about keeping all the bills paid. Making the home run right is your wife's domain, right?

When my kids were younger and I'd earned a week of vacation, I'd feel frustrated because I had to spend a *whole week* with my family trying to keep everyone entertained. My idea of a vacation was to stay home and use that time to work on one of my own projects, like writing a book. So when we had a vacation and we went to a motel, I'd say to my wife, "Listen, honey, why don't you and the kids go down to the pool without me. I'll just stay in the room and work on my book. Then after dinner we'll do something together. OK?" The way I looked at it, if I could just get my space, we could all be happy. Besides, I felt the kids were really my wife's responsibility.

My wife put up with this abdication on my part, making the best of the situation, but I was robbing everyone (including myself) of a healthy family life. It wasn't until later that I realized my failure to be involved in having fun with my kids would decrease my effectiveness when we reached the teenage zone.

Sure, I believed in doing those "fatherly things," but there never seemed enough time for my own fun. So I found myself taking vacations from my family responsibilities so that I could slip in those writing projects and football games and . . . well, you know what I mean. Then one day, before my oldest daughter, Rebecca, had even hit age thirteen, the adolescent storm broke.

Even in elementary school, my oldest daughter had been a handful. Several times she had threatened to run away when things got tough, and it had been obvious almost from the beginning that we had our work cut out for us. But as she approached the threshold of adolescence, it seemed that a hurricane had broken in and threatened to sweep away the family. I remember when Rebecca informed me that *she* didn't like to go on vacations because she didn't want to be away from her friends. (Now, where had she learned *that?!*) Suddenly the illusion I had managed to maintain of being a good father came crashing down with all the force of an uprooted tree. I was faced with not a single crisis, but a battle of wills that was destined to last for years—and I really wasn't prepared to handle it. Why had this problem come upon me?

Just like Dad

In my own stormy adolescent period, my relationship with my father had gone from frustrating to hopeless. Things got so bad that I remember thinking, *I don't ever want to be like my father.* When I reached college, I began to confide in my best friend (who was a married man, ten years my senior) about my frustrations with my father. One day he knocked me off my chair with a rather rude remark: "John, you know, you're just like your father."

Jack's words really upset me. *I was not like my father!* "Jack, you're wrong. How can you say that? I don't smoke or drink. My father isn't even a Christian; I'm not anything like him."

But my friend dispensed one of those condescending smiles we all hate. "John, I'm not talking about outward things. What I'm saying is that you have the same *attitudes* he has."

Jack was crazy. How could he say such a thing, especially with him being my best friend and all? I was nothing like my father. But you know, as much as I could not see it at the time, he was right.

About the time my daughter began to rebel, I participated in a discussion meeting in which several men in my church revealed the impact their fathers had on them. As the men shared how they felt toward their fathers, the tears began to flow. Even several men in their sixties broke up emotionally when they talked about their fathers' inability to show love. Each man had reached out only to be rejected and pushed aside. It seemed that most of the fathers had not wanted to spend any real time with their sons, and certainly none had left their boys with any sense of approval. Of the twenty men in that room, *only one* had good memories of his father!

I wish I could say that I was that one, but my father seemed unable to communicate his love for me. On those rare occasions when we did anything together, our outings would collapse under the strain of his impatience. My father never took the time to understand me, let alone get to like me. He made me a prisoner to his unexpressed expectations. I never knew where I stood or what he really wanted from me. I desired his love and approval, but instead I received his criticism and eventually his disapproval. Sitting through that meeting that day helped me understand that I wasn't the only one who had a frustrating relationship with his father. Almost every man in the room was still hurting because of the way his father had treated him. Think back to your father. How did he impact you? Did you have a good relationship with him? Or did he seem distant, aloof, and preoccupied? Was he critical and unloving?

As I thought about my own daughter's struggles with me, I wondered if she would one day have the kind of adolescent memories I possessed. *But I can't be as bad as my father was toward me,* I reasoned. *The problem is with her, not me.* But then I wondered if my father thought the same about me when I was growing up. Somehow, life seemed to be coming full circle. The concluding words of Harry Chapin's song "Cats in the Cradle" come now to my mind: "And as I hung up the phone, it occurred to me, he'd grown up just like me; my boy was just like me."

Over the years I've come to realize that I've treated my kids the same way I felt my father had treated me. My natural tendency has been to pull away into my own world, ignoring them. "I haven't got time right now," I would often say. But when did I ever have time? Without realizing it, I was programming them to be as insensitive to me as I was being to them.

God reveals the impact of this kind of behavior. "The Lord . . . forgives iniquity, transgression and sin; yet He will by no means leave the guilty unpunished, visiting the iniquity of fathers on the children and on the grandchildren to the third and fourth generations" (Exodus 34:6-7). Our sin reaps consequences not only in our lives, but also in the lives of our children. Now that passage does not say that God will punish our offspring for the sins we commit; it says that God will visit our iniquity upon them. In other words, if we don't repent, God will allow them to follow in our sinful footsteps. Our iniquity will soon become their iniquity. So the cycle will continue; kids become just like their sinful parents and will train their kids to follow in their rebellious ways.

What's your situation? Are you "just like your father"? Did he leave a negative imprint upon your heart that haunts you even now? Even if this has happened, don't use this as an excuse for inappropriate behavior. I am still responsible for my own actions. I can break this cycle, especially now that I see the pattern for what it is. You and I still have to deal with our own rebellion toward our less-than-perfect fathers. We have to neutralize our negative focus toward Dad. We have to put ourselves in the place of forgiveness in order to allow God the opportunity to heal our bitterness. And when that happens, we will have a much better relationship with our own teenagers.

Reaping What We Sow

When my daughter's rebellion began to surface, my instinctive answer was to get tougher on her. But it became quickly obvious that we were like an irresistible force meeting an immovable object. Such a clash seldom solves anything; I could see that we were only polarizing into two sharply divided camps. At the time I failed to understand that one of the reasons Rebecca and I were having such problems was that we were so much alike. And let me ask you, how can a self-centered, critical father hope to improve his child's character? (Tough assignment).

Fortunately, at this time in my life, God sent an older man to point out some of the things I was doing through my attitudes. That man sat me down and painted the big picture for me. With his help, I began to move in the right direction, becoming much more aware of my importance in this fathering process.

I wish I could say today that I now have all the answers and am a perfect father. No such luck. But I have learned a few things simply by my willingness to face my own weaknesses. With two of my own teenagers still in the house, a foster teenager, and one more coming a few years from now, I still have some excellent opportunities to practice what I'm preaching.

What Does God Want?

When you search the Bible for examples of good father figures, it is interesting how hard it is to find them. In fact, the majority of fathers presented in the Scriptures are actually examples of how *not* to do the job. Think of Eli, the high priest who would not discipline his rebellious sons, no matter how God railed upon him. Consider Isaac, who preferred one son over the other and caused a great historical division (between Arab and Jew). And picture David, who produced offspring who committed rape, murder, and treason within his own house. Whoa! If David, a man "after God's own heart," has such results, certainly we lesser mortals have our work cut out for us.

Although the Bible tells us how to father, it doesn't give many tangible examples of men doing a great job. Part of the reason for that, I believe, is because of the difficulty of the task. But my guess is that God did not want to set up an example we could translate into some mythical image in our minds for the "ideal father." If we had such a role model, we could all "play the game," doing only those things we had to do to qualify for the "Good Father Seal of Approval." God certainly knows how adept men are at faking family involvement.

So how can we know if we're on target? What's our

standard or image? Let me make three suggestions: 1) We need to study the Scriptures to see how God tells us to behave as a husband and father; 2) we should obtain feedback from our own family about how well we're performing our job; and 3) we might want to get input from other fathers so that we'll have some basis of encouragement from outside our family.

Obviously, there isn't enough space in this chapter to adequately discuss everything the Bible says about being a husband and father, but let me touch on a few things to stimulate your thinking about becoming a spiritual leader in your household.

Follow the Leader?

One of the most common complaints of many Christian wives is that their husbands do not fulfill their role as spiritual leaders in their homes. This does not necessarily mean that your wife wants you to pull out your Bible in an attempt to act spiritual. You can only be the spiritual leader if you have a close walk with the Lord and you understand the spirit of those you're supposed to be leading. *But I'm leading,* you may be thinking. *It isn't my fault that my family doesn't follow me.* Not necessarily. Good leaders will be followed.

In the last chapter we discussed the need to commit ourselves to God's plan of order for our family. That order involves children who obey, a wife who is a submissive helper, and a husband who provides spiritual leadership. But for the family to function like God designed it to, your wife and children must *want* to submit to your leadership. Demanding submission and obedience will only increase the frustration level in your family and intensify any rebellion breeding under the surface.

In your wife's case, the key to her submission is for *you,* her husband, to fulfill your role as God intended. We are to treat our wives like Christ treated the church. As the head of the church, Christ certainly didn't act like a dictator; instead, he voluntarily allowed himself to be crucified in place of the church. (*Whoa!*) If you treat your wife like that, putting her ahead of your own wants and being willing to die for her, I'll bet all kinds of good things will start happening in your house. God wants you to protect, nurture, and love your wife so that you'll be the type of leader she and the kids want to follow.

Do You Love Your Kids' Mother?

The Bible has a lot to say about how a man should treat his wife. It is interesting that several passages tell men to love their wives, but I'm aware of only one passage where women are encouraged to love their husbands. I believe that is because women are naturally more loving, while men have to be reminded and encouraged to actively perform the task of loving our wives. Love is something that you *do*. It doesn't really matter if you feel like doing it; you've committed to doing it (at your wedding). God encourages you to do it, and it's in everyone's best interests for you to practice doing it.

Now to some, loving your wife may seem like the easiest assignment a father has, but many surveys of teenagers indicate that their biggest wish is that their father would love their mother. They desire this because everything in their home ultimately depends upon their father's and mother's relationship. *Well, I definitely love my wife, so there's no problem here,* you might be thinking. But how do you show that love? Do you love her on *her level*, giving her the kinds of things she wants out of the relationship? Or are you so preoccupied with your own world that anniversaries and birthdays just slip by? Do you give her occasional love notes? Do you send her cards every once in a while with touching comments written in them? Do you ever show her a little physical affection when you're not negotiating for a "return on your investment" in the bedroom? Do you have any times of intimate communication when she receives your undivided love and attention?

Probably the hardest verse in the entire Bible for a man is 1 Peter 3:7: "You husbands likewise, live with your wives in an understanding way, as with a weaker vessel, since she is a woman; and grant her honor as a fellow heir of the grace of life, so that your prayers may not be hindered."

Understanding a woman has to be one of the most difficult jobs for any man. Many men ask, Why can't women be more like us? But can you imagine what it would be like to be married to someone as insensitive as you are? *Yuck!* But if you can come to a deeper understanding of what makes your wife tick, you will be able to love her more perfectly and meet some of her deepest inner spiritual needs. And that, my friend, is an investment in effort that will bring a great return with it.

Most women live life on a different level than most men. They are usually more sensitive and therefore less direct. This confuses many men. For example, when a woman asks, "How do I look," what is she saying? Most men think, *She wants me to evaluate how she looks.* Wrong. If a husband hears that question and studies his wife's appearance, he will totally misunderstand her. She is definitely *not* asking for an evaluation. Having spent a long time dressing and making herself up for you, she now wants a compliment. Women often ask such questions because their husbands aren't generous enough with their verbal reassurance of their love. Don't say, "Well, that skirt makes you look bottom-heavy, and I really don't like those earrings." No, no. Instead, tell her how beautiful she

is. Focus on what will minister to her spirit. Make her feel
as special as you did the day you asked her to marry you.

Sometimes we men are so realistic and honest we just
can't keep our observations to ourselves. "Honey, I was
just noticing how your wrinkles—" *Bite your tongue!*
Your wife knows all about her flaws, and she's constantly
working against the ravages of time just to please you. Certainly she isn't what she once was, but neither are you.
Focus on the things about her that you have always loved
so much. What she needs is to be cherished. Find out what
she wants most to hear about herself, and then see it in her.
(I'm not suggesting you lie; I'm suggesting you work to see
in her those very traits). Every wife knows there are many
other attractive women in this world. But she wants the
assurance that you find her attractive, that you would
rather be with her than any other woman. What she wants
to hear and feel is that your heart belongs completely to
her.

Coming to love your wife like she wants to be loved is a
lifetime process for most men. Be sensitive to her, remembering what she puts up with every day. If you can truly understand and appreciate your mate on a daily basis, you
will be a much more effective spiritual leader in your
home. And believe me when I tell you that your kids will
pick up on the quality of your marriage relationship, and it
will favorably impact their future.

Don't underestimate how important this is. A man who
does not know how to effectively love his wife is likely to
end up treating his entire family in an abusive manner. He
will cause his daughters great problems in their future relationships with men. A girl who has never been around a
well-balanced male authority figure won't know what to
look for in the boys she dates. And if a girl feels rejected by
her father, she will select the kind of guys who are a lot
like Dad, perhaps because she's trying to win his accep-

tance through them. I believe a girl's choice of spouse will often be directly impacted both by how her father responds to her and by how he treats her mother. I'm fascinated by how often I've encountered women whose trouble with their husbands, or just men in general, stems from earlier problems with their fathers. But if fathers have a healthy love relationship with their wives, they will be in a good position to assist their children in making wise decisions in dating and later in their choice of a spouse.

Showing the appropriate amount of love and affection to your wife, then, is important on more than one level. You want to love your wife for her own sake, but you must also be aware that how you express that love and affection will dramatically impact your entire family.

The Fathering Attitude

There are a few passages in the Bible directed just to fathers. Colossians 3:21 says, "Fathers, do not exasperate your children, that they may not lose heart." How easy it seems to be for fathers to ruffle their teens. We men have the natural ability to frustrate our adolescent children by our black-and-white, I'm-not-going-to-take-any-guff attitude. Why are we so intolerant and critical of our kids when we hate it when other people treat us that way?

Did your father encourage you? Did he support your interests, or did he push his own likes and dislikes upon you? I know of a father who attempted to thrust his hobby on the entire family, even paying his teenagers to get involved; hence, that man's children felt manipulated. Don't use your position as a father to manipulate, dominate, or coerce your children into fitting your particular mold. Your children are not an extension of your own life; they are separate individuals who must make their own choices in life. Your task is to help them make wise decisions. If you try to make their choices for them, they will probably feel forced to rebel against you.

Ephesians 6:4 says, "And, fathers, do not provoke your children to anger." God never says that to mothers—just fathers. Again, God singles us out because of our natural (carnal) ability to provoke angry responses from our children. We have our chair, and nobody better sit in it. What we say is law, and woe to any child who crosses us. Our withering words can humiliate anyone who steps over the line we've drawn in the carpet. A man's way of dealing with unruly behavior or silliness in his kids is often so harsh that he blows the offense all out of proportion. When a father refuses to listen to his teenagers or accept their point of view as having any validity, he can create great bitterness in his kids. Remember that you alone can spawn a household full of angry, hostile teenagers. It is imperative that we men learn how *not* to provoke our children to wrath. (In chapters 8 and 9 I will give you more help in building trust and communication with your teenagers.)

Ephesians 6:4 goes on to say that you are to bring up your children "in the discipline and instruction of the Lord." God lays upon us, the fathers, the task of providing these two things: discipline and Christian instruction. If we expect our wives to do either of them, we are abdicating responsibility that God has given specifically to us.

In a later chapter we'll talk in detail about how to discipline our teens, but for a moment I want to focus on the second half of that command. Bringing up your kids in the instruction of the Lord is a long-term task that takes a great deal of commitment. We can't wimp out on this responsibility, depending on our church to do the job, nor can we lean on our wives to teach our kids about the Lord. Let me say it plain and simple: If we do that, we will be blowing our responsibility. God called us, not them, to do this job.

Having ministered both as a youth pastor and as a senior pastor, I can tell you it is a great mistake to expect your church to do this job for you. A church simply cannot be consistent enough to impart a proper love for God and the necessary character that every Christian should have. The church just doesn't have enough resources to do that job for you; besides, it is only meant to assist you. God has ordained *you* to raise your children in the instruction of the Lord.

Perhaps you never thought that this was your responsibility. But it is. God wants you to impart to your children a healthy concept of what Christianity is all about. It is important that parents (especially fathers) know how to lead their kids to the Lord and from there into a balanced walk with Christ. (Chapter 14 deals with helping your kids find Christ.) Helping them live for God will be greatly dependent upon the kind of Christianity they see lived in you. So again, your own life-style, your personal walk with the Lord, will be of utmost importance to raising your kids in the instruction of the Lord, because they'll catch what you are faster than they'll hear what you say.

If you fulfill this assignment like God asks you to, several things should happen in your life. You'll become more proficient in knowing the Word of God; you'll have a greater sense of your own purpose in life; and you'll become a better Christian because you'll have to practice what you're preaching. It takes a real man to live out the calling of God in his life as a father. A truly spiritual dad cannot be a man who tries to hide behind some macho act. (I'm convinced that anyone who tries to play the macho role is really hiding a bankrupt spirit). Your family will measure your manhood not by how much money you make or how nice a house you buy, but by how well you fulfill God's calling for your life. Are you sensitive to the

Lord, to your wife, and to your kids? Live your life in that way, and God will bless your house.

SUMMARY OF KEY POINTS

1. Being an effective father takes a lot more effort than most fathers think.
2. Many fathers act like they believe it is their wife's job to take care of the kids.
3. If you are self-centered, your kids will tend to copy that behavior in you. A father's sins will be learned by his kids and acted out in their lives.
4. A man must overcome any bitterness he has toward his own father if he is going to break the sin cycle being passed down from one generation to another.
5. A father's natural tendency is to force his children to obey him, but that will provoke his children to rebellion.
6. God didn't give us an "ideal father" model in the Scriptures, probably because we need to seek our own understanding of how to do this important job.
7. A father isn't leading his family properly if they don't want to follow him.
8. For a man's wife to want to submit to him, he must treat her like Christ treated the church.
9. It is important to teenagers that their father loves his wife in a way that meets her emotional and spiritual needs.
10. Truly understanding a woman takes much time and sensitivity from any husband; a wife wants to sense that she is the most important woman in the world to him.
11. A father should never use his position to manipulate, dominate, or coerce his children into fitting into his mold.

12. Fathers are commanded to bring up their children in the instruction of the Lord, showing them what true Christianity is all about by their teaching and their example.

4

ANY "CHARACTERS" HERE?

"Fame is vapor, popularity an accident, riches take wings. Only one thing endures and that is character."
~Horace Greeley

....

Teenagers are so unpredictable; you never know what inconsistency they are going to catch you in next. How a parent handles his sins in front of his children will have a great deal to do with how authentic their faith will become. If Mom and Dad only make excuses for their own excesses, what can we expect from our kids?

Let me emphasize an important point: *Your character is extremely important to your success as a parent.* One of the most effective ways for parents to help their teenagers grow up is for them to first improve their own character. Character is making the proper choices when we would rather not. Whatever selfishness we exhibit will be seen and imitated by our children, so one of the best things we can do for them is to give them a tangible example of how life ought to be lived. In other words, we must practice what we preach. Alphonse Karr said, "Every man has three characters—that which he exhibits, that which he has, and that which he thinks he has." What others see in us is certainly different from what we see in ourselves. And both of those views of us are different from the person God sees inside of us.

Looking Forward to Judgment Day

I would like to encourage you to take a few moments to

get away by yourself. The material I will be presenting in just a moment is very important to your ongoing success as a parent, and you should have the luxury of being able to think through this next assignment without having to worry about being sociable. So pull away from your family and read the next few pages when you can be uninterrupted.

Someday all Christians will stand before the judgment seat of Jesus Christ. At that judgment our good works will be separated from the works done in the flesh. Imagine in your mind what that scene might be like. Picture yourself entering the throne room of Jesus Christ, with angels all aflutter. The Lord is just about ready to hear your case. Our all-knowing Master will need no testimony about you, but let's just say that he has decided to have those that love you most testify about your competence as a spouse and parent.

Try to picture this scene honestly in your mind; it's very important to be candid with yourself if you are going to benefit fully from this exercise. As you sit before this huge audience composed of scores of people, myriads of angels, and, most important, the King of kings himself, you begin to feel a little nervous, knowing that people you loved and spent your life with are about to testify about your behavior down on earth.

First, your spouse steps up and begins to speak about how you treated her (or him). You can hear the familiar voice; you listen to the words. What does she (or he) say? Are you ashamed of what you're hearing? Can you hold your head up high, or are you kicking yourself for the way you've treated her (or him)? Your spouse cannot lie on your behalf. She (or he) is telling the naked truth. Do you like what's being said? Your spouse sits down, and one by one you see your children approaching the microphone. Your firstborn takes it and begins to talk, honestly extolling your virtues and laying out your weaknesses. What is being said? How are you feeling about what's being said, about seeing your words, behavior, and attitudes played back for everyone to see? Is the look in your son's (or daughter's) eyes one of gratefulness and love? Or is he speaking from deep wounds that you caused? What accusations or praises are being spoken?

For this assignment to be truly effective, you must be brutally honest with yourself. You must not think about how *you* would answer for your spouse and kids; you must think how *they* would answer about your behavior, your consistency, and your love, based upon how they are feeling toward you right now. If you are really honest, you probably will hear some things that you don't want to hear. But this is good; it will help you see things as they do. Now if you are not happy with what you think that they would say, stop for a moment and picture them testifying about you in the way that you would like to be remembered. What nice things would they say about you? What nice memories would they have? What would be their overall impression of how you treated and loved them?

Take a moment and write down those thoughts. Even if they are a long way from what you think your family would say at this moment, those imagined thoughts are a good goal. If you would like to have your children remember your love and gentle direction, that's important. Write it down. The way you would like to be remembered is a key to your behavior today.

Taking Our "Response-Ability"

Your family is what it is today because of the choices you and your spouse made yesterday. A child's behavior is extremely dependent upon the kind of input he receives from his parents. If he turns out less than perfect, you can bet that he will be a reflection of what he's learned by observing his own parents. This is why we're told that the sins of the fathers are visited upon the sons. Our kids learn from us. If we don't like what we see in them, we have to look back at ourselves and ask where we've failed.

Stephen Covey, in *Seven Habits of Highly Effective People* (New York: Simon and Schuster, 1989), called taking responsibility for our own actions *response-ability*. I am responsible for how I reply to life. I can decide to respond in any way I choose. The Bible is the best book ever written to help people take responsibility for their own actions. In fact, that principle is at the foundation of our relationship with God. If we don't take responsibility for our own actions, God can never really save us from our sins. If we're too busy blaming others for our faults, we'll never see the reality of our own transgressions.

The Bible has countless examples of men and women who were willing to take personal responsibility for their own sins. Remember Daniel? He was a man of great personal integrity who always seemed to do what was right. We don't have any recorded example of him sinning, yet when he began to pray for his people, the first thing he confessed was his own sin and shame. And he also took personal responsibility for the actions of his own people. This pattern of accepting personal responsibility is found repeatedly in the Scriptures.

Remember Joseph in Genesis? His father assigned him a cushy job and gave him the preferred coat of many colors. His brothers reacted jealously and sold Joseph into slavery. Instead of blaming them, he took responsibility for his own life, right where he found himself. Being taken from an easy position in a comparatively well-to-do family and made to become another man's slave could have been extremely depressing. In his situation, many people would have just given up on life. After all, he had been betrayed by his own family. Yet, he made the best of his new situation as a slave. He soon worked his way up to being in charge of his master's entire house. But when the master's wife tried to seduce him, he rejected her advances, and for that she accused him of trying to rape her. Once again, fate seemed to be against him; he was sent to prison for a crime he did not commit.

If ever there was a time when he could have felt justified in feeling sorry for himself, it was at that moment. But Joseph was a man of action. Instead of cursing his destiny, he went to work to become the model prisoner. It didn't take long before he was in charge of the entire prison, but he stayed in that prison for several years until by the hand of God he stepped up to become the prime minister of all Egypt. We must not miss that it was God who blessed Joseph and made him successful. But could God have blessed him if he had moped around in his slave's quarters or his prison cell and cried all day? I don't think so. God was able to bless him because he took responsibility for his own life. He accepted his situation for what it was and refused to wallow in the bitterness that often comes to people when they fail; he didn't waste his time blaming others. He remained faithful to God throughout his long ordeal. He raised his sights and began to look, not at what he could not control, but at what he could change.

So don't wallow in frustration because of the problems in your family. Focus, not upon what you cannot change, but upon the areas of your life over which you have control. But you'll never be able to make any changes unless you start moving. Even if you're on the right track, you'll just end up being run over if you keep sitting there. Putting off an easy task makes it hard, but putting off a hard task makes it nearly impossible. So determine in your heart, right now, that you will start making some changes in your own attitudes.

Those Little Traps

"If only my teenager was more productive." "If only my daughter would clean up her room." "If only my son had better friends." "If only my kids would obey." The problem with all these "if only" statements is that they put our problems *out there*. The implication of such expressions is that you can do nothing to solve those problems. Maybe you've even thought, *I could be a good parent if I just had decent kids.* What a silly (but common) thought.

Good parents *make* good kids. Good kids don't just happen—they're created. As you become more of what God wants you to become, your teenagers will also. But all of you will do that one step at a time. Great works are performed not by strength, but by perseverance. And I can't think of any greater work than raising a household full of children to be godly adults. It is good to be concerned about your teenagers, but don't ever tell yourself that there's nothing you can do to help them change their character. You have a great deal of influence over them. No one else has or will have more influence over your kids than you do. Focus on what you can do to change the things about your kids that you don't like. Identify the problems, and ask yourself how *you* could have caused those difficulties. Then work out a plan for solving those problems.

For example, let's give a hypothetical problem that you might someday face. Suppose that your adolescent child sits passively around the house watching television all day long. He eats constantly but never cleans up after himself. What causes a teenager to behave this way? Parents are responsible for allowing their child to vegetate by not expecting enough of him. They have provided too many passive activities, such as TV and video games, that have stiffled much of his creativity. What should you do now?

My first suggestion would be to remove some of the passive entertainments in your home. Put both of your TVs (Americans average 2.1 sets per family) in the garage for a while; pack up the video machines; take the computer games off your computer.

"But, *Dad!* What am I gonna do now?" That's a great question. And it's one you mustn't answer for your teen. Don't let yourself be caught in the trap of trying to keep your kids entertained. They must learn to entertain themselves. Certainly you can and should suggest a few possibilities. Reading is an excellent diversion that will help the average teenager grow mentally. Most teens don't really know how to read anything substantial because they have always had the TV turned on. When my daughters were in elementary school, we lived in the country and decided not to own a television set. That was probably one of the wisest decisions we ever made. Because of it, our children learned how to read and how to creatively entertain themselves. In Rebecca's senior year, she surprised her English teacher by how fast she read all of the books on the extra-credit list.

For most parents, the thought of removing the television set, even for a while, probably seems pretty scary. I've heard of families who were promised large sums of money if they would just eliminate their television-watching for a month. Apparently, most of those families experienced "withdrawal" and after only a few days claimed it just wasn't worth the money.

You fathers are probably thinking, *But if we get rid of the television, I won't be able to watch the play-offs.* Well, whoever said that life didn't take sacrifices? Besides, is something like that really necessary? Bruce Barton (quoted in *Seven Habits,* p. 287) said, "Sometimes when I consider what tremendous consequences come from little things . . . I am tempted to think . . . there are no little things." Is a closer, tighter family worth this kind of a personal sacrifice? Of course it is.

I have tremendous control over my own destiny and a relatively large amount of influence over what happens to my family. I can choose to act in a situation, or I can let the situation act upon me. What a shame that most of us let our environment be manipulated by the entertainment media. Why don't we take charge of our own lives for a change? (After writing this paragraph, I sold our television set. And you know what? None of us really miss it).

I know that this is a dramatic concept for most people. It is so much easier to blame other people or things for the situation we find ourselves in. But we have to face the reality that we can change our lives and the lives of our families by our choices. We can make things better. We are not powerless victims; we have control over our lives. Your thoughts, actions, and habits determine the future.

Latchkey Kids

In our society many women have entered the work force, often because of financial circumstances. Working parents look forward to the day when their offspring will be old enough not to have to be supervised. However, because these (two million estimated) latchkey kids have a great deal of unsupervised time on their hands, they get into all sorts of trouble. Studies have been done that show that the majority of teenage mischief happens when teens are unsupervised. A great deal of sexual promiscuity, drug abuse, and crime occurs during the interval between when a student arrives home from school and the time when his parents show up.

"But there's nothing I can do about this situation," you may say. "We just can't *afford* to do it any other way." But you have made choices, and you are responsible for the

consequences of them. If you are unhappy about those consequences, it is in your power to work out solutions.

By nature, I'm a workaholic. As a writer I can spend all
of my time working on some project to the exclusion of
my family. And if our finances are tight, I can easily justify
why I just *have* to work late to get some project finished.
But really, if I'm honest, I don't have to—I want to. There
are many excuses but only one real reason for why we do
things. If I work late, it is because I *choose* to. If I cause
other people to suffer because of that, I must see my behavior for what it is. Working hard all night won't really bring
anyone prosperity. We must learn to work smarter. Wealth
consists not of our income but of what we're worth. Most
young families want to raise their income so that they can
own more things. Yet Jesus made it plain that our lives do
not consist of the things we possess.

If both husband and wife are working, and you don't
like the consequences you are seeing in your family, ask
yourself why you are doing that. If you're merely trying to
get ahead, perhaps you need to reexamine that commitment. Downscale your financial sights, and take more
thought to planning for your family's spiritual future. I
have never met a man (or woman) who reached the end of
his (or her) life and said, "You know, I wish I had spent
more time working on the job and less time with my kids."
When our teenagers are finally grown and gone, there is
no way we can recapture those potentially fun-filled days.
When they have passed, they will be gone forever.

Many people work hard to achieve the things that they
thought were so important when they were younger, only
to realize that they have lost their family in the process.
Everything we do has consequences. What are the consequences of working too hard? Losing your family? What
are the consequences of taking more time off? A little less
income? Are you laboring for some goal, perhaps even the

salvation of the masses, to the exclusion of your own spouse and kids? You have the choice to spend your life on anything you want. No one can impose that choice upon you without your approval.

Have You Grown Up?

Many parents have a difficult time bringing up their kids precisely because they have not yet grown up themselves. I remember a counselor we had on staff in my church saying he couldn't help a particular young mother with her discipline problems because "she'll have to change her whole life-style." That mother used television to baby-sit her young children so that she could talk for hours on the telephone with her friends. The counselor knew that she had to get her own undisciplined ways under control before she could rein in her kids.

If you want your children to be honest, sincere, and tolerant, you should examine your own behavior to see if you are living out those very same character qualities. I recently read about a father whose grown son was arrested for tax evasion. When the father asked why his son did such a thing, he replied, "Now Dad, where do you think I learned how to be such a cheat? Remember all those times when you said, 'What they don't know won't hurt them'? Dad, it was you who taught me everything I know."

Jesus told us that we are responsible for every idle word, and sometimes those words will come back to haunt us. I remember once hearing a speaker make the statement that "parents hate it when they see themselves in their children—especially their character qualities." How true.

Often, when I have attempted to reprimand one of my teenagers, I will hear, "But Dad, you do that same thing all the time." Oh, how I hate to hear those words! But when the shoe fits, I have to wear it. Although I won't let my own slothfulness become an excuse for my children, I certainly have to admit when I'm not practicing what I've been preaching. I know anything less will warp my kids. And my attempts to become consistent will help my children do the same.

What Fills Your Heart?

Much of our problem with character boils down to what's at the center of our lives. Most of us are living for something, even if we have never given it much thought. Let me suggest several possible "focus centers" for our lives.

When we think of someone who lives for work, we generally think of a workaholic. This is quite common, especially for men. A person who loves his work and finds it difficult to take time off makes his job his most important priority. Many so-called workaholics are really just into making money. I heard one man sum it up when he said, "It's not the money I'm after; it's only that money is a way of keeping score." Close kin are those who are being consumed by the desire to own things. "I can afford it; why not the best?" is their philosophy.

The pursuit of pleasure can become someone's center if that's all they think about. Some men live for sports, waiting anxiously for the weekends. Some women live for soap operas or romance novels. When pleasure is at the heart of people's lives, they will usually do whatever is necessary to make certain that their fun level stays high. Related to this hedonism is the me-first attitude; people who possess this selfish attitude think that nothing and no one else is more important than how they feel.

Many women and some men live their lives focused upon the needs of their family. On the surface, this would seem good, but these people often become slaves to their family's every need. Friends can easily become the focus of many teenagers, who become overly dependent on pleasing them. (I call this "peer dependence," and I've devoted chapter 10 to it). Even church can become the center of a person's life, taking him away from a proper perspective. Living for your family, your spouse, or your church may seem like a noble goal, but God has made it plain that he wants no other gods before him. Anything that becomes a ruling passion in our lives—except for Jesus Christ alone— is wrong. Anything that takes possession of our heart and thought-life becomes a form of idolatry.

Now we think of idols as being statues to which people bow down, but our idols are cars, people, pleasure, sports, romance, etc. Usually, you can tell what your idol is by looking at what you do with your available free time. At different times in my life I have found that good activities like writing a Christian book or performing a ministry have become the center of my life, to the point where nothing else mattered. The Word of God tells us to destroy everything that raises itself up against the knowledge of God; we are even told to take "every thought captive to the obedience of Christ" (2 Corinthians 10:5).

Your Purpose in Life

I attended a Christian college, intending to go into full-time ministry. One afternoon I visited my best friend's apartment (the man who told me how much I was like my father). During a break in our study time he asked me a question.

"John, what are you studying for? What's the purpose of your education?"

I thought for a moment, then proceeded to tell Jack all about my goal to become the best youth pastor I could possibly be.

"John, that's good. But I don't think you understand my

question. What's the purpose of your life? Where are you going?"

"Jack, maybe you didn't hear me." A little frustrated, I proceeded to repeat myself. But Jack only shook his head.

"John, what you're sharing is good, but that's only a short-term goal. I'm talking about your life's purpose. It seems to me," he said, "that your purpose in life as a Christian should be to get to know Jesus Christ in the fullest possible way." He then opened his New Testament and read Philippians 3:7-10, where the apostle Paul talks about his desire to know Christ. Then he said, "Knowing Christ should come first. Everything else should come second."

I had to agree with what Jack said. Although wanting to be a youth pastor was high on my priority list at that time, it certainly was only an immediate goal. Knowing Christ had to be my long-term purpose in life.

The secret to good character is putting Jesus Christ at the center of your life. And good character is at the foundation of a good relationship with your teenagers. Everything, including your spouse and your children, must be brought into captivity to his will. As we make the conscious effort to put each day under the Lord's control, it is amazing how God can help us focus on performing all those tasks necessary for a smooth-running family.

Are You Willing to Pay the Price?

When my daughter had begun to rebel, it was really only a signal that something was wrong in my own heart. As I mentioned, God sent a counselor to help me see my own character more clearly. It was at that point in my life that I knew I needed to make some major changes if I was going to win back my daughter and keep my family from self-destructing.

Together, my wife and I decided that the best antidote

for my daughter's peer dependence would be for us to home school. We decided to enroll with the Advanced Training Institute of America because it had such a strong Scripture-based curriculum. This decision required that we attend two week-long conferences (at great expense). ATIA also required that I would have to daily teach my teenagers from God's Word. All of this had a positive impact on both my character and that of my daughters. It was a big price to pay, but over the next few years the wisdom of that commitment proved itself.

I heard about a concert pianist who performed a beautiful mini-concert in front of a small audience. After the performance, a man came up to the pianist and said: "You were absolutely great. I'd give half my life to be able to play the piano like you do." The artist smiled. "You know, that's exactly what I gave—half my life."

Sometimes we're oblivious to what must go on behind the scenes to make things happen up on the stage. I heard of a man who had been hired to play his trumpet professionally in one of those studio orchestras. When asked if he still practiced, his answer was: "Of course, I always practice. But recently I've managed to get it down to where I only have to practice *six hours a day.*"

Success always has a price tag. The question we have to ask ourselves is, Are we willing to pay the price to have godly teenagers? It takes work to see our offspring through the trying times to the goal of becoming godly adults. William Penn once said, "No pain, no palm; no thorns, no throne; no gall, no glory; no cross, no crown." It takes pain, thorns, gall, and often even a visit to the Cross. But it's worth it because the palms, the throne, the glory, and the crown follow.

Let me stand on the sidelines and be your cheering section. I want to encourage you that God can help you rise to the occasion to make your family everything that God wants it to be. Don't give up. Don't look at the pain, the thorns, the gall, and the cross and forget where you're headed. As your kids turn out right, you'll be able to hold up your head someday knowing that you took the higher road—the road less traveled—but the one that made all the difference for your kids.

Ask yourself, "How can I do a better job with this family?" Then pray, "God, you know my limitations; you made me. Tell me what I should stop doing with my kids. Tell me what I should start doing." As you pray about your family situation and reflect upon it, God will give you the direction that you need. I'm also certain that he will use books like this one to stimulate you into seeing the potential and possibilities that are easily within your grasp.

SUMMARY OF KEY POINTS

1. A person's character is extremely important to his success as a parent.
2. A person's family is what it is today because of choices made yesterday; each parent is responsible for the ramifications of his own behavior.
3. Parents should not try to blame anyone else for problems in their family.
4. Good parents make good kids; good kids don't just happen—they are created.
5. Parents must make temporary sacrifices of their own happiness in order to effect change in their children.
6. A parent might come up with an excuse for why he *has* to do something that is not in his family's best interests, but ultimately we make most of our own choices for selfish reasons.
7. All our life choices have consequences for our family. We must take responsibility for our own actions.

8. Despite their numerical age, many parents need to work at "growing up" for the sake of their kids.
9. Whatever consumes our thoughts and our time is usually the "focus center" of our lives.
10. God wants us to bring every thought captive to Christ.
11. The secret to truly good character is in having Jesus Christ at the center of your life.
12. There is always a price for success, and that is especially so in the life of any family.

5
WHERE ARE YOU GOING?

"*Our plans miscarry because they have no aim. When a man does not know what harbor he is making for, no wind is the right wind.*" ~Seneca

Ever embarked upon a family journey, not really sure of how to get to your destination?

"You got the directions, didn't you?" you ask as you accelerate up onto the interstate.

"No. I thought *you* had them," replies your better half.

"So we don't know where we're going?"

"Hey, it's not *my* fault. I handed them to you."

From there, the road just seems to go downhill. And if by some fluke the family car arrives in the general vicinity of the target, it begins to circle aimlessly. After about seven loops around the same block, the inevitable suggestion comes—usually from Mom. "Let's pull into a gas station and ask for directions."

"No," replies Dad, applying his superior logic, "we're too late for that."

What is it about us dads, anyway, that we don't believe in stopping for directions when we're lost? Is it because we feel that to stop would only make us later? Or could it be that we just hate to admit that we are actually lost? My wife and I have probably had more arguments over directions than all of our other arguments combined. The usual subject of most of those arguments is to figure out who should be blamed for our being lost. And that's followed, a close second, by the arguments over my unwillingness to stop and ask for directions.

Road trips are a lot like life. We all think we know where we're going, but we spend a lot of time being lost simply because we didn't consider it necessary to take the time to look at a map to make certain we knew the way to our destination.

What Plans Have You Made?

If you don't know where you're going, the odds are you won't end up anywhere you want to be. This is an important concept in your family's overall success: *Know where it is that you want your family to go.* Few of us ever take the time to sit down and plan our family's future.

I once heard a mother comment to her grown son that she was pleased that he and his sister had turned out so well. The young man responded: "Yeah, you and Dad were *sure lucky!*" That's the way it is with most families. If the kids turn out fine, it probably has very little to do with any planning the parents did. While today's couples engage in the all-consuming pursuit of the American dream, it seems that most kids just have to figure life out on their own. What little prodding most parents do give their kids often seems pointless. The typical parent reminds me of someone straightening deck chairs on the *Titanic.* The chairs may look great all lined up, but that isn't going to make much of a difference because of the liner's ultimate destination.

In the last chapter we talked about picturing yourself at the judgment seat of Christ, hearing the members of your immediate family reveal how they see your success as a parent. One of the reasons that exercise is important is that it helps you think about your personal destination and resolve to be more in control of it. But what about the destination of your family? Where are you taking this family, and how will you know when you have arrived?

They say that one of the biggest reasons new businesses fail is because the entrepreneur fails to produce an effective business plan; he neglects to define his market or determine the amount of capital he'll need to make the enterprise work. If a businessman has only a vague idea about where he's going, his company will usually fold before he's even had the opportunity to breathe life into it.

So where are you headed as a family? Do you know? Have you really thought it out? If you're like most of us— probably not. We tell ourselves that it really isn't necessary to nail down our ultimate goals because "we all know where we're going." Yet if we had to put it down on paper, we might have a difficult time doing so. This failure to plan ahead is one of the most common ingredients for failure at all levels. A great French surgeon by the name of Nelatin once said that if he only had four minutes to perform an operation, he would use the first of those minutes to plan how to perform the surgery.

A couple of years ago my wife and I designed and built a home. We decided to make our final drawing (before our contractor drew up the blueprints) to a specific scale so that we could see just how our furniture would fit inside the rooms. In doing this, we discovered, among other things, that we hadn't allowed enough space for our dining-room table. How glad we were later when everything fit inside our house. Just as we're wise to plan ahead when constructing a house, how much more when we build the family living inside the house? But before you figure out where your family is going, let's talk about being certain you know where you're going in life. One of the best ways, I believe, that this can be done is to sit down and write what I'll call a personal mission statement.

A Guiding Direction for Life

When I composed my own personal mission statement, I didn't include any of my short-range goals, like finishing some project I've been working on. Those things go on my daily "do list." Instead, I focused on things that will still be on my list when I've reached the final days of my life. I printed it up on my computer so that it is now on the wall above my office desk—right where I can see it every day. Now on a pretty regular basis I look up at those words and ask myself how well I'm doing. (A copy of my mission statement is in appendix A.)

The first point on my statement reads: "My primary goal in life is to glorify God." As a Christian I've always been committed to that goal, but as I live my life, I get caught up just being busy, so busy that I don't give much thought to what God might want me to do. I have found that when I have a lot of work to do, getting up and working earlier usually doesn't help much. On the other hand, when I give the most important part of my day (the morning) to ask God for his direction and help in maximizing my time, everything seems to go better.

The second point on my personal mission statement reads: "My goal is to love and nurture my wife, Susan." I know from the Scriptures that I am to cleave to her—I'm to put her high up on my list of personal priorities. Whenever I read that statement, I ask myself what I should be doing for her and what I should stop doing. How can I nurture the love that is within her and encourage her to keep on loving both me and the kids? These are questions I should never stop asking myself.

My third statement reads: "My children will receive thorough love, consistent direction, and adequate time." Because every child is different, the intensity of their need for love will probably also vary. But I do know that I don't want my kids to have any doubts about my love. My kids need my love and attention. I want that love to be thorough, not from my point of view, but from theirs. That means I also have to give them adequate time. I need to stop what I am doing when my teenage daughters come into my office and want to talk to me. I need to look them straight in the eyes and listen. I want to help fulfill their needs by being available to them when they need me. I put down "consistent direction" because I felt that my children need to be pointed back to God's standard. We all need some driving force in our lives, and if it isn't God, it will usually end up being our own selfish desires. I recognize that one of my major roles as a parent is to help point my teens in the right direction.

I continue to see, each day, the value of having a mission statement in life summed up in plain sight. It helps me keep things in focus; it helps me force myself to stay on the track. These are the things that I value most, and they're right where I can see them. I'm not as consistent as I would like to be in implementing them, but the presence of that statement makes me constantly reevaluate what I'm doing and, even more important, what I'm *not* doing on a moment-by-moment basis.

I have to admit that sometimes when I look up at that statement, I realize that it contradicts my current behavior. But nobody has imposed that statement upon me. It is my choice. And I know if I am not fulfilling it in my day-to-day performance, I'm not working in my own best interests. "The secret to success," said the famous British statesman Benjamin Disraeli, "is constancy to purpose."

Another thing I like about my mission statement is that I can revise it at any time. As I go on in life, I'm certain that I will feel that parts of it are inadequate for my life or that it does not hit the nail for me like it used to. Fortunately, I can change it to say whatever it needs to say. Only God should write on stone.

Your Own Mission Statement

I'm certain your mission statement will be much different from mine. You might want to write down far more than I have. I saw one statement that consisted of a long list of character qualities that the person wanted to be known for. This is a custom document that should be personalized to your own needs.

If the focus of your life is still pleasure, sports, or work, you might find that this statement will contradict your life-style. If you honestly develop a well-balanced statement of your personal mission, it will probably challenge you to reevaluate any self-centered behavior. That's the beauty of such a paper—it becomes a measuring stick to help you see how consistent your beliefs are with your behavior.

As you write out your statement, take care to include your family in the statement, especially in relationship to how you will be ministering to each member. And don't worry about this document being perfect. You'll probably go through many drafts before you're happy with every-thing it says. Although this is a personal exercise, you might find it helpful to talk through the process with your spouse. As you share your aspirations with the one that you love most, you will no doubt have a much stronger motivation to fulfill your calling.

Now, don't procrastinate. Set this book aside and grab a piece of paper—and *do it!* Get something on paper before you move on any further in your reading.

A Larger Frame of Reference

Setting down your personal mission statement is valuable because it gives you a bigger view of how you fit into life as a whole; looking at life from a higher vantage point tends to make things appear clearer. But for this to be truly effective, it must continue to be perfected as you contrast it with that of other people in your family.

A few years ago I called a national airline to reserve two tickets. The woman at the other end of the line was extremely short with me. No matter what I said, she seemed to react. She seemed to have no understanding that the customer is supposed to be right. Now I like to think that it's difficult to arouse my anger, but this woman had definitely succeeded. Finally, in frustration, I demanded to talk to her supervisor. She was so hostile toward me at that point that I was surprised she didn't just hang up on me. I have to admit it wouldn't have bothered me one bit to get this woman fired. When the supervisor came on the line, I complained about how poorly I had been treated.

"I'm sorry," she said. "Our sales representatives seldom treat people like this, and I'll take care of the situation. There's no excuse for this, but it might help you to understand that this morning Miss Jones found out she has cancer."

The moment I heard that, guilt feelings swept over me, especially considering how I had reacted toward the woman. Had I been more sensitive to her, I would have realized that her overreaction to me was based not on me but on some turmoil in her life. Seeing things from a larger frame of reference often helps clarify other people's behavior.

How do you get this larger view of life? I believe that one of the best ways to expand our frame of reference is through communicating with other people, especially those in your own family (chapter 9 will deal with this subject in depth). But I believe the single most important way to expand your horizons is through prayer, because the larger frame of reference we want to develop ultimately comes from God.

Martin Luther said that he had so much to do in a typical day that he had to spend at least three hours praying before he began his day. Now what was he doing during such a long prayer time? He certainly couldn't have spent that time asking for things. None of us have *that* many things that we need. What he was doing in such a long time of prayer was building his relationship with God and learning God's mind on how he should run his day (and ultimately his life).

If I have some important decision to make or if my family is going through some major trial, I like to take an hour (usually after everyone else has gone to sleep) and begin to pray and pace in our kitchen. I like to use the Lord's Prayer, because Jesus gave it to us as a model prayer. It is a framework upon which I build my time with God. "Our Father, who art in heaven . . . ," I say as I begin, and for a while I'll pray to my Father and focus in on him and his goodness. I've found that after about ten or fifteen minutes of such praying, asking for whatever things I might want to request for myself and my family dissolves into asking God what he wants of me. That's when it seems that my frame of reference really gets stretched; it's at that moment that I start reevaluating my situation in the light of God's will for our lives.

Usually when I'm going through a crisis, I don't have enough information to make correct decisions because my mind is awash with all sorts of concerns. But as I take my mind off myself and begin to pray God's Word back to him, soon I can see things from a whole different perspective. My frame of reference expands. I'm no longer limited to seeing things from my own mundane point of view.

Over the past several years, we've developed a little tradition in our home of praying together with our teenagers before they go off to school. This has been a good experience because we get to hear about each other's concerns and learn to take an interest in what someone else is going through. I can't think of any activity that is more important to the well-being of your family than to pray regularly—both with the kids, together with your spouse, and by yourself.

How many times have we heard stories from grown men and women who considered that the secret to their later success in life was that one or both of their parents spent a lot of time on their knees on their behalf? Keeping a small prayer notebook for each of your kids is not a bad idea. List out the things that you would like to see happen in their lives, and then pray consistently for those character traits. But don't allow yourself to pray "hopeless prayers" that you are certain God won't answer. The Lord made it plain that he cannot answer faithless prayers. You must believe that the Lord wants to answer your prayers, or you're better off not asking (see James 1:6-8).

Praying for the salvation of some of our kids is a little like trying to run and leap a flight of stairs in one big jump. We'll never get to the top of a set of stairs like that, so why try to pray that way? Instead, make your requests to God in proportion to the size of your faith. Ask for little things like a change of attitude here or a behavior there. Get results in your little prayers that move your son or daughter in the right direction, all the time keeping your ultimate goals for them in mind.

It is important to pray for specific areas of character growth in your kids. What character quality would you like to see develop? Perhaps you'd like to see your teen get his temper under control, or develop a more loving spirit, or be a more productive member of the family. As you pray about specific things on your prayer list, God will no doubt give you project ideas that you can use to help your kids achieve those qualities.

One of the important keys to successful praying is the intensity of your prayers. Do you remember the parable Jesus gave about the woman who persisted in pestering an unrighteous judge until she received help? (See Luke 18:2-8). And then there is the story of the man who kept knocking on his friend's door in the middle of the night for help (Luke 11:5-13). The Lord wants us to know that persistence in prayer will be rewarded (of course, our prayers must also be in line with God's will).

How badly do you want to see changes in your family? The degree to which you are serious about your family and determine you will be consistent in praying for them is the degree to which you will be rewarded. Remember, prayer is a long-term ministry. But then raising your kids is also a long-term project, isn't it?

Those Important Family Times

As your children enter the teenage zone, one of the best things you can do for them is to have a regular family hour each week. Plan this as a night reserved exclusively for the family. On this evening plan ahead to do things like playing games at home or going on outings (ice cream, skating, bowling, jogging, out for dinner, etc.). The focus should be on working together and having fun; it should also be on giving your family input that helps negate the garbage that they are receiving every day in the world.

If your teenagers are trying to avoid this evening, one of their common excuses may be that they have too much homework. With this in mind, you may need to select a weekend evening. But you must be willing to be flexible if your family time is scheduled on a regular basis for a Friday, Saturday, or Sunday night because so many irregular school and church events fall on those nights. It might be a good idea to establish at the beginning of each week when your normal family night will be held. Periodically, everyone will have to bend schedules so the entire family can come together. To keep your teens from grumbling, make certain that they're not always the ones who have to be flexible.

One of the major keys to the success of the family night is that your teenagers *want* to be there. If they do not, such a time can easily turn into a boring, ho-hum evening where they are just putting up with you. The family hour should be seen as a time set up just for them, to cater to their needs and wants. If your teens feel that this meeting is for them, they'll be much more receptive to the idea. As you develop it, a family night can become a powerful time to give your kids the input they need. This night should always include an opportunity for family discussion. Use it to discuss anyone's concerns and to establish the principles by which you want your family to live. This is the time when you can help your family develop its own game plan.

Your Family Character Blueprint

Before we leave this chapter, I would like to encourage you to do one final project, which can be accomplished through the family hour. Over a several-week period, develop your own blueprint of family character. This is an important exercise that should bring great dividends for everyone.

Your family should have some kind of character blueprint that can become the ultimate measuring stick for your teens' behavior (especially when they are out of your view). The Jews, of course, had the Ten Commandments and the Torah that they diligently taught to their children (see Deuteronomy 6:4-9). As Christians, of course, we have the entire Scripture as our rule of life. Unfortunately, many adults and most teenagers are ignorant of most of its teachings. We can't live by them unless we know what they teach.

It's a good idea to sum up some of the key scriptural teachings you would like on your family's character blueprint so that everyone knows what the standards are. Always refer to the Scripture that clarifies God's standard so your teens can see that this is not some arbitrary rule you've established; let them see that God gave us the standard.

For example, you might want to put down the Golden Rule on the top of your list. "However you want people to treat you, so treat them" (Matthew 7:12). You might also want to include "Love your neighbor as yourself" (Matthew 19:19). Try paraphrasing the Ten Commandments (Exodus 20) into a vernacular your teens can understand (e.g., "bearing false witness" becomes "lying," "covet" becomes "lust after," etc.).

It's not a bad idea to include a statement about the use of illegal drugs, condemned in Galatians 5:20. The word translated "sorcery" there is the Greek word *pharmakia,* which is the root from which we get our English *pharmacy.* (See also 1 Corinthians 6:19-20.) Avoiding alcohol (Proverbs 20:1) and sex outside of marriage (1 Thessalonians 4:3) would also be good values to add to your blueprint. You'll probably want to work at polishing this blueprint by adding and clarifying things until you have a clear guideline that will help give your kids direction in life. (See appendix B for a sample character blueprint).

If this seems like a difficult assignment for your family, try bringing up one character value each week. You might want to feature one value, discussing the Scripture passage it's based upon during your family hour, then assigning everyone to live it out the following week.

When your teens make a personal commitment to live

by this character blueprint, it will clarify many issues for them. When they are offered alcohol or illegal drugs, they won't have to decide whether or not they should say no. They will already have decided that they don't do drugs; they won't disobey God or their parents because they will already have committed their lives to biblical character. Decision making is always easier if a person's character is clearly defined.

If on your family character blueprint you've stated you desire to live by the laws of the land (Romans 13:1-3), you won't have to decide whether you should slow down or speed up whenever the street signal turns yellow; you won't have to decide whether or not you are going to go sixty-five on the freeway when the speed limit is fifty-five. Your behavior will be determined by the character you have already mentally (and prayerfully) adopted.

Remember that your own consistency in living by this character blueprint will encourage your teenagers in being consistent in their lives. We all have a need to live in a predictable world, and when you are consistent in your behavior, your teens will find it easier to trust you. There are also many personal benefits you will receive from being consistent (such as being able to look at yourself in the mirror). Your kids need to know what you stand for. People always respect someone who stands for something; being wishy-washy is always a big turnoff. Whatever your character and the standards you adopt—stick with them, and you'll find that you will win the respect of your own family.

Counting the Cost

As you can see, knowing where you are going in this parenting stuff takes a lot of planning. If you have read these suggestions at one sitting, they may seem a little overwhelming (and like a lot of work). But whoever said being a godly parent was going to be easy? Believe me, in the end it will be worth all the work you put into the job.

Jesus encouraged his followers to count the cost. He used the illustration of a man who is about to build a tower, and the first thing he does is sit down and calculate the cost of the project before he begins construction. The builder knows if he starts something he can't finish, he'll be ridiculed by everyone who passes by. Fail to plan, and you're planning to fail. Jesus also gave the parable of a rich man who planned ahead, but left God out of those plans. As a result, the Lord called him a fool.

It is probably the rule that most parents don't give much thought to where their family is headed. Family teamwork has to be learned. And if we don't train our kids when they are children, it will be much more difficult to train them when they are teenagers. But it can and should be done. Don't let anyone tell you you can't be a successful parent. Even if your house seems way out of control, you can influence your family to move in the right direction. You can be what God wants you to be and end up with a family that creates a meaningful legacy—if you want it badly enough.

Remember those classic verses in Proverbs 3:5-6? "Trust in the Lord with all your heart," said Solomon. When you don't have the answers, when things are not going the way you know they should, trust in the Lord with all your heart. What better advice can you get than that? As you trust in the Lord, either he will change your situation or he will change *you*. And that's often the key to changing the situation.

"Do not lean on your own understanding." Teens just don't act like they used to, or like they should, or like we want them to, and we can't figure them out. That's precisely why this verse is such good advice for parents. If you lean on your own understanding you will be, in a word, *frustrated*. How much better to lean on him.

"In all your ways acknowledge him, and he will make your paths straight." If you depend upon the Lord, always pointing your life in his direction, he will direct your paths. Or, as the passage says literally, he will make your paths *smooth*. Isn't that what any parent of a teenager needs—a smooth path!

Life is not so much what happens to you with your teenager as it is how you respond to what happens. Every parent gets a little rain in his life now and then. But can you smile in the face of it? Now, that's the question. If your dependence is upon the Lord, you'll be able to do so. Count on it. Practice it. It works because *he works*.

SUMMARY OF KEY POINTS

1. Every parent should know where it is that his or her family is supposed to be headed.
2. Most families have failed to plan their future because it seems so unnecessary and understood.
3. A personal mission statement helps a parent focus on where he (or she) wants his (or her) own life to head.
4. All parents need a higher vantage point if they are going to see their family's needs more clearly.
5. Our prayer time with God is the single most important way of expanding our horizons.
6. Consistent family and personal prayer times are a vital part of a family's growth.
7. A regular weekly family time is an effective way to build relationships with your teenagers.
8. Families should work on establishing a blueprint of family character in which they write out what they believe and especially what character values they want to live by.
9. Parents need to trust the Lord and lean not on their own understanding but on him.

6

TEMPORARY INSANITY

"Youth have exalted notions because they have not yet been humbled by life. . . . They love too much, they hate too much; they think they know everything; that is why they overdo everything." ~Aristotle

....

Samuel Beckett said, "We are all born mad. Some remain so." Was he right? Are we all a little off? Is there anyone truly sane, who never does anything that's a little off-balanced? Mark Twain quipped in his notebook, "When we remember that we are all mad, the mysteries disappear and life stands explained."

Whenever a church needs workers to teach the kids, everyone volunteers to lead the elementary kids or the high schoolers, but nobody (in his right mind) volunteers to enter the cage where the junior high group is kept. Most young teachers discover that spending an hour a week with these early teens will cure them of ever wanting kids of their own.

If ever a parent becomes convinced that we are all mad, it will probably come when his children reach their early teen years. Although your children will go through more changes between twelve and nineteen than at any other period of their lives, there can't be any other age group that drives more parents crazy (except perhaps the "terrible twos"). In fact, one expert, psychologist Thomas Olkowski, described teenagers as "toddlers grown up."[1]

....

[1] "Early teen years are tough for parents, kids," *Redding Record Searchlight*, September 30, 1992.

What they do is very much like the eighteen-month-old to two-and-a-half-year-old phase of the infant. First they want you for a little while, then it's, "Go away, I wanna do it by myself." Yet they still want the assurance of knowing you are nearby just in case they get into trouble.

What words can we use to describe kids during this time frame? Select the adjectives that best describe your kid: Squirrelly? Wired? Motor-mouthed? Unbalanced? Hyper? Silly? Sex-obsessed? Foolish? Boy crazy? Zany? Witless? Insane? All of the above?

The Difficult Years

While an elementary boy is likely to bring home a frog after school, your junior-high teen is more likely to sneak into his room with a dirty magazine. Up to this point, your son may have preferred to paint his face with clown's makeup; now he wants to put a bandage on to cover up his latest zit (that's slang for pimple). Your elementary daughter may have been into pigtails and white socks, but now you may not be able to pry your junior-high girl away from the bathroom mirror. Your teenybopper may suddenly shift from Barbie dolls to *Seventeen* magazine and rock-and-roll idols.

This is a time when a boy discovers his genitals; for the first time he has to undress in front of other boys his age. The locker room can become a crucible in which such things as the presence or lack of pubic hair and the size of one's penis become an occasion for group ridicule. A girl encounters her "monthly fun" and may beg for a padded bra if nature has not immediately granted her the endowments of her rivals.

All of life is suddenly in a turmoil; everything about teens is changing. But because every other young teen in their school is going through the same changes, they are all conscious of their differences. Whenever someone's body grows unusually fast in any area—whether it be in height, facial hair, or the size of one's breasts—you can be sure that someone, somewhere, has noticed and will comment about those changes in public.

Your teen daughter may draw into her shell so no one will single her out as different. Your teenage boy may gravitate toward a small group at school that offers him at least some insulation from the caustic comments of his peers. About this time your kids may even beg you to remove them from school so they can be taught at home, away from prying eyes. On the other hand, you may suddenly become disgustingly old because someone in your family has just turned thirteen.

Many experts believe that thirteen is the toughest teen year for girls. For boys, it is believed that fourteen is often the most difficult year. Wanda Draper, a child development expert at the University of Oklahoma, says, "The early teen years are harder than the middle or late adolescent years because the teen is making a dramatic shift from childhood into youth."[2] The young person experiences so many changes on so many levels (physical, psychological, social, and even intellectual) that it is difficult for him or her to cope with the reality of it all.

Early-Warning Signs

Before a child enters into the adolescent years, he slides into what the experts call the preadolescent period. At this stage, both sexes will increase in physical activity, due in part to an increase in energy and in part to an increase in anxiety about the bodily changes that are imminently approaching. Suddenly there may be a wild growth in

....

[2]Ibid.

appetite, certainly caused by their growth needs, but often also a way to release tension.

Children approaching adolescence begin a fast period of growth, starting at about age ten-and-a-half and continuing until about age fourteen. The peak of this growth will usually come at age twelve; at this peak, a boy's height will have an average increase of up to four inches per year, while a girl's increase will average about three-and-a-quarter inches.

During this stage, the preteen will often have mixed emotions about the opposite sex. The preadolescent feels both eagerness and apprehension. A guy is apt to be uneasy whenever he has to be around girls and may tend to seek the reassuring company of other males. A boy at this age has definitely begun to notice girls; he has also noticed their interest in him—but he may feign indifference, especially if the other boys his age are still making fun of girls. His feelings are usually masked by teasing and aggressive behavior. Through fifth and sixth grades I had a crush on a girl named Sharon. During a sixth-grade square dance, Eric and I both asked her to dance at the same time. Since neither of us would back down, we ended up fighting over her after school. This type of behavior is typical right before the onset of puberty.

During this period a girl is typically aggressive and not very feminine in her pursuit of attention from boys. Some girls find a temporary solution in the compromise of becoming a tomboy, developing an interest in horses, or advancing more quickly toward adolescence in roles that are more feminine, such as ballet dancing.

On one hand there is an intense curiosity for sexual information and that need is often filled by peer discussions, perusing erotic magazines, and the sexual exploration of their own bodies. On the other hand, a preadolescent often has a tendency to forget sexual facts and information recently presented by adults. This may be caused either by his own mixed emotions or by compliance to our cultural double standards.

The Puberty Explosion

You can tell that a boy has hit puberty when he stops walking through puddles and begins to walk around them. Girls at this age lose their faith in fairy tales but suddenly embrace the concept of love. Puberty is that in-between age when a youngster is too old to say something cute but too young to say something truly sensible.

Puberty may seem like an explosion to adults, who invariably notice the onset of the symptoms but don't think much about them until one of their kids suddenly seems to "explode" in front of them. Technically, adolescence really begins at the onset of puberty, but when is that? Puberty comes to a child in stages, similar to the coming of bad weather. When the barometer and thermometer fall and the humidity is rising, we begin to look for other signs of the approaching storm, like an increase in clouds and wind. So it is with puberty; the symptoms are all there if we will just notice them.

Puberty marks the "official" beginning of the onset of hormone activity under the influence of the central nervous system (especially the hypothalamus and the pituitary glands, which stimulate physical growth). As sexual and growth hormones begin to flow, the child's body undergoes dramatic changes that originate even before puberty and last well afterward. In girls, the budding of the breasts and the beginning growth of pubic hair occur on the average between ten and eleven years of age, while menstruation commences between eleven and thirteen. In boys, the pubic hair first appears and the testicles begin to enlarge between twelve and sixteen. Enlargement of the penis and the first ejaculation come between thirteen and seventeen.

In addition to these primary sexual changes, a host of other secondary changes occur, which include size, weight, body proportions, muscular development, strength, coordination, and skill. In some adolescents this will take place over a five- to six-year period, while in others, the transformation will happen rapidly in one or two years. It is interesting that the earlier the growth occurs in either sex, the more rapidly the other associated changes also take place. Usually, the more rapid the growth, the more difficulty the young person will have dealing with it on a psychological level.

One of the big problems adolescents face, especially males, is that different parts of his body grow at different rates. His head, hands, and feet reach their adult size soonest, and the legs grow faster than the torso and have to wait for the rest of the body to catch up. Of course, this produces a gangling appearance and adds to coordination problems and a feeling that he does not quite fit in. Another problem for boys is that their growth spurt often lags behind the girls'. I can remember feeling stupid looking up at several girls when I was in sixth and seventh grades. Of course, a boy's peers are certainly no help; if he hasn't kept up with the others, he'll quickly be labeled "shrimp" or some similar title.

During this period the larynx in both sexes begins to enlarge, and the vocal cords become longer, thicker, and further apart so that the sounds produced are lower in pitch. This is especially noticeable in boys, who may, to their embarrassment, suddenly switch from high to low pitch, as much as an octave. But even worse for a boy is when his voice doesn't keep pace with his body. How humiliating it is for a guy to speak on the telephone and have the operator say, "Yes ma'am." Being confused for a woman has to be the ultimate slam on a male's ego, and it certainly couldn't come at a worse time—when he's in doubt about his involvement in the human race.

The New Sexual Identity

Overnight (or so it seems), the early teenager develops a brand-new sexual identity. Because a male's primary sex organs are external, he often becomes much more concerned by their size and difference from those of his peers. Although the development of female sexual organs is internal and therefore not seen, a girl still faces the onset of menstruation, which signals to her, her parents, and her contemporaries that she has become sexually mature.

The experts refer to secondary sex characteristics as the distinguishing physical features of masculinity and femininity that are less visible to the casual observers. But those traits are hardly secondary to teenagers. The male adolescent is quite concerned about his stature, the slimness of his hips, the size of his muscles, and the breadth of his shoulders. The appearance of body hair is also a great concern to a young teen, especially if his contemporaries have started to develop a slight mustache and he still hasn't generated the slightest peach fuzz. The female, on the other hand, carefully observes (and measures) the development of her breasts and worries that her hips will broaden too much or that she will grow too tall. The advent of cosmetic surgery and the promotion of an ideal of feminine beauty in magazine star-searches and fashion catalogs have greatly contributed to a high standard for women's looks that is seldom attainable by girls of average diet and heredity.

With some adolescents these signs may be confusing. Both the male androgenic and female estrogenic hormones are present in both sexes. Not only can there be great variations between when and how kids of the same age develop (or fail to develop); many body changes are based upon the fluctuation between the balance of these secretions. Boys who acquire a good deal of fat during early adolescence are likely to have a broadening of the hips that will give them a somewhat feminine appearance, and about a third of the boys will have an enlargement of their breasts. Add to this a high voice, and males with such traits are likely to suffer cruel teasing from their peers.

Another phenomenon that comes with these sexual changes is the sudden rejection of intimacy toward a teen's parents. Your cuddly elementary child is transformed from a loving, affectionate "mama's boy" to a teen who won't be caught dead being with his mother, let alone be seen hugging, kissing, or telling her of his love. Peer pressure is only part of this problem. As a teenager develops a whole new body, there is often mutual uneasiness between parents and their offspring. When a father first notices his young daughter's blossoming figure, he may abruptly withdraw his hugs in an attempt to fight off his own sexual feelings. At the very time a girl needs to have a strong relationship with her father, both may be backing off, attempting to sort out their feelings.

The Acne Invasion

At this age the apocrine sweat glands enlarge in both boys and girls, and of course this brings on the increased odor of perspiration. The sebaceous glands also enlarge and become more active; but because the ducts of these glands do not enlarge in proportion to deal with their increased secretions, they often become plugged and are easily infected. The result is acne.

The tremendous increase in hormonal secretions, especially androgens (the male hormones), stimulates the rise of acne in both sexes. There are not too many things that a teenager finds more embarrassing than to feel the oncoming rise of a red pimple. And when a pus-filled whitehead threatens to erupt like Mount St. Helens, it's pretty hard not to be self-conscious about it. At any age, blemishes are a problem, but when they first appear, marring that once-flawless childhood skin, the results to a kid's equilibrium can be devastating. And why does a brand-new crop always reach harvest time right before school pictures are scheduled to be taken? Any kid can feel cursed by God when an enormous red blotch attacks the end of his nose.

The Moody Blues

The early adolescent years are often considered to be the most difficult period of a person's life. These years are marked by emotional instability; a teenager is torn between feeling and acting like a child one moment and the pressure to be a full-grown adult the next. A junior higher is often so spontaneous that, to his parents, he appears to be out of control.

Such moods swings make the junior-high kid difficult to live with. According to one major survey, kids between thirteen and fifteen feel that school life is their number-one problem. This probably has much to do with the teenagers' willingness to make slashing comments to one another. Second on the list was getting along with their own brothers and sisters. Parents should expect peer rivalry to be a major source of pain for their adolescents.[3]

All the physical changes the junior higher goes through certainly contribute to definite alterations in his or her personality. If you remember that the natural drugs a teen's body is now producing are highly likely to throw

....

[3]*The Private Life of the American Teenager,* by Jane Norman (New York: Rawson, Wade, 1981), p. 177.

your kid out of balance, it will be easier for you to offer a little more grace. Knowing why those mood swings are coming should help you to cope with them more creatively, without losing your temper or your sense of humor.

Because of all the physical and emotional changes a junior higher goes through, he becomes a candidate for depression, probably for the first time in his life. In our society, teenage depression runs at epidemic proportions, and because this problem can lead to suicide, it is important to know what signs to look for. Adolescent depression is a complex and subtle phenomenon. Parents and even friends are often stunned when a teenager has reached the point of suicide, never guessing that there was even a problem.

Teenage depression is often so difficult to spot because the symptoms are usually different from those adults experience. Depression in an adult would be strongly felt and communicated, while teenagers seldom show their symptoms and sometimes even mask their moods, in what is called "smiling depression." When teenagers often talk about morbid subjects, such as death or the latest crisis in the world, or constantly harp on their problems, they may be moderately depressed. In the case of smiling depression, teens will put on a good front until they are alone, when their true feelings can be displayed. Other symptoms might include a shortened attention span, poor grades, daydreaming, boredom, and withdrawal.

A teenager may act out his depression by becoming involved in crime, such as breaking and entering, shoplifting, and drug abuse. Depression may be revealed in sexual promiscuity. And of course, the ultimate sign is a suicide attempt. It is important for parents to keep their eyes open to discern any of these various mood or behavior patterns.

What's a Parent to Do?

In discussing the changes your child will go through as he enters puberty, it hasn't been my intention to scare you. But the nice thing about expecting the worst is the fun of being disappointed when your kid doesn't have so many problems. I would rather assume the worst and be pleasantly disappointed than expect the best and be frustrated. If you know what's happening within your child's mind and body, you'll be less likely to make his problems worse and more likely to help him through his own valley of despair.

How should you respond when your child develops all of these symptoms of teenage instability? Be assured that most teenagers will only ride this emotional roller coaster for a few years. Things should eventually level out. If you play your parenting role properly, you can help him make the transition into adulthood with far less trauma (for everyone in your family). Here are some suggestions:

1. Provide a safe environment for your teenagers. It is extremely important for your teens to feel that home is a safe harbor from the storms of life. While they are being verbally assaulted by peers at school, they must feel that Mom and Dad understand them and are on their side. A safe atmosphere is created with love and acceptance. (The next two chapters will discuss these in more detail). Junior-high adolescents are striving to find themselves in a world that seems to be upside down. If they feel you love and accept them—if they feel supported and encouraged—they are much more likely to confide in you and keep from falling victim to peer pressure and rebellion.

Part of providing a safe environment must be the assurance to your teenagers that they are safe from abuse. Sexual and emotional abuse are reaching epidemic levels in our country, and it is important that parents understand the destructive nature that such trauma creates for teen-agers. If you know that you have tendencies toward abus-ing your kids, for everyone's sake, seek counsel. Don't play down the problem—seek help.

2. *Give your teenagers all the encouragement and praise you can.* Nothing encourages us more than being appreci-ated and praised. Now this may sometimes be difficult, especially if you think everything your teenagers do is wrong. But believe me, there are things you can find to praise your teens for if you'll take the time to look for them. Remember, the behavior you praise is much more likely to be the behavior you'll continue to see. So look for everything you are happy with and make that the center of your encouragement. And whenever you have to do any correcting, make certain that you first point out those things you like about what they are doing. Make them want to obey by whetting their desire to please you.

3. *Don't draw attention to the physical changes your adolescents are going through.* Whenever you notice some-thing different about them, it will be easy to point it out with some apparently innocent remark. Don't. It's too easy to make those little complaints about how fast they're growing, especially when you have to replace recently pur-chased clothes. If you're not careful, they may begin to feel like freaks. Instead, look for subtle ways to praise their maturity.

And whatever you do, don't give any lectures about how to get rid of pimples. Your teens already know if they have a problem. Instead, purchase the latest acne remedy and quietly place it where they can find it. No matter what anyone says, there is no foolproof acne remedy, and paren-tal lectures on the subject do far more harm than good.

4. *Keep the lines of communication open.* This may seem like a difficult chore if they are already beginning to break down. But there are definite ways to keep your com-

munication open. (See chapters 8 and 9.) Open communication is the best way to determine what problems your young people are facing. It can help you determine the extent of teens' despondency and let them talk about their fears and frustrations. Communication is even more important because your children are going through so many physical and emotional changes. They will need someone to talk to, and if they feel they can't communicate with you, they will likely turn away from you to their peers. At this age, peer pressure will soon become one of your biggest concerns, so work at keeping good communication open to head off losing your kids to peer dependence.

5. *Don't give your teenagers a vacation from the family.* It's important that a parent not allow adolescents to have a vacation from reality just because they are feeling boxed in or bored. They must lovingly be encouraged to fulfill their part in the family. You must expect them to continue to take part in family activities and meals; they must not be allowed to withdraw into their own world.

SUMMARY OF KEY POINTS

1. To parents, junior-high students can seem almost crazy.
2. There are many varied changes that mark the passage of the elementary years and the beginning of puberty.
3. Early teenagers are often easily embarrassed and have a difficult time coping with the changes going on in their bodies.
4. The preadolescent period (beginning as early as ten-and-a-half years of age) is usually marked by a physical growth and activity spurt. For the first time they take note of the opposite sex.
5. There are many signs of puberty; hormonal activity causes primary body changes to take place, including breast enlargement and the development of pubic hair.

6. Puberty brings on a host of secondary changes, such as size, body proportions, and coordination, that may occur for one or two years or up to six years.

7. The sexual and physical changes are a great concern to teenagers, especially if they lag behind their contemporaries.

8. These sexual changes may have a direct bearing on the teen/parent physical relationships as both back away in embarrassment from earlier hugging and kissing behavior.

9. Skin problems can become a major humiliation for teenagers.

10. Junior highers are often spontaneous and may appear to be out of control to parents; a big problem will be getting along with siblings.

11. Teenage depression is a common problem that parents should watch for and monitor because of the potential seriousness.

12. Parents should work at providing a safe environment, an atmosphere that affirms their teenagers, where communication is kept open and their growth changes are not made into a big issue.

7

DO YOU REALLY LOVE
YOUR KIDS?

*"To love as Christ loves is to let our
love be a practical and not a sentimental thing."* ~Charles Villiers Stanford

....

Do you remember that classic song in *Fiddler on the Roof* between Tevye and his wife? Each asks the other, "Do you love me?" Both spouses reply by introducing the evidence that proves their love (like the fact that she darns his socks). But the question keeps coming back all the louder, *"But do you love me?"* There is only one correct answer to that question, isn't there? *"Yes,* I love you!"

Most of us just assume that our children appreciate our love, perhaps because of all we do for them. But if you were to survey your family and ask for their evaluation of your love on a scale of one to ten, how would you be rated?

My father used to ask, "John, do you love me?" On the surface that sounds like an innocent and well-meaning question, but it always disturbed me. It communicated doubt and made me feel that my father must be unsure of my affection. My reply was always, "Dad, you *know* that I love you."

There probably isn't anything more important for parents to communicate to their teenagers than their love. Everyone needs to know that he or she is loved. I may not like everything my teenagers do, but I will always love them. And they need to know that. Our love should be a copy of the Lord's love for us. His love is unconditional, and he certainly doesn't like everything we do.

I have learned how important it is to say those three simple words: "I love you." I've also found that no one ever seems to tire of hearing that positive affirmation. If you haven't developed the habit of verbally communicating your love, it's probable that your offspring will have doubts about your feelings. This is something they should never have to take for granted; love is the foundation stone of our existence. Without knowing that we are loved, none of us will be able to survive emotionally. I believe that love should be communicated through words as well as deeds.

But I'm just not a demonstrative person, you might be thinking. *It would be impossible for me to verbalize my love for my kids. I'll just have to show it through my deeds.* Certainly our behavior and the things we do for our family are quite important. But often what we do is not motivated by love so much as by our circumstances. For example, a man works because he has to or because he wants to. To expect your teenagers to appreciate that you go to work—as a demonstration of your love—is a bit unrealistic.

Some people are embarrassed to say I love you simply because they rarely say the words. Speaking that phrase may take practice for some people. And if you did not make that statement a part of your everyday language when your children were young, you'll probably struggle to get those words into circulation when they're older. The harder you feel it will be to declare your love, the easier it will be to convince yourself that such affirmations of affection are not necessary for your family. But I would encourage you to *learn* how to communicate your affection openly. Studies have been done that indicate that if we verbalize something, we will be much more likely to follow through with our actions.

Grown-ups can master many things they were not taught as children. Anyone can learn to say loving words, even when it doesn't come naturally. Remember, *love is a verb*. It's something you do—an activity you perform. It is not just a state of being. Love starts in our hearts; it is communicated through our mouths and then finally expressed through our deeds. The things we say or do for our kids don't ultimately prove that we love them, but they certainly go a long way toward confirming that love is present. If you don't have a desire to do loving acts for your kids, you should question why you do not. If we really love our kids, it will come out in our words and our deeds.

Do You Really Love Your Kids?

Of course I love my kids, you might be thinking. *Who doesn't love his own kids?*

Unfortunately, lots of parents don't love their kids. Maybe they won't figure that out until their children enter puberty and begin to mirror back to them their own lack of affection. But when it comes right down to it, many parents just put up with their kids. The fact that you have this book in your hands is a positive sign that you care about your teenagers, but I think it's still a wise idea to question your affections so you can determine the areas in which your love needs to grow stronger.

Why do you love your kids? Most of us have a built-in love that comes the first day we see that incredible bundle of life. But for some, especially fathers, those natural feelings are simply not present. When a friend of mine first saw his newborn daughter through the glass of the hospital nursery window, he said to himself, *I don't love it.* Alex had expected to have an overwhelming affection for the child, but it just wasn't there. He felt detached from that little infant, and he had to work on arousing those parental feelings. Fortunately, he succeeded quite well, but how many men don't? My guess is a lot.

Most mothers usually feel closer to their children than fathers because they have carried the infant for nine months before birth. Afterwards, they have more opportunities to bond with the child through the feeding and nurturing process. But mothers too may find their love waning when the child begins to make additional demands upon their lives. It always amazes me when I hear about a mother who abuses a small infant because she can't get the child to stop crying. I wish I could tell you that such behavior is rare, but it's not.

Because many kids come into this world accidentally, because their presence can stress an already weak marriage, and because children often break a family's meager budget, parents may quickly grow to resent their offspring. Picture a father who didn't want the child, who encouraged his wife to get an abortion. A kid coming into a family in this situation may not know that his birth has been viewed as a calamity, but he will sense it. However faulty the reasons may be behind a parent's coolness, it becomes increasingly difficult for any young person to live in a home devoid of love. I know a high-school girl who is in this type of situation. Whenever she's happy, her father becomes upset with her, telling her she doesn't deserve to be happy. If she leaves her Bible where he can find it, it will be destroyed when she comes home. No matter what she does, he remains agitated and judgmental. Simply put, he does not love her.

The day inevitably comes when most youths grow up and begin to understand how their parents really feel. When they begin to compare the limited love that comes from Mom and Dad to what they perceive coming from their friends and their friends' parents, resentment starts to take over. This attitude aggravates their parents' feelings, and soon everyone is lashing out. As the meager love dwindles and dies, the cycle of iniquity continues on into the next generation, just as Moses predicted it would.

Rebuilding Our Love

If this is your situation, how can you bring the love back into your family? Probably the most important need in reigniting our love is to first admit that it has grown cold. This is harder than it might seem on the surface because we will always find it easier to complain about our teens, perhaps hoping to make ourselves appear more like victims than failures. But that only magnifies the lack of love in the house. It is always easier to blame others, isn't it, than to take responsibility for our own sins?

If your teenager has turned rebellious, it is even easy to blame God. *Lord, why did you let these kids rebel like this? After all I've done for them, they rebel. Lord, it's just not fair! Why couldn't I have gotten good kids like my sister did?*

How incredible, when you think about it, that we could ever blame God, yet that is exactly what we do so often. If you blame God, you'll never be able to deal with your own lack of love for your teenagers. In the book of James (1:13) we're told that no one should blame God for the temptations that come our way because God doesn't tempt anyone. The passage continues on to say, "But each one is tempted when he is carried away and enticed by his *own* lust" (James 1:14). *The Discovery Bible* points out that the emphasis in the original is on the word *own*. In other words, we have no one to blame but ourselves when we succumb to temptation, especially the temptation to stop loving our kids.

As we talked about in an earlier chapter, facing our own transgressions and inadequacies is at the core of our rela-

tionship with God. If we cannot agree with him about our
condition, we're calling him a liar (see 1 John 1:8, 10). Fortunately, once we admit that we do not always love as we
should, *then* we're ready to begin solving the root problems that come into our family relationships as a result of
our failure to love.

We are told, "Above all, keep fervent in your love for
one another, because love covers a multitude of sins"
(1 Peter 4:8). If your teenagers know that you love them,
they will find it much easier to listen to your words than if
they can't feel your love. This is so basic that we must not
miss it. If your teenagers feel that you don't love them,
they will not listen to your correction. Why? Because they
won't be convinced that you are doing it for their benefit.
They will see your actions as cruel and unusual punishment. So the key in how they see your deeds comes back to
how well you've communicated your love to them. And, of
course, with that comes the sixty-four-thousand-dollar
question: Do you have any love to communicate?

Fortunately, God does not leave us to our own devices
after we've admitted the inadequacy of our love. Incredibly, he supplies to us what is missing in our lives. When we
allow God access to our lives, he builds within us *a new
capacity to love.* He injects us with a spiritual love beyond
our own natural love instincts (which may or may not be
present when our kids are born). In other words, when we
become Christians, we also get (at no additional charge)
the ability to love other people with the kind of love God
has for us. What a deal!

But, unfortunately, for many Christians this capability
often remains dormant because they don't even know it's
there. This reminds me of a sophisticated software program for a personal computer. Most users typically use
only a fraction of the power of such a program; they learn
just enough to make the program work, and then they

never learn any more. There is often so much more that the program can do, if they only knew how to make use of it. This is what happens in our relationship with God. When we become Christians, Jesus Christ comes to live within our heart. When he comes in, we get all of the divine character qualities (also called the "fruit of the Spirit" in Galatians 5:22-23). The more we study and pray about these traits as they are presented to us in the Bible, the easier we make it for God to develop them in us. Like all of the rest of these fruits of the Spirit, love is a choice. You and I must *choose* to love, then we must let God teach us *how* to love. No one else can do this for us. We must do it ourselves.

God's Unique Love

When we think of love, many concepts flood into mind. Because this English word means so many things—from the way we feel about our dog to a score in tennis—it is often difficult to pin down exactly what is meant by this term.

The New Testament was written in Greek, a language that is much more precise than English. In the New Testament, the Greek word describing God's love for us is *agape*. God uses this word to indicate a higher level of love than we experience in our everyday lives. *Agape* has a supernatural character to it; it describes God's capacity to love the sinful world, even when it has defied his wishes. It is the unconditional, unending love God has for us even though we don't deserve it. This is the word used to describe that fruit of the Spirit that God injects into us when we become Christians.

If we are going to understand what this love is all about, we can't compare it to anything we know from our own experience. It is unlike our natural love, which usually has strings attached it. We say, "I'll love you *if. . . .*" But God's love is unconditional. He keeps loving us despite the fact that we keep disobeying him. Because this love comes from God, it is supernatural, just like he is. Its capacity goes beyond our ability to fully understand or comprehend it. In fact, this love cannot be used independently of God. He must exercise this love through us, so that we become pipelines (the Bible uses the term "vessels") through which his love flows. Of course, that's exactly what God wants us to do—to depend upon him to provide us with the love we need to love everyone with whom we come in contact, especially the members of our own family.

An example of this is found in *The Hiding Place.* Corrie ten Boom and her Dutch family suffered unimaginable torture at the hands of the Nazis. But after the war, she forced herself to travel back into Germany to speak in a church. Imagine her emotions when one of the very SS men who had stood guard over them and perpetrated the suffering she and her sister had experienced in Ravensbrück walked up to her after the service.

"How grateful I am for your message, fraülein," he said. "To think that, as you say, he has washed my sins away!"

As he stuck out his hand to shake hers, she found herself frozen and unwilling to forgive him. She could not raise her hand; she couldn't even smile. But a quick, silent prayer to Jesus suddenly transformed her heart. And then she felt an overwhelming love suddenly flowing through her.

Every parent could certainly use such a love—a love so powerful it looks beyond the child's behavior and into his soul with the eyes of God. Such a pure love seeks the best for the one being loved. And not only does it change the one loved, it changes the lover as well, as the very power of God flows through us and gives us a bigger frame of reference toward those in our life. How can we come into contact with the flow of God's love and not be transformed?

The Love Chapter

The classic passage in the Bible explaining this love is 1 Corinthians 13. The first thing we notice (see 13:1-3) is that love is contrasted with other Christian works, such as having faith to move mountains, giving our possessions to the poor, or suffering a martyr's death. But then we're told that if we do all of these great works without love, the impact is worthless.

The nice things we do for our children are not as important as the attitude and the power (God's power) in which we do them. Teenagers are certainly capable of looking right past our good intentions to the true motives behind our deeds. If the reason we want our kids to behave is so that *we* will look good, they'll pick up on that fact. Even if we were to die for our kids, God says that such a deed won't count for much if it isn't motivated by his supernatural love flowing through us.

This passage in Corinthians goes on to provide what amounts to a definition of how this supernatural love will manifest itself when it flows through our lives (13:4-8).

Love is patient (or long-suffering). Oh, how necessary this character quality will be when your squirmy junior higher is bouncing off the walls. Long-suffering, some have said, literally means *to choose to suffer long.* Now that's a radical concept, because no one in his or her right mind wants to suffer. But if you have teenagers in your home—I hate to say this—you have already made the decision to suffer. (Is he kidding?) So you might as well get "spiritual credit" for that by learning how to let God's love increase your ability to suffer for the sake of righteousness. I'm not talking about some masochistic ritual in which you are supposed to torture yourself; this is suffering by not reacting to your teenager's weaknesses so that you can help him change his behavior.

I've heard messages from well-meaning preachers who have said, "Don't ever pray for patience, because the Bible tells us 'tribulation works patience.'" That's ridiculous. Do you think that God is going to single you out for more problems just because you want patience? No way. You already have enough tribulation in your life (*especially* if you have a teenager). What you need is the patience to deal with the problems you already have. And that is exactly what God gives us through *agape* love. Take advantage of it. When you feel yourself fraying around the edges, tell God how you feel and ask him to be lovingly patient through your mouth. Then when he tells you what to say, make certain you yield to that loving impulse.

Love is kind. How easy it is to be unkind to your teenagers when they do something you consider stupid or silly. But remember, their peers are already looking for ways to make fun of them; the last thing they need is for their parents to be unkind. Ask God to show you ways you can be kind to your kids. Most of us have difficulty thinking up ways of being kind to our kids. If you had to do five kind things for them—what would they be? You could pick up after them (but would you be encouraging their irresponsibility?). You could give them something (but would they see that as an attempt to buy their love?). I'm convinced that the best thing you can do for them is to give your time and interest. Those little signs of affection, those words of praise, and those offers to do things with them are so important. If the love level with your teens is low, you may have to work at finding kind things to do that *they* will feel good about. Let *your teens* plan the next vacation; let them have a say in things you know will mean a lot to them.

Love is not jealous. Beginning with this phrase, it is interesting to note that many of the coming parts of love's definition are spoken in the negative; we're told what love *is not* instead of what love *is*. Why? I think the reason God does this is that we have so little experience with this kind of love that he decided to teach us by contrasting the negative emotions we're all familiar with.

It might seem impossible for parents ever to be jealous of their teenagers, but do you remember the true news story (and later the TV movie) about the mother who wanted to murder another girl so her teenage daughter could succeed as a cheerleader? That's jealousy gone wild. Many parents try to live out their lives through their teenagers (hopefully not in such bizarre ways). Because they want their kids to achieve what they were unable to accomplish in school, they drive their adolescents to satisfy their own private agendas.

Jealousy has been defined as the fear of being replaced by someone else. Often parents have a difficult time when their teenagers begin to grow up and get interested in outside activities and people. Suddenly the parents may feel unnecessary and unwanted. We must be careful that we do not find ourselves exhibiting jealousy over something that is inevitable. Our kids must be given the freedom to grow up and move away.

Love does not brag. I've always hated those bumper stickers that say: "Proud Parent of an Honor Roll Student." You've probably seen them. Over the years we've had our kids at Christian schools filled with overachievers, and it's been difficult for them to achieve such stature—*until this year!* (Oops! Was I just bragging?) We certainly have the desire to see our kids succeed. But have you ever noticed that bragging isn't any fun if everyone else manages the same accomplishments? Bragging is enjoyable precisely because it makes us feel better than the next fellow—and that, I'm afraid, is just another form of pride. When we display such an attitude, we can end up pushing our kids beyond what is necessary or prudent. We must make certain that we appreciate our kids' accomplishments for their own sake, not for how good they make us look.

Love is not arrogant. Arrogance is taking responsibility for something that has never been given to us. Most of us resent it when someone elects himself to be our boss. Although God has given you responsibility over your children, it is important to recognize at what point that responsibility ends. You are not ultimately responsible for their eternal destiny. You are not the one who will stand in judgment over them. Most of us are too sinful to do a good imitation of God—and besides, the position is already filled. It is important for parents to keep a sense of reserve toward the authority delegated to them. Don't pontificate. You can't determine your adolescents' future. Shape and guide them, but don't try to control their every move. Leave room for God to act independent of you.

Love does not act unbecomingly. Are you rude to your own children? If they're now rude toward you, it could be an echo of the way you've treated them. Never shoot at a teenager's basic self-worth. Even in the way you discipline him, it is important to focus on the offense instead of pointing at the offender. You don't want to exasperate your children. Statements like "You're *always* doing that" can be self-fulfilling prophecies. Even if your teens seem incorrigible, treat them like you would like to be treated—with respect and dignity.

Love does not seek its own. God never does anything for us that isn't in our best interests. Unfortunately, we human beings fall far short of that standard with our own offspring. Usually we are more motivated by how their behavior irritates us than by how they might be hurting themselves. But if we can look at our teenagers through God's eyes, we will be much more willing to enter into the shaping process our teenagers need to help improve their character. Love creates in us the desire to attend the school open house, or to go watch the play they're in, or to spend those hours helping with their homework. Instead of seeking our own comfort, love motivates us to perform those activities that are in our teens' best interests.

Love is not provoked. Ouch! Now if ever a character quality was written for parents of teenagers, this is it! How easily we are provoked by the dumb things our kids say and do. Yet God says love does not allow itself the freedom to react. Instead, we need to take the time to ponder our response. If we *react* instead of *respond,* we can count on having problems. In most cases, parents react because they look at a teenager's offense from their own perspective. Parents should focus upon an adolescent's needs. Love doesn't let itself be irritable or touchy. Jesus showed us how he handles major provocations. In fact, we're told that we should learn to suffer just like he did (1 Peter 2:19-23), but few people are capable of taking such abuse. It is my opinion that what God wants us to do is to let Jesus suffer *through us.* So the next time your teenager causes the hair on the back of your neck to stand on end, ask the Lord to do the suffering for you.

Love does not take into account a wrong suffered. Have your children done things that have alienated you? Many parents have lost respect for a particular teenager because of what he or she has done. Our brains often act like a computer; whenever any new offense takes place, our adolescent's "file" pops up and we are immediately reminded of the many past violations. It is virtually impossible for a young person to dig himself out of such a hole. God tells us not to do that to those who love us. We must not lock in on the wrongs (real or imagined) that a kid does in an attempt to make him wallow in it. Jesus went so far as to say that if we cannot forgive those who have transgressed against us, our Father will not forgive our transgressions (Matthew 6:14-15). That means our very salvation is dependent upon our forgiving our children's offenses and not storing them up in our brain. If you have some offenses stored away, I would highly recommend that you deal with them.

Love does not rejoice in unrighteousness. I believe this means that we are never happy when bad things happen to our children, even if we warned them. Because we want what is best for them, we will not rejoice whenever they resist God's will. This means that you should not look the other way if your adolescent desires to do something that is wrong. Sometimes *agape* love will make us unpopular in the short run. But we must not be worried about winning popularity contests. We have greater concerns; we cannot approve of behavior we know is against God's will.

Love rejoices with the truth. We rejoice with the truth even when that is not what we would like to hear. Ephesians 4:15 tells us to speak "the truth in love." Truth that doesn't come from a loving heart can be like a cudgel across a person's head. We must be so in favor of the truth that we support it at all times because we know it is in our child's best interests.

Love bears all things, believes all things, hopes all things, and endures all things. To bear up under injustices against us, to believe our children are capable of the best, to never lose hope for them (no matter how far away they might stray), and to endure all that they put us through is what *agape* love is prepared to do. Certainly this is not natural or normal; only God can enable us to bear up like this. When Jesus went to the cross, he certainly acted out all of the above characteristics for us. Now he wants to do that through us. This is a tall order, but because he is up to it, we are up to it.

Love never fails. Again, only God never fails. That is why we must make certain that we depend upon him to let his love flow through us. No matter how we might want to give up on a teenager, God never does. That lets us know that we will always have resources from which to draw. Whenever we desire to give up in this fight with our flesh, we must lean back on Christ, tapping into his abundant resources.

We all need God's *agape* love to survive in this fast-paced world. But even more, we need it to survive the teenage zone. To let God's love flow through us to change our teenagers, it is imperative that we work at learning how God thinks and what he wants us to do. I believe the purpose of *agape* love is to motivate us to be committed to developing God's character in our lives and to show us that love is by far the best way to deal with our teenagers.

SUMMARY OF KEY POINTS

1. We must create a family atmosphere in which all know that they are loved, regardless of their behavior.
2. Love is best communicated with both words and deeds.
3. Teens won't see the fact that their parents hold down jobs as an expression of their love; they need something more tangible.
4. If we have a difficult time loving people, we inevitably will have a difficult time loving God.
5. God gives Christians a special kind of love called *agape*, with which we should love our offspring.
6. God's love changes us and causes us to love our children in a new, supernatural way.

7. God tells us what love *is not* because we're more familiar with what it isn't than what it is.
8. Parental *agape* chooses to suffer for the sake of its teenagers in order to heal them.
9. *Agape* love will cause a parent not to react to his teenagers, but to respond to them.
10. Love does not focus on the wrongs of a teen or make him wallow in them.
11. God's love never fails; parental love for children should be just as everlasting.

8

BUILDING YOUR "TRUST ACCOUNT"

"To be trusted is a greater compliment than to be loved." ~James MacDonald

....

One of the most important words in the Bible is *faith*. It is the vehicle God uses to establish a relationship with us. That term is so important because it opens us up to God; if we do not have faith in him, we cannot begin to please him. Martin Luther was so impressed by Romans 1:17, which says, "The righteous man shall live by faith," that he wrote in the margin of his Bible, "Plus *nothing.*"

Now if faith is the beginning of our relationship with God, we can also be certain that it is the foundation of our relationship with everyone else. *Faith* is another word for *trust*. Whether or not you trust someone is ultimately a key element in your desire to build a union with them.

Has Our Relationship Broken Down?

A child passing through puberty suddenly begins to see things he has never seen before. No longer does he blindly accept everything his parents tell him. Perhaps for the first time in his life he begins to question their judgment and love. If he doubts them, he will stop trusting. If he stops trusting, he will stop listening. And from there, everything goes from bad to worse.

If you don't trust someone, and they're trying to talk to

you, how do you listen? You will probably be skeptical, detached, and maybe even a little hostile. Most adults know how to camouflage such feelings, but that doesn't change what goes on inside our head. If we don't trust someone, we simply can't listen attentively to him, no matter how right and true his statements may be. This is simply human nature. Now put that shoe on the other foot. If your teenage son or daughter is finding it difficult to listen to you, it could very well be that the reason for his inability to hear is that he no longer trusts you. In a family setting, trust is a long-term proposition. It is built (or torn down) over the years.

> *If a teenager lives with:*
> criticism, he will learn to condemn;
> yelling, he will learn to cringe;
> ridicule, he will learn to be shy;
> condemnation, he will learn to feel guilty;
> hostility, he will learn to fight.
>
> *But if a teenager lives with:*
> tolerance, he will learn to be patient;
> encouragement, he will learn confidence;
> praise, he will learn to appreciate;
> fairness, he will learn justice;
> security, he will learn to have faith;
> approval, he will learn to like himself;
> acceptance, he will find love in this world.

Every emotion seems to reproduce after its own kind. When you give love, you will receive love in return. If you become angry, you will provoke your teenager to anger. If you are constantly uptight, you will inevitably produce stressed-out kids. Hostility produces hostility; hatred arouses hatred; patience begets patience. So ask yourself what kind of emotional lessons you are teaching your children.

The Invisible "Trust Account"

Imagine that every person in your family has an invisible emotional account with you. Let's call this a "trust account." Every time you treat someone well, you make a deposit into that account, improving your relationship. But every time you treat someone poorly, you make a withdrawal. Over the years, parents are used to telling their children what they must do: "Take out the trash." "Clean up your room." "Stop complaining." But we also make many statements that are really more like judgment calls: "Go away; can't you see I'm busy?" "You're such a slob." "Wipe that look off your face." We must realize that such belittling words become withdrawals in our trust account with them.

Suppose I see a problem with one of my teens. My stomach tenses and I prepare for battle. I'm not thinking about our long-term relationship; I'm thinking only about what he's doing that I don't like. So I demand obedience. I use my superior size and authority to intimidate or threaten. And I win. I receive outward obedience, but in the process I drive my kid's feelings underground. In such a situation, I really haven't solved anything. The rebellion that I have suppressed will only return later, perhaps in an uglier way.

Every person has different ideas of what constitutes a withdrawal, but you can be certain most teenagers resent the demeaning words with which they have grown up. When a teenager feels that his relationship with you has reached the point of bankruptcy, getting him to trust you again will take a lot of effort. He's seen enough. The mere sound of your "good advice" will cause him suddenly to lapse into a catatonic state resembling death. A family that is experiencing a generation gap is really having a crisis in trust.

Building Up Your Account

In any family, relationships are forged over a long span of time and are susceptible to misunderstandings and wounded feelings. Bringing trust back into your teenager's account is not always an easy task, but reestablishing this trust is vitally important.

Think for a moment how God builds our faith in him. He is so utterly consistent and faithful it's hard not to trust in him. He means what he says and says what he means. He has written down for us, in his Word, exactly what he expects of us. He understands and accepts us, even when we don't deserve it. And of course, he wins us because he was willing to make the ultimate sacrifice of himself on our behalf. The way God deals with us is a pattern we can use to build back our trust with our teenagers. Let's look at some ways we can do this:

1. Seek to understand your teenagers.

One of the biggest struggles that most of us face is that of feeling misunderstood. How frustrating it is when no one really understands what we're trying to do. Few things hurt worse than having our motives misjudged. Many teenagers find themselves feeling misinterpreted by their parents. One of the greatest commitments you can make toward building your trust account with them is to learn to listen carefully so you can truly understand what it is your teenagers are saying. Because this has to be one of the hardest lessons for any person to learn, the next chapter is devoted to this vital subject of communication.

2. Be interested in what appeals to your teenager.

Now I'm not saying that you should try to be one of the boys (so to speak), but it is important to show an interest in what excites them. Make time to let them talk to you about their concerns.

When I was in junior high, I became extremely interested in newspapers and journalism. When I was about to sign up for print shop, my father told me, "Don't take print shop. I took it and hated it. Take electronics; it's much better." But my Dad and I had different interests. What was right for him wasn't right for me. I took three-and-a-half years of print shop and loved it. I only wished my father had been more supportive of my interests.

I know of a girl who fell in love with a boy who was an engineering student. When he gave her an architectural book that had greatly influenced him, it was his way of saying, "You mean a lot to me." And you know what? Even though she found the book extremely dull reading, she was interested in it anyway—because she was interested in him. If you love someone, you find a way to get interested in that person's passions.

When my daughter Rebecca started to like country music, I nearly choked. (I've never liked country music.) But I realized she was serious about developing her own tastes, and I knew it was important for me to respect her opinions. Because I did, we were able to have some good conversations on the subject without having to protect our own emotional landscape. Whenever I heard a singer that had something to say, I could comment positively about him. (Just a few weeks ago, Rebecca told me that she had stopped listening to country music because many of the words had begun to offend her—but that was her decision, not mine.)

Every teenager has a few subjects about which he or she would like to talk. Most males want to converse about sports, a hobby, cars, or some girl. Girls will want to relay what's going on with their friends, their music, and the boy of their dreams. If you aren't interested in talking to them about their subjects, you can be certain that they will find others who are. You may find much of what interests your teenagers to be boring stuff. Yet it is worth becoming involved in because such conversations, if they are done right, will certainly please your teens and make big deposits in your account. And remember, when your kids have problems, it is much more likely that they'll come to you if they feel you are approachable.

3. Pay attention to those little kindnesses.

Most parents have a tendency to take their teenagers for granted (even more than they do their spouses). If your trust account is overdrawn, this is certainly an area where you can make some nice deposits. Sometimes it's much easier to make grand statements or grandiose gifts, but true trust is built in the consistency of little things. Compliments, the gift of a flower, or the touch of a hand on a shoulder will often reap greater long-term dividends than big-ticket gifts. Little kindnesses make life so much more meaningful; they show we care. It's wise to look for occasional little gifts that reveal you are thinking about your kids. It is the unexpected and truly thoughtful surprise that usually creates the nicest deposits.

When my oldest daughter was thirteen and we were having a difficult time getting along, I decided to take her out for a night on the town in an attempt to build back our relationship. We ate at her choice of fast-food places and then went shopping for clothes. Can you imagine any teenage girl in her right mind not wanting to shop for clothes? Neither can I. But our relationship was so strained that she really wasn't certain going shopping with me was a good idea. I'm sure part of her fear was that old dad would make her buy something that was horrendously out of style or too grown-up for her tastes. Now I hate to go shopping, *especially* for clothes, so for me this was a big sacrifice. But I couldn't command my daughter to have fun; I had to work at letting her make her own decisions about the clothes she bought. I had to enjoy letting her do what she wanted to do and keep most of my opinions to myself. That day certainly helped our relationship and moved us in the right direction.

4. Be a person of your word; keep your commitments.

If you promise your employer that you will have some job done by a specific time, you will make certain that it gets done as promised. But for some reason, perhaps because we think we can get away with being inconsistent with our family, our commitments to them often seem much less binding. In reality, they should be *more* binding; employers come and go, but our family will always be our family. When we make a commitment to our teenagers, we should move heaven and earth to fulfill it. We all hate it when people don't come through on their promises to us. The last thing you want to have your own kids believe is that you are not a person of your word. If you promise to take them somewhere—do it. If you promise to do something with them—follow through.

Many fathers have allowed some ministry to sidetrack them from commitments to their family. I know of one pastor who was interrupted in the middle of the evening he had set aside for his family by an urgent call from someone in the midst of domestic strife. He told the caller, "I'm sorry, but I can't come. If I preempt my family time for you, it is only a matter of time before I'll find myself in your situation. I'll have to see you tomorrow." What a wise decision. By showing his family they were more important than another family's emergency, he made great deposits in everyone's trust accounts, including his wife's.

Dag Hammarskjöld, the former secretary-general of the United Nations, made an interesting statement that I find challenging: "It is more noble to give yourself completely to one individual than to labor diligently for the salvation of the masses." How true. As a Christian, you will never have any higher priority than those God has personally entrusted to you. And God has called you to your family before any ministry to the outside world. If you fail here, you will also fail in whatever ministry you might have "out there."

So keep your commitments to your teenagers. Be a person of your word, and it will make large deposits in your teenager's trust account. If you are not used to being a person of your word, you may find that you will have to make less commitments. But your word should always be good for something. No matter what it takes—or what it costs—follow through on your promises.

5. Clarify expectations and work at meeting them.

This is a major problem in many families and one to which parents are usually oblivious. So often parents have expectations they have not communicated to their children. They just assume their children know what they want.

I know of a father who had a difficult time clarifying his expectations. One night at the dinner table he gazed across at his son and commanded: "Pass it." The family had been eating for several minutes, and he obviously wanted a refill of some item.

"Pass what?" the son asked.

"You should be able to tell," was the father's only reply.

The son had no idea what his dad wanted. Like everyone else at the table, he had been too busy cleaning his own plate to anticipate what it was his father might be running short of. The son sensed this was another opportunity for his father to condemn him. The exchange ended in an argument that made a deep withdrawal in the father's trust account. If we have some imaginary line over which our teenagers cannot cross, the least we can do is explain where it is and why we have drawn it. Few things are as frustrating for a teenager as trying to please a parent and not knowing how to do it.

Talk about what you expect from your kids. Tell them if you want them to follow the Lord with their whole hearts. Verbalize to them if it is your desire for them to remain chaste. And don't tell them these things once; talk about your concerns on a regular basis. Keep the lines of communication open so that they will understand how important your concerns are.

Also, put some effort into meeting the expectations your kids have. Find out what their desires are and discuss with them how their expectations can realistically be met. Usually teenagers' expectations are based on the commitments you have made to them. Of course you don't want to let them manipulate you with their desires, but you also don't want to disappoint them in areas where you have built up expectations.

"You remember I'm going to spend the night with Stephanie," a daughter states.

"When did we decide that?" I ask.

"You said, 'If you get your homework done,' I could go."

"Wait a minute. That's not what I said. I said: 'Maybe, if you get your homework done, you can go. We'll talk about it later.' And we haven't talked about it yet. So let's talk."

Because teenagers often read into what we say and come up with their own interpretations, it is important to keep the air clear by clarifying everyone's expectations. It is much more likely that everyone will be kept happy if things are talked out.

6. Attempt to treat everyone by the same standards.

I was a second-born child, two years younger than my sister. People who study birth order claim that most second-born children work harder at trying to be accepted. I certainly felt that my older sibling was the favored child and became absolutely convinced she got away with murder simply because she was a girl.

Partially because of my experiences growing up, I became committed to the idea of attempting to treat my kids equally. But, let me tell you from experience that this is difficult to do. Parents often have favorites. It would be my guess that the most compliant child will get the golden spoon. But just because a child seems to do what we want, this is no real gauge of what's going on inside his head. Remember the Prodigal Son? He decided to venture out on his own and lost his inheritance as a result of his foolishness. It would appear that he was the least obedient of his father's two sons, but the older brother revealed his intolerance once the prodigal returned home. Even though the firstborn outwardly obeyed, inwardly he was not as close to his father as the prodigal ended up being. If we favor one child over another because of behavior, we may discover that we are fooling ourselves. Often, the more obedient children appear to be, the easier it is for them to hide their true feelings. At least with openly defiant teenagers, you know what's on their minds.

I've tried to be fair in my dealings with my daughters, but inevitably I have heard them make comparisons. "That's not fair; you let her do that when she was my age." Or, "When I was her age, you wouldn't let me do that!"

Over the years, parents often slide on their standards. But believe me, when the next child comes up, the older siblings will remember in detail the stricter code that was imposed upon them. Some rules lend themselves toward complete consistency—others do not. We have to be willing to change if they point out our inconsistencies. And if we have decided to change the rules, we'd better have a good reason for it. I've said, "I'm treating you differently because you are different. What was good for your sister won't necessarily be good for you. Because your needs are unique, I cannot approach you with all the same rules." But this should be the exception.

We're talking about the need for integrity. Having integrity causes parents to do what is consistent, even if they would rather not do so. The opposite of this is expedient behavior, which is doing what will bring the fastest short-term reward. In the end, gains from expedient behavior may be lost. Maintaining integrity with your kids will produce long-range deposits that cannot be achieved any other way.

7. Be willing to acknowledge your inconsistencies and ask for forgiveness.

Everyone makes mistakes. Your teenagers certainly know this is true for their parents. But if you are unwilling to admit your errors and ask for their forgiveness, your trust account will go down immeasurably. This is often difficult for parents because they tend to view their children as being below them. To admit a flaw seems a little like an umpire changing his decision in the middle of a ball game. It just isn't done. But if you don't do it, you'll only be creating a cardboard image of yourself. Everyone sins. Everyone says wrong things from time to time. Even the Bible tells us to confess our faults to one another (James 5:16).

Your kids will easily forgive mistakes of the mind or failures of judgment, but they will have a harder time forgiving errors of the heart. If your motives are bad or your pride causes you to cover up your mistakes, realize that your kids will have a difficult time responding positively to you. Those sins cut to the heart of the problem and reveal that you *intended* to hurt them or were unwilling to take any of the blame for your actions. Trust is difficult to achieve when someone premeditatedly hurts you. But when you ask for a teenager's forgiveness, it makes for a powerful deposit and erases the previous withdrawal you caused by the original offense. But there's a right and a wrong way to do this.

If a deep division has developed between you and your teenager, you may have to sit down and take care of your 10 percent of the problem. I say 10 percent because most of us are certain that 90 percent of the problem belongs to the other person. But from the other's point of view, you are 90 percent at fault. Forgiveness and healing can usually only come when one of the two factions opens the door and admits his own blame.

As a kid I remember telling my father I was sorry for something I did. He replied, "Why are you sorry? You're such a sorry person." I also remember apologizing to him, and he would say to me, "You're always apologizing. Don't be so apologetic. *Change!*" I wanted to change, but because I didn't know how to get an emotional release from his expectations, it seemed we were destined to stay on a bad footing. The situation between my father and me was never really dealt with until after I was married. One afternoon, I determined to change our situation. I shaved off my beard, put the portable television I had borrowed from my parents in the car, checked out the meager savings my wife and I had managed to accumulate, and drove over to my parents' house. There, with mixed emotions, I sat down in front of my father, mentally preparing for the worst. Although, from my perspective, my father had perhaps "caused" much of my rebellion, I was a Christian and he was not. I therefore knew that if he was ever going to come to the Lord, I had to get out of the way. I could see now that he would never come to Christ as long as he didn't think much of my Christianity.

"Dad, I've come to ask for your forgiveness for my lack of love toward you," I said. I admitted that I had been self righteous, rebellious, and disobedient. As I listed all the basic offenses I could think of, my mind told me that I was wasting my time. The gulf between us was just too great. He never talked to me; he just grunted whenever my wife and I came over to the house.

"It's not that easy, John," he said. "I remember when you sat right there in that same chair and said to me—" He then repeated my exact words from an incident in the past that had remained pretty fresh in his mind.

"I know, Dad. You're exactly right. And that's why I've come to ask you to forgive me. I was very unloving when I said that, and I don't want to be that way anymore. So that's why I've come."

"But it's not that easy, John. You owe me some money."

I had withdrawn all the money we had in the bank, even though it wasn't enough to cover my debt to him, but I wanted him to see that I meant business. I wanted to take care of any outstanding problem between the two of us. But this wasn't easy for him. From the time we first sat down, an hour and a half passed before he was finally willing to utter the words I had come to hear: "I forgive you." Those words released both of us so that we could finally begin to enjoy a real relationship together.

That day I made a powerful deposit into his trust account. As a result of that encounter, my father started to go to church and eventually resurrected his childhood commitment to Christ (which I had never even known about).

The results of that afternoon were certainly worth all of
the pain that goes with admitting you're at fault. Although
I instigated the reconciliation as the son, not the parent, I
have also done this with my own children, as they have
done with me. What is important is that one person, prefer-
ably you, take the first step.

When a parent initiates this process of asking for forgiveness, a teenager will often admit his part in the problem
and also ask for forgiveness. My wife and I have attempted
to let this become a part of our relationship with our teenagers so we can regularly solve our differences. When I'm
willing to admit to my kids that old Dad has blown it, you
can be certain that they are much more willing to come
clean with their part of a problem. Just a few days ago my
daughter reacted to something I said in the morning. After
thinking about it all day at school, she came home and
asked me to forgive her. What a blessing when your kids
are not afraid to admit their faults and ask for forgiveness!
But that only happens if you are willing to start the ball
rolling by giving them the example they need to see.

Several important guidelines might help you here. First,
if you ask for forgiveness, don't say, "I've made some mistakes, *but so have you!*" That will only push the other person away. Second, don't apologize or say that you're sorry.
That approach doesn't give the other person the opportunity to release you from their bitterness. Third, don't item-
ize specific sins. Instead, summarize your basic offenses so
that you won't resurrect past sins. Finally, press for forgiveness no matter what is brought up. Both people need to
hear those words, "I forgive you."

You should know that if your offenses toward your teenagers have been great enough, they may refuse to forgive
you. This is certainly painful, especially after you have
humbled yourself in front of them. But this only under-
scores the depth of your crimes. (Whatever you do, don't

get mad if they refuse to forgive; that will only "prove" that you haven't really changed.) Another reason your teenagers might not want to forgive you is because they know if they do, they will have to take care of their own sins. If they're unprepared to do that, you may have to be patient with them. (And remember, love chooses to suffer long.) Also, keep in mind that hearing a parent repeatedly asking for forgiveness for the same offenses is difficult for any teenager. Such apologies are interpreted as insincere because the same offenses continue as before. If this is your situation, your adolescent will wonder why you don't change your behavior and will therefore have a much harder time absolving you.

All of the seven suggestions above should help you build up your trust account with your teenagers, but if you have become estranged from them, asking for forgiveness may be mandatory before the others become truly effective. Remember that trust can't be won overnight if it has been lost over the years. There are no quick fixes when it comes to building long-term relationships. It takes time and work and consistency to establish with them that you really do care about their feelings. Your focus should be to make consistent deposits with fewer withdrawals.

SUMMARY OF KEY POINTS

1. Faith or trust is a key character quality on which any relationship is built.
2. If a person doesn't trust someone, he will find it difficult to have a relationship with him.
3. Everyone has, inside his head, an invisible "trust account" for other people.
4. Deposits are made in people's trust accounts when we

treat them nicely; poor treatment causes withdrawals to be made.

5. A relationship breaks down when our account gets overdrawn.

6. We can build up our account by seeking to understand our teenager.

7. It is important to show an interest in what concerns your teenager.

8. Trust is built with those little kindnesses that show parents really care.

9. When parents keep their commitments with their teen, it builds trust.

10. Trust is also kept by clearly communicating our expectations.

11. Treating everyone by the same standards builds trust.

12. Acknowledging parental inconsistencies and asking for forgiveness increases trust.

9

"WHY CAN'T HE HEAR ME?"

"The most successful parents are those who have the skill to get behind the eyes of the child, seeing what he sees, thinking what he thinks, feeling what he feels." ~James Dobson

Have you noticed that the communication level changed when your kid hit adolescence? Why is it that your once-talkative child has reduced his answers to a series of noncommittal, monosyllabic grunts? And if he does actually speak, you'll probably only hear a few intelligible words. A truly erudite teenager seems to have at least eight stock answers at his disposal: "Huh," "Maybe," "I dunno," "I forget," "Nope," "Yeah," "It's not my fault," and "Who—me?"

Home seems to be one place where you can say anything you want—because nobody is going to pay any attention to you anyway. Isn't that the problem? Your kids don't seem to be listening to you anymore? Developing communication with a non-talking teenager can be an art form. If he is doing his best to say nothing, you have to do your best to keep from exploding. The result is the beginning of a generation gap of major-league proportions.

How do you respond to this wall of silence? Mothers often back off and attempt to be a little more chatty, hoping somehow for a breakthrough. Fathers, on the other hand, usually opt for the direct approach—make the kid sit there until he gives you some "straight answers." Either way, things don't look too promising.

Good communication is essential in any good relationship. But often, parents (especially fathers) assume that if teens aren't talking, everything must be OK. But just because no one is complaining does not mean that there aren't problems under the surface, like weeds breeding underneath black plastic in the garden. If one or both sides fail to talk, communication isn't happening. Where there is no talking, relationships are weak.

The less you are able to communicate with your kids, the less influence you have over them. And it is precisely during the teenage years that our influence begins to wane as our kids are dramatically impacted by outsiders—especially their peers. (We'll discuss peer pressure at length in the next chapter.) It is important that you maintain good communication with your teens if you ever hope to keep your influence on a high level.

The Importance of Credibility

The early Greeks developed a philosophy of communication that is still taught in speech classes today. It can be summed up in three sequentially arranged words: *ethos, pathos,* and *logos.* The first rule of being able to communicate effectively is how we are viewed by our audience. This is *ethos*—our personal credibility. The first half of this book has been spent discussing parental character growth concepts, precisely because it is this that will cause your kids to look up to you. If your character is great, but your kids don't think so, you've got a problem. If your teenager views you as caring more for yourself, or thinks that you hate him, or if he feels you are unloving, your message will be shot down before it even passes your lips. Therefore, recreating your image in his eyes is of prime importance to reopening the lines of communication.

In the last chapter we discussed the importance of building up your trust account with your adolescent children. This is one of the most important issues in effective communication. If your kids don't trust you, they will not *be able* to listen to what you have to say.

The next time you have a parent-teen conversation, try to watch the impact of your words on your adolescent. Try to look at what you're saying from *his* point of view. Is he construing your words as deposits or withdrawals? Too often we make emotional withdrawals, not because we intend to be hurtful, but because we do not realize the impact of our words. If he reacts negatively to the simplest of input, you can guess that you have an overdrawn trust account. If so, it might be good to reread the last chapter and work on building back his trust. Your goal is not just to develop some artificial techniques designed to manipulate your kid; your goal is to care enough about him to see and feel things from his point of view. Because you love him, you want to build your relationship with him so that you can help him become a godly person.

Think about how other people have inspired you over the years. Perhaps you have been impacted by your pastor, your parents, a coach, or even a close friend. When you're around that person, you have such faith in his or her integrity and character that it inspires you to want to be a better person. That's the way you want to inspire your children. You want to live your life in such a way that they continue to look up to you (even after they have grown up and can see your sin more plainly). You do this, not by being perfect, but by living as consistently (with God's help) as you can. I've known many parents who were able to maintain their children's love and respect. And by God's grace, I am endeavoring to be another one who has succeeded in inspiring my kids to live a godly life.

Do You Really Understand Your Kid?

This brings us to the second rule of communication—being able to empathize with our kids and feel what they feel. The Greeks called this *pathos*. To step inside another person's head and feel what is happening there is difficult for most people. But this is a definite aid to effective communication.

Keep in mind that communication is based upon more than just words. Under pressure, most teenagers can fake the answers they know their parents want to hear. Words are tools to be used in getting a message across, but their mere use does not mean a real connection is taking place. I once worked with an assistant pastor who had an uncanny ability to hear beyond what people were really saying. He would often correctly interpret someone's meaning, even when they struggled to get the proper words out. He taught me that people often use imprecise words in an attempt to express themselves.

How does that statement go? "I know you think you know what I said; but what I said isn't what I really meant." Isn't that how teenagers often seem to communicate? The subject they bring up may have nothing to do with what they really want to talk about. Your daughter might bring up some innocent subject, when what she really wants to talk about is hidden behind the words. She may hope that you'll show enough interest to find out what's really bothering her. But if you're not sensitive to *her*, you'll never discover the real problem.

Are You Really Listening?

Now all this seems simple enough, doesn't it? Just watch and listen to your kids and you'll be all right. But unfortunately, good listening is a deceptively difficult skill, and most people never develop much ability in practicing it.

Have you ever been deeply involved in a conversation with someone only to discover that the person you're talking to really isn't interested and is barely listening to what you're saying? This can be frustrating. You want your ideas to be appreciated and understood, but instead you feel rejected. Well, that's what many parents do to their kids.

Often when we "listen" to our teenagers, we are secretly ignoring them. (Of course, we try not to be too obvious about it.) Perhaps we've had a long, difficult day, and our kid wants to talk about something that seems so silly to us. Because we don't want to appear rude, we pretend to listen, periodically looking up from what we're doing, punctuating our silence with occasional *uh-huh*s and *I sees*. And as long as no one quizzes us on what we heard, everything will be OK.)

Actually we are trying to listen selectively, keeping our antenna up just in case something "really important" happens to creep unnoticed into the conversation—like a request by a teenager to go out on a first date, or to borrow some of our hard-earned money, or even to use the car. A typical conversation might be completely one-sided until a magic word is suddenly uttered by your teenager:

"Dad, Mom doesn't have enough money for my dress."

"Ah . . . what was that you just said?"

"Mom needs some money," she says.

"I mean . . . what did you say about a dress?"

"For my prom dress. You promised."

"Prom? When did we talk about you going to the prom?"

"Remember? We talked about me needing a new formal. We talked about how I wanted to go to the prom with David Anderson?"

"David Anderson? He hadn't even *asked* you."

"That was days ago, Dad. Now we're going for sure."

"Oh, you are, are you? When did we talk about this anyway?"

"You remember, Dad. You were reading the paper? I asked you if it was OK if I went if David asked me, and you shook your head yes."

"Oh, I see. Ah-huh."

Busted! We don't remember much because we were listening selectively. Why is it that our kids so quickly learn the most effective times to manipulate us? We really shouldn't be surprised if they discern when we're not listening.

Even if we do get serious in our attempts to listen to what they're saying, it's often difficult for us to hear what's really being said. When your teens begin to talk, don't you really feel you know what they're going to say before they say it? You were their age once, and when they talk about their experiences, you immediately reflect back to similar encounters you've had. You can't wait for them to finish talking so you can tell them how you handled a similar situation. If we listen only so we can talk—we're not really listening. We're too busy running their words through our internal computer in an attempt to get our answer on-line.

As an example, suppose a daughter seems down in the dumps.

"What's bothering you, dear?" asks mother.

"Oh, nothing, Mom."

"Now sweetheart, I can tell that something is wrong. You know you can tell me."

"But, Mom, you'd think I was silly."

"Of course I won't. You can tell me, dear. No one cares about you like your mother."

"Well, . . . it's Mary Anne. Every time I tell her something she blabs it all over the school. Yesterday, I told her I had a crush on Freddy and she went and *told him!* Mom, she humiliated me!"

"Now sweetheart, I've told you before, you can't have such a thin skin. I know Mary Anne would never try to hurt you like that on purpose. And besides, that Freddy isn't much of a catch for a nice girl like you anyway." Mom pauses. "Now, go ahead and tell me what else you're feeling."

Now tell me, do you think that daughter is going to want to continue the conversation? Probably not. Her mother didn't validate anything she was saying. Instead, what the daughter received was an unrequested lecture.

Most of us parents, wiser though we might be, have a strong need to rush in and fix things before we're really sure what's wrong. You can't fix something if your teenager is convinced nothing's broken. Proverbs says, "He who gives an answer before he hears, it is folly and shame to him" (Proverbs 18:13). The problem with most of us is that we really haven't learned to listen. We're so busy formulating our answer that we don't pay any attention to what our kids are saying.

This happens because we all have a tendency to look at other people through our own glasses. We evaluate their words and actions through the filter of our beliefs and experiences. We come to conclusions about them based upon how they measure up to our own personal book of rules. What we're doing is nothing more than judging or passing sentence on them. Judgment says, "You're not as good as I am. In fact, you'll never measure up to my standard. Why are you wasting my time?" Parents often don't realize that they view their offspring judgmentally. But their words and mannerisms communicate it all the same.

Perhaps this is why Jesus said, "He who has ears to hear, let him hear" (Matthew 11:15). He knew most people already had things "figured out" in their own minds and would have a difficult time really hearing what he had to say. We all have ears, but we seldom use them effectively because we're too busy coming to conclusions about what people are saying. We may hear a person's words, but seldom do we hear what he is really saying.

Practice Some Listening Skills

Being understood is one of the most exciting things that ever happens to us. So seldom do people really seem to comprehend what we're saying that we usually brighten when we sense that someone is on our same emotional level.

To listen with an understanding ear is difficult. It means we have to fight our natural tendency to hear from our own vantage point. It also means we will avoid passing judgment on what another person is saying. Of course, this is all the more difficult because we often feel it's necessary to give our teenagers an occasional piece of our minds. (Most of us have no pieces to spare.)

The challenge here is to see what is being said from their point of view, working hard at hearing what they mean to say (not just what their words say). You will also be working equally hard not to evaluate it from your own point of view, which will probably be the hardest part of such an exercise. To do this, here are five helpful suggestions.

1. Try listening with all your senses.

The experts claim that only 10 percent of a person's message is communicated by words. The way we say something (sounds, inflection, attitude, etc.) communicates about 30 percent of a message. And, amazingly, our body language communicates approximately *60 percent* of our message.

Even if you have never read a book about body language, most parents can instinctively read the outward signals indicating how their teenagers are feeling. When they won't look you in the eyes, you can literally see the uncomfortableness and guilt. You've seen so many other signals: the shrugging of the shoulders, the hands perched defiantly on the hips, the mouth covered by fingers, and the giddy expectant countenance. All of these are signs indicating how a person is feeling, of which you should take note. Be aware of what their bodies are telling you. Be sensitive to their moods without reacting to them. You can usually tell if tears are about to explode from your daughter's eyes. You can spot anger rising to flush the surface of the skin. Stop, look, and listen before proceeding. These things are important signals you need to notice if you want to stay sensitive to your adolescents' feelings.

2. Repeat the essence of what they're saying back to them.

This may feel uncomfortable for us at first, especially if it sounds like we're mimicking them. But this will help you hear what your kids are saying, and it will also encourage them to continue speaking.

"Mom, I'm so frustrated with Mr. Jones."

"You're frustrated with your history teacher."

"Yeah, he really makes me mad."

"You're mad at him."

You haven't passed out any opinions of what your daughter is saying. Nor have you agreed with her about anything; you've just affirmed that you heard what she was saying.

3. Rephrase the meaning in your own words.

This technique takes more concentration and a little interpreting of what they've said. But remember, you are not evaluating content; you're just interpreting it to determine what's being said.

"He really made me mad."

"You're angry with Mr. Jones."

"Yeah. He's the worst teacher I have."

"You're upset with Mr. Jones, and you don't like him as much as you like your other teachers."

Again, it is important to note that you are neither condemning nor approving of what she is saying. You are only seeking to understand it by rephrasing her words.

4. Reflect upon the feeling that's being communicated.

Feelings show us what our teenagers are going through and are important clues to better communication. Look beyond the words and actions to what your sons or daughters are feeling. Try to understand what your teens say by reflecting upon and then summing up the emotion that's being communicated to you.

"I can't believe how he tricked us on our test," says the teenager. "He always let us use our notes before, but this time he wouldn't let us use them."

"So you feel that Mr. Jones didn't treat the class fairly."

"No. He should have told us we wouldn't be able to use our notes on this test."

"You feel that the class wasn't prepared for the test because he didn't tell you what kind of test was coming."

"Yeah, Mom. And a lot of people got bad grades."

"So, it's Mr. Jones's fault that so many kids got bad grades."

Your goal is to understand what your teenagers are thinking and feeling, to give them a nonjudgmental, listening ear. The beauty of this is that if you miss the mark, your teens will surely clarify what they mean because they will sense your honest interest.

What often happens in this kind of dialogue is that the barrier between what is going on inside their heads and what's being communicated to you often disappears. This opens a free exchange of information so they feel the liberty to communicate exactly what's hidden below the surface.

"I don't know why he did that, Mom. Half the class failed the test."

"So his failure to warn everyone about how he was changing his test is the reason so many people failed?"

"Yeah. I guess so. And . . . Mom, you won't tell Dad, will you? I was one of the ones who failed the test."

"You're angry with Mr. Jones for flunking you unfairly."

"Well . . . I guess I could have studied better."

"You feel that if you had studied harder you wouldn't have flunked?"

"Yeah. Mom, do you think you could help me study for his next test?"

5. Double-check and clarify your perceptions.

Another useful technique is to double-check the feeling you perceive with simple questions. Here you will attempt to express your understanding of your teens' feelings in an effort to confirm that you are hearing correctly.

"I hear you saying that you are upset with your best friend for spending so much time with Jim. Am I right?"

This approach is much more direct, but it is also easier to give offense. Here you want to clarify and confirm what you're hearing. You are asking for verbal confirmation of your perceptions. This approach is especially useful if you want to get your teenagers thinking about what they're actually saying.

I used this approach recently with a high-school girl. I repeated back to her the two conflicting statements she was making and then asked, "Is that what you're saying?"

"Well, no," she said. "I mean, yes. I don't know what I mean."

Another way to double-check your perceptions might be to ask questions like: "Do you feel angry about what I just said?" "I'm uncertain why you are responding this way. Did my statement hurt you?" "Can you explain that better to me by giving me some illustrations of what you mean?"

This latter approach will help your teenagers be a little more tangible in what they're feeling. If they say things like, "You *always* do that," you'll want to ask for a few examples. They may not be able to come up with any, but the question will help them focus upon what it is that they're trying to say. If they perceive that you always do something, it is important to take the time to listen to why they feel that way.

Nonjudgmental Communication

All of the approaches above are designed to communicate with your teenagers without passing sentence on their words. How much more effective it is for a teenager to come to a wise conclusion without your having to hand it to him on a platter. Think how exciting that is. That's exactly what you want your children to do—to learn to make wise decisions. Even if one of your lectures would accomplish the same results, it wouldn't be as rewarding as watching your kids make the decisions on their own. Our goal as parents is to point them in the right direction and train them to make their own decisions because we know we won't always be there to help them.

I heard about four men who came together in an attempt to really understand each other. The communication was so good that one by one the men started to confess their sins to each other.

"You've all been so supportive," said one man, "and I have a confession to make. I . . . I've been unfaithful to my wife."

As the others shook their heads in mutual sympathy and understanding, another spoke up. "I guess I should make my own confession. I've been struggling with gambling. It's really been a problem for me."

A third man nodded. "I can't be still any longer. I also have a secret sin. I have this terrible drinking problem that nobody knows about."

Not to be outdone, the fourth fellow finally spoke up. "You know, this has been an incredible meeting. But I guess I should make a confession too. My sin is that of gossip—and I just can't *wait* to leave this room."

Certainly none of us would consciously gossip about our kids. But think about the fact that gossip is a form of passing judgment on other people. And we would probably all have the tendency to pass sentence on our kids if they were to make a confession to us. Unfortunately, that's the very judgmental spirit that will probably put off our adolescents and keep them from opening up to us.

The older they grow, the more their actions will fall upon their own heads. And it is important for us to begin to give our teenagers more of an opportunity to take upon themselves the responsibility for their own actions. As they earn their freedom, we must be willing to back off and not pass judgment on their behavior. If we can do this with our kids by keeping open a nonjudgmental form of communication with them, we are much more likely to see them grow up and admit their own sins to themselves.

Seeking to Be Understood

In this communication process, it is important to seek first to understand your kids before you seek to be understood. If you really understand what your teenagers are feeling and saying—not passing judgment—you will find it much more likely that they will listen to and appreciate what you have to say.

The Greeks called this third level of communication *logos,* the logic and reasoning part of your presentation. This Greek term summed up the presentation of a message.

Whenever you have something important to say to your teens, it is a wise idea to prepare yourself for that presentation. Plan where and when you'll have the talk, and who will be there. It is also important for both parents to discuss and agree upon the goals of any major presentation; you certainly want to work as a team.

Select your words carefully. This is very important. Take out of your vocabulary those words that imply negative conclusions about your teens. Use only the language of respect; avoid sarcasm. You might even want to write down the exact points you want to communicate or the wording you want to use. This can certainly help you clarify your thinking.

As you begin to communicate your message, work at making it appropriate to the situation. Emphasize your interest in what's best for your teens. Even if the message you want to communicate is something you know your teenagers will struggle with, they will be far more likely to respond favorably if they feel you love them and that you are working on understanding and appreciating them.

I'm finding that my communication with my teenagers is far more effective today than it used to be, simply because my communication level is better with my kids. Just yesterday Rebecca said to me, "Who would have thought that I would be wanting to come in to talk to you at least three times a week about my problems?" Now that was exciting for me to hear, especially considering the troubled waters through which we've come together.

Family Communication Times

One other suggestion on this subject that might work for you is to try a "family communication time" during your weekly family hour. When I was in elementary school, my father established a weekly get-together in which each of us would stand up in front of the others and talk about whatever we wanted. That exercise really excited me about my family because I knew that I would have an opportunity each week to get everyone's undivided attention.

If your teens know that they have the opportunity to say whatever they want, and that you will definitely be listening, this can become a productive time of relationship building. But make certain that you establish a few rules. Respectful language must be used; we must honor everyone else's opinion; and we must not interrupt each other. Have a plan. Know what you are trying to accomplish. This could be a great way of drawing your family closer together.

SUMMARY OF KEY POINTS

1. Good communication is essential to a good relationship.
2. The less you communicate with your teenagers, the less relationship you will have with them.
3. Your personal credibility with your teenagers is based upon how they perceive your character.
4. It is important for parents to be able to understand their teenagers to effectively communicate with them.
5. Too often parents only half-listen to what their teens are saying; this is a poor form of communication.
6. Listening only with the intent of giving out advice hurts true communication; avoid forming conclusions about your teens based on limited information.
7. Listening to really understand is a difficult skill that must be learned.

8. Observe teenagers' body language to determine what they are feeling.
9. Seek first to understand before attempting to be understood.
10. A skill that will help listening is to repeat the essence of what teens say to assure them that they're being listened to.
11. While listening, rephrase the meaning of their words and repeat them back as part of the conversation.
12. Listen by reflecting upon the feeling of what's being spoken.
13. By removing judgment from a conversation, parents can help teenagers judge their own thoughts and feelings.
14. Remove negative or disrespectful words when you are seeking to be understood.

10

FEAR THE PEER DEPENDENCE

"The conformist is in no way a free man. He has to follow the herd."
~Norman Vincent Peale

....

It was Mark Twain who said, "We are discreet sheep; we wait to see how the drove is going, and then go with the drove."

Peer pressure. It's probably the single biggest cause of teenagers' straying away from the influence of their parents. It is extremely important that you recognize this pressure for what it is and know how it will impact your adolescents. Few things are more frustrating than to wake up and realize that you have lost your children to the influence of their friends.

The Whys of Peer Pressure

Somewhere in the beginning of the adolescent years, a teenager discovers the importance of fitting in. Peer pressure can quickly take control of a teenager's life, dictating such things as his behavior, clothes, music, games, conversation, and even food. A kid will learn to like something simply because he sees that "everyone else likes doing it." Because this pressure is so intense, it often pushes a young person into things that he once thought were completely unacceptable. Smoking, drugs, and premarital sex usually all begin as a result of peer pressure.

Parents often have a difficult time understanding this

from an adult perspective, thinking or even saying, "Why do you care what anyone else thinks?" But don't ever underestimate the power of a group's acceptance (or rejection) to force everyone into conforming. Unless you grew up on a desert isle, you probably had similar experiences when you were thirteen.

In the summer between elementary school and seventh grade, I had a paper route. Every day I would ride my bicycle past the junior high school to pick up newspapers. Before I entered seventh grade, my older sister asked how I was going to get to school.

"I'll ride my bike," I replied confidently. *Besides,* I thought, *I need it for my paper route. I'll just keep right on going after school to get my papers.* It made sense.

"You'll never ride your bicycle to school," she responded prophetically. "No one rides their bicycle to school. It just isn't done."

In my fiercely independent mind, I thought, *No one is going to tell me that I can't ride my bicycle to school!* But just to be safe, I didn't ride it that first day of seventh grade. And you know what? After I saw that no one else (except the nerds) brought their bicycles, I never once rode it to school. Never mind that I had to walk *a mile and a half* from school to get home so I could ride my bicycle back past the same school to pick up my newspapers. At least at that time, no one was looking. And no one would make fun of me for using such an "out-of-it" method of transportation.

Every early teenager knows that being singled out as different is the kiss of death. Young adolescents respond intensely to this peer pressure when they realize their acceptance or rejection is based upon how they measure up next to other teens. Because acceptance is seen as the key to survival, teenagers will go to great lengths not to be marked as different or weird.

Bonding rituals emerge as part of their rites of passage that declare that they are now part of a group. These may include such things as the use of slang and jargon. This shouldn't be difficult to understand, as almost every group has its own in-group jargon; human beings have a deep-felt need to identify those who are part of their subculture, and this is often done though language. Doctors, lawyers, and even spies all have their in-crowd terminology they bandy about to keep the uninitiated from understanding or breaking into their group.

Teenagers quickly develop a language that is designed, primarily, to shove adults to the outside edge of their universe. Much of this jargon comes from the latest hit movie or television show, but a good deal is always local in nature and dependent upon what has risen up on the "in" list of school cliché words and phrases. Parents who adopt all the current teenage jargon may be tolerated, but they'll never be truly accepted (especially by their own kids) because they've missed the *purpose* of such language: an adolescent is trying to distance himself from the realm of adults so he'll be accepted. Remember, being an adult is simply never in.

It's important for parents to realize that there are many different groups with which a teenager can become involved. Ask your kids and they'll tell you that dress, language, and behavior are different from one group to another. For years in California schools, the "stoners" have been those who have long hair, listen to rock-and-roll music, and basically have an antiauthority attitude. But in most schools there are at least two types of stoners—those that actually do drugs and those that don't. Every campus is fragmented into a wide variety of such peer groups, and it is not a bad idea to find out which group your teens aspire to join.

Clothes Make the Kid

Another route to acceptance for many teens is through having correct clothing. Teenagers perceive that the quickest way to be accepted is to follow the trends and buy popular brand names. To most teens, brand allegiance is an expression of self-identity, and where the clothing is purchased is as important as the brand name itself. This is why a four-teen-year-old may want a pair of Levi's from the Gap, but will reject a similar pair of jeans manufactured by an inferior company or even the same jeans sold in a substandard store. Every young person knows that the world would end if his friends pointed out that he had purchased a cheap imitation of the accepted brand of choice.

To understand the importance of clothes, parents must appreciate nuances. Most adults think all teens dress alike. In reality there are usually marked differences between young people aged thirteen to fifteen and those sixteen to nineteen. On the surface, there are similarities, but details set the two groups apart. Teenagers feel that they are dressing individually because they have made subtle changes as minute as the placement of a hair clip or the size of an earring. Such differences are as important to them as the width of a tie might be to a businessman. They are fitting in while still proclaiming some sense of independence.

When I was in ninth grade, I remember, it was cool to buy Levi's jeans, which we would then alter by removing the leather tag, the belt loops, and the orange thread that circled the top edge of the pants. Another group in my school never washed their pants so that they would stay dark blue and end up quite stiff.

Think back to some of your experiences when you were a teenager. I'll bet you became involved in similar trends. What made us all succumb to such silly dress styles? We so desperately wanted to fit in that we didn't dare do anything that might be considered uncool. We would never have been caught dead as part of the "nerd herd." Even today, most of us are aware of the proper clothes to wear. Such books as *Dress for Success* have made it clear that the pressure of our peers continues on through life, even if not to the same degree.

What's hot in clothes, like everything else in the teenage world, changes quickly. Not only is it important *who is* wearing something, it's equally important *who isn't*. If parents—heaven forbid—should start wearing the latest teen fad, you can be sure that the trend will move quickly in a different direction.

The mystery to all this hot and cool stuff is that it's all manufactured, advertised, and sold by men in wingtips and pinstripes. How can these geeky grown-ups figure out what kids will find desirable in the next six months? Simple. They keep asking the kids. The marketing men hang out at the local mall and interview thousands of teenagers to see what the latest fickle trend has ushered in. (If they just hung out at your house they'd probably get the *real* low-down, right?)

All of this pressure to be up with the trends, of course, is much more intense than in later life because the early teen is thrown into a totally foreign environment in the typical school. Unlike the elementary grades, where they had one or two accepting teachers, now they must compete with multitudes of other students for the attention of many and varied teachers who aren't nearly as sympathetic to their needs.

Because so many of the standards of any peer group are localized, young teenagers will feel very threatened by the thought of having to move away. The task of fighting their way into some new group and being accepted is so hard that they will usually be extremely rebellious over the idea of having to start all over again at some new location. Parents discover that changes during these years are much more fiercely challenged than they ever were during the elementary years.

How Should You Respond?

At first, most parents tend to chuckle at the genuflections of their teenagers in response to all this peer pressure. But recognize that the more your child scurries to meet this pressure, the more likely it will be that he will eventually come under the control of his peers.

This is a good reason for not winking at all these silly fads. It is important not to cater to your young person's fears. He may insist that you run around town purchasing the "right" clothes or demand additional freedoms and privileges so he can fit in with the gang. But if you allow him to make your life subservient to his, you are acknowledging not only that these artificial group standards are OK, but also that you approve of his pursuit of them.

Indulge your teen, and you'll harvest a spoiled kid who requires megabucks to satisfy the whim of the moment. Nothing will ruin your kid faster or send him down the road to a self-serving life-style more quickly than this. No one owes him anything, and the sooner he learns that lesson, the better off everyone will be.

Also, don't ever try to insulate your teenager from peer rejection. If he is never rejected, he'll end up allowing the group to become his cultural god. Nothing brings us back to reality more quickly than being burned by our so-called friends, especially if it happens just because we don't measure up to their petty preferences. No lecture from you will ever eclipse the lesson he'll receive about the fickleness of his friends. It is difficult for a teenager to see that friends don't last forever. And the sooner he figures that out, the sooner he'll move up on the ladder of maturity. He'll also appreciate his parents more, because you'll still be there long after the friends have moved on.

Now, of course, you don't want to be insensitive to him so that he views you as the enemy, trying to get him away from all his friends. But you certainly don't want to cater to them, either. This is probably one of your biggest challenges in the battle against peer pressure—keeping your trust account open and rising. The desire for a young person to bend to peer pressures is often so strong that your teens will begin to dramatically resist your attempts at parental control. By the middle teenage years (ages fourteen to sixteen) your child may fiercely challenge any attempts to control his life. During this time, a teenager is feeling increasingly "grown-up" and will demand more freedom. Of course, a wise parent knows that his younger adolescent has not reached the time for independence. In fact, the opposite is true. If a teenager is given too much freedom at this point in his or her life, all sorts of problems will be created, with ongoing results.

Independence must be earned. Over the years I've made it plain to my kids that the more maturity they show, the more responsibility and freedom they'll receive. The less maturity we see, the less freedom. If a young person asks, "When am I going to get to do ————?" my answer has always been, "When Mom and Dad think you're ready." Sure, that's a judgment call on our part, and my kids have sometimes challenged me on it. But I always point back to their attitudes. Any teen who is demanding independence is certainly not ready for it. For the most part, a young person is approaching adult status when he is no longer trying to "prove" he's an adult.

What Is Peer Dependence?

"There are times," said Peter DeVries, "when parenthood seems nothing more than feeding the hand that bites you." He must have been talking about what happens when a teenager becomes peer dependent.

Most teens don't mind having parental approval for their actions as long as it doesn't conflict with that of their peer group. But a teenager who has declared war against his parents has moved from peer pressure to *peer dependence*. The group has replaced his parents and will always be chosen over them because of the erroneous belief that they understand him better and care more about him then his parents do. Peer dependence is one of the key reasons parents lose their teenagers emotionally. When teens are more interested in pleasing their friends than their parents, you've got a dependence that *must* be broken.

Our oldest daughter, Rebecca, was always greatly influenced by other children. From the day (as a three-year-old) that she wandered from our yard and caught the big kids' bus to school, we knew she loved socializing with other kids. Her sixth-grade teacher told us that Rebecca was a leader in her class. Rebecca's response? "Oh, no. I like to do what the other kids are doing." None of this really seemed that important until she reached the teenage zone. Suddenly we began to hear statements like: "Why do you always have to tell me what to do? My friends' parents don't do that to them." "Why do I always have to be so 'good'? Why couldn't I have been born in a normal family instead of being a pastor's daughter?" "My friends mean more to me than you do. If I had my way, I'd just leave home and go live at my best friend's house."

When you start to hear statements like these, you know

that you are facing a crisis that just won't go away overnight. Your young adolescent has become peer dependent, and weathering this storm will take careful planning, a little spiritual strategy, and a lot of long-term follow-through. The Bible makes it clear that "bad company corrupts good morals" (1 Corinthians 15:33). The Word also has instructions to young men not to spend time with those who are prone to violence (Proverbs 1:10-19). But just because other kids have encouraged your son or daughter in his or her rebelliousness, don't assume that it is they who are corrupting your kid. Your teen may actually be the one doing the corrupting. Generally, such teens are attracted to each other because they have found someone whose rebellion is equal to their own.

If your teen is into a relationship that is dramatically influencing him away from both you and the Lord, it is extremely important that you take corrective action. Here are some suggestions that might prove helpful:

1. Don't play the "I'm Bigger" game.

This is where you tell your teen (in words or actions), "I'm bigger than you are; therefore you must obey me." Do you believe that your kids are obligated to do what you say just because you are their parent? My guess is that if you have that attitude, they are only obeying you on the outside. But a young person will only play the role for so long. Sooner or later every young person will react to this parental attitude with something like, "I don't care if you are bigger because I don't really care about you anymore." When kids have been ruled like this, they will end up rejecting all their parents' values and beliefs because they will have concluded that what you believe must not be any good or else your beliefs would have made a difference in your life.

2. Work at rebuilding broken relationships.

I don't want to sound like a broken record, but we must have an emphasis upon constructing *relationships*. You must be much more committed to long-term growth than to quick fixes. Your teenagers must see you as loving parents who truly care about them. This takes time, especially if you have allowed the weeds to grow up into your relationships.

Adding to what we've said so far, I would ask you if you do any fun things with your kids. Do you do things that your kids would like to do? Take them places they want to go? Play games? Talk openly? And so on. If you don't, start working on doing some things with them.

3. Work on building relationships with your teens' friends.

If you can't make the mountain come to you—go to it. Most of your teens' friends will not have the same kind of rebellion toward you as your own kids do (simply because you probably haven't offended them yet). By having them come in and do things with your teen while you are around, it will be much easier for you to get to know each other, and also dispel some of the animosity building up in your absence. It is always easier to be against someone you don't know. Bringing your teens' friends into your own sphere of influence will tend to neutralize them and maybe even get them on your side. Hopefully, when your adolescents are griping, they'll someday say, "Your parents aren't so bad." You also may want to get to know your teens' friends' parents. Good communication between families can often dissipate much of the rebellion fomenting as households talk back and forth about their mutual problems.

When we moved to a new community last year, we knew that our teens would have a difficult time finding

friends at their new high school. We therefore decided to
run our own youth group out of our house to help them
get to know their friends better and also to lead some of
them to the Lord. This worked well and gave us an opportunity to have more input into the friends of our teenagers.
It also made us allies because our teenagers desired our
help in winning their friends to Jesus.

4. When necessary, separate the young person from his/her friends.

This is a more drastic solution that should be taken only if
absolutely necessary, but often radical problems require
radical solutions. If you are not able to combat the influence of your teenager's friends, it might be time to limit the
relationship or even separate your kid from those friends.

You can say something like, "We don't like the attitudes
we're picking up from you whenever you spend time with
that friend. If we don't see some changes, we'll simply have
to restrict the amount of time you spend with him. The
future of your relationship with him is up to you." Certainly, if this isn't done properly, you may create great
rebellion in the heart of your teenager, so great care must
be used in handling this kind of situation. If possible, let
any restrictions become a cause-and-effect situation. You
explain what you expect and give him the options. If positive changes don't take place (or the problems continue),
your teenager will know what to expect. He made the
choices, not you; therefore he will reap the consequences.

In really difficult situations, consider changing schools
or even churches. Moving around is certainly hard on kids,
but it is definitely preferable to losing your kids altogether.
I've watched too many parents lose their teens because
they didn't keep on top of the peer problems that were
brewing right under their noses.

5. Remove all outside input from your home.

This would include anything that has a message other than what you are completely happy with: television, radio, recorded music, secular teen magazines—anything that can possibly impact your teenagers in a negative way.

For several years I did not watch television, listen to the radio, or subscribe to a local newspaper. There was certainly a lot I missed out on, yet I can say that, overall, both my family and I were much better off as a result of the lack of media input. If a teenager is too dependent on his music (cassettes, radio, and CDs), just remove the listening device for a period of time. This doesn't have to be done as punishment (although that is certainly a possibility). It can be done simply because of the impact that all this "garbage" has upon the family as a whole. But make certain the restrictions apply equally to everyone, or your kids will certainly rebel. Don't allow yourself to create a double standard, as it will do more harm than good.

6. Try home schooling.

With my oldest daughter we encountered an attachment to her friends that was way out of proportion to what it should have been. It wasn't just one or two friends; it was the socialization in the entire secular school system that she seemed to be feeding on to replace her parents.

Of course, as I've discussed earlier, the problems weren't all with Rebecca; I certainly had my own share of blame in our deteriorating relationship. But we determined that the best solution for her at the time was to place both of our daughters into a home-schooling environment. On two separate occasions we did this, at great personal sacrifice (especially on my wife's part). But the changes we saw in our daughter's behavior were certainly worth the extra commitment.

Because of the problems in our secular school system, many parents (including many non-Christian parents) are moving away from the secular schools and into home-schooling programs. It has been proven that students often perform much better academically in a one-on-one environment. Certainly, such a situation will help your child relate better to you in the long run (after he gets used to the idea).

If you are anticipating home schooling, I strongly encourage you to go with a recognized program, especially one that can work with a local school that is accredited in your state. In the years that we were involved in home schooling, we used several different programs, but found that the Advanced Training Institute of America (under the auspices of the Institute in Basic Life Conflicts) was best for us. The program was quite extensive and required my wife and me to go to several week-long seminars to qualify, but we were convinced they had the best Bible-based curriculum available.

Because such programs are becoming increasingly popular, there are home-schooling groups in many cities, where parents have come together to give each other support and plan activities together. Such groups can be a great resource in sharing educational programs beyond the level of most parents.

7. Finally, pray regularly for your kids.

We've talked about prayer several times in previous chapters, but if you are running into major peer dependence, you will (hopefully) be even more willing to pray for your kids on a regular basis as you encounter these major behavior problems. We all know that praying for our kids is important, but it certainly isn't the easiest thing to do consistently. Never forget that prayer moves the hand of God, but it also changes us. When we pray over our teenagers, we will inevitably think through our relationship with them from God's point of view. That can't help but make great changes in how we deal with them.

SUMMARY OF KEY POINTS

1. Peer pressure is probably the single biggest cause of teenagers' straying from the influence of their parents.
2. Every teenager knows that to be singled out as different is the "kiss of death."
3. A major purpose of teenage jargon is to maintain distance between adults and their own world.
4. Although adolescents may all seem to dress alike, teenagers mark their part in an elite group by the clothes they wear.
5. Most teenagers struggle with the thought of moving away from their school because they have invested so much effort in fitting in.
6. It is important that parents do not cater to their teenagers' fear of peer pressure by helping them meet the whim of the moment.
7. Parents need to help teenagers keep a balance with this pressure, knowing that the group is often at cross-purposes with them.
8. It is important to teach teens that independence must be earned, not demanded.
9. Peer dependence is when the group becomes more important to a teenager than his parents.
10. To overcome peer dependence, don't demand obedience because you're bigger.
11. Work at reconstructing broken relationships.
12. Build relationships with your teens' friends.

13. When necessary, separate your young people from
    their friends.
14. Try removing all outside media input from your home.
15. A parent with a difficult situation might try home
    schooling.

11

GETTING THE SITUATION UNDER CONTROL

"The parent must convince himself that discipline is not something he does to the child; it is something he does for the child." ~James Dobson

....

As a father wandered down the crowded aisles of Wal-Mart, a squirmy adolescent boy followed behind him, constantly touching the merchandise and adding his own running commentary on each new discovery.

"Will you look at those stupid ties. I mean, *get real!*" And then a few moments later, "Hey, Dad, buy me my own portable telephone!"

At each new indignity to his quiet persona, the father merely looked at his son and replied quietly: "Wilbur, maintain."

Throughout the store the noisy teenager continued to draw attention to himself. Whether he talked loudly across the aisles to friends he spotted or attempted to balance a stack of women's hats on his head, his father continued to remain calm and collected. "Wilbur, maintain" were his only words.

Another parent, having observed the father's lack of reaction to his exuberant teenager, spoke to him when they both stepped into the same checkout line. "I've been watching you in the store, and I must say I admire the calm way you handle your son, Wilbur."

The man looked at him with a blank expression for a moment. "Oh," he said, finally comprehending what the stranger was saying. He nodded towards his junior higher. "He's not Wilbur—*I am!*"

It doesn't take most of us long to discover the lack of correlation between our elementary angels and our junior-high demons. The names remain the same, but almost everything else changes—and nothing is kept secret so that no one is protected! It makes you wonder if your kid somehow found the chemical concoction that mutated Dr. Jekyll into Mr. Hyde. Before your very eyes, he has undergone this strange transformation. But the biggest problem is that you know the changes will never wear off, just as with the good doctor. You're stuck with your very own teenage aberration.

Most of the methods you used in bygone days to secure the obedience of your kids have suddenly been rendered as obsolete as a ten-year-old fashion magazine. Can you imagine a five-foot-tall mother attempting to spank a five-foot-eight-inch, one-hundred-and-fifty-pound teenage boy? With teenagers, threats become useless, and spanking virtually loses its impact. Junior-high parents need a whole new arsenal of tools. You'll have to change your tactics if you want to stay out of the institution for the parentally insane.

Punishment vs. Discipline

We're talking about how to discipline our teenagers. But what is discipline? One tongue-in-cheek definition claims that discipline is giving your teenager *everything he deserves.* As parents of teenagers, you soon discover that obedience is something only dogs do. And if by some incredible chance encounter, your son should ever utter those alien words, "Yes, Dad," the shock of hearing them might cause you a nervous breakdown.

Good early discipline in the elementary years is at the heart of your relationship with your teenagers. If you have failed to discipline or if you have punished your kids harshly during their early years, your task will be harder when they reach the teenage zone. Good discipline is far more than making our kids cower in fear, and it is far more even than establishing outward obedience. To understand what is effective you must reflect upon the difference between punishment and discipline. The purpose of punishment is to inflict pain for offenses that have been committed; it focuses upon past misdeeds, has a hostile attitude, and produces fear and guilt in the one being punished. I agree with Don Marquis when he said, "Many a man spanks his children for the things his own father should have spanked out of him." In contrast to this is discipline, the purpose of which is to train a child for correction and maturity. Discipline focuses on creating good behavior. Its basic attitude is one of love and concern, and it produces security in the one being disciplined.

Fleas can be trained. If you put several in a Mason jar, you will hear them pop up against the lid for several minutes as they attempt to spring out of the jar. But then they get wise and stop jumping so high, presumably because it hurts to hit the lid. Apparently, this is the way that the famous trained flea circuses were created years ago. Many parents train their kids in a similar way. By the use of harsh punishment or shouting episodes whenever a child disobeys, these adults educate their children—in the fine art of avoiding parental wrath. But they haven't really changed the child's thinking about what is wrong; they have merely taught him to avoid punishment.

Punishment is therefore not an effective tool in curbing undesirable conduct because its results are only temporary in nature. It does not teach the long-term need for changed character. The fear of punishment is like the presence of a state trooper or highway patrol vehicle on the interchange. Everyone slows down as long as the officer is visible. But the moment the officer pulls off the highway, all the nearby autos immediately accelerate back up to their "normal" cruising speed. That's the type of changed behavior punishment produces in most kids. Only outward behavior has been affected, and that only temporarily.

The Problem of Guilt

Closely allied with punishment is the use of guilt. Although making a child feel guilty about his offenses will also temporarily change his behavior, in the long run such a tactic ruins parent-adolescent relationships. A load of guilt is such a heavy burden that most of us will flee from anything or anyone who makes us feel guilty. How many grown children are embittered against their parents because they were made to feel that they could never measure up? Probably millions. That's the legacy guilt leaves behind, and believe me, you don't want to use it to control your kids.

Wait a minute, you might be thinking, *my kids are guilty when they do something wrong. Aren't I supposed to make them feel ashamed about their misbehavior?* To answer that, let's probe deeper into the nature of guilt. I believe there are two kinds of guilt. *True guilt* is what happens when we sin; we stand before God guilty as charged for our transgressions. Fortunately, we are told that "there is therefore now no condemnation for those who are in Christ Jesus" (Romans 8:1). All our sins are under the blood of Christ (1 John 1:7), and it is the devil who tries to condemn us in an attempt to make us feel guilty and to deny the Lord's forgiveness. For a parent to condemn his child on this level is to take the position of almighty God, or, worse, of Satan himself. Instead, our task should be to encourage our children's understanding of how we are forgiven when we turn away from our sins. If we fail to do this, our offspring will never know where they stand either with us or with God.

But we must distinguish true guilt from *guilt feelings.* Our sense of feeling guilty may be appropriate to our sin; then again, it may also be inappropriate. People often feel overly guilty for imaginary offenses that God doesn't condemn. Think of the Tin Man in *The Wizard of Oz*; he would step on a bug and feel so guilty that he would cry until he rusted. That would be an example of remorse that is out of proportion to a real (or imagined) sin. On the other hand, people can feel no guilt when they are truly guilty of some offense. A few years ago I met a "Christian" inmate who was serving time for being a professional killer—he had murdered over fifty people. The man wanted me to write his life story. (*Get serious!*) I could see no remorse and wondered what might happen if we ever had a disagreement or he backslid. The fact that people feel no remorse about their sins doesn't mean that they are not truly guilty before God. Many have succeeded in numbing their conscience even though they never really repented.

Guilt feelings should be in proportion to our transgressions; we should feel as bad about our sin as God does. The purpose of those feelings is to lead us to repentance, not to punish us. It is appropriate for a parent to help a child feel the pain his sin causes God (and others) so that he will repent of it and turn back to God. But you shouldn't make a teen feel guilty by condemning him; you should help him feel the pain that his sin causes by explaining to him what he has done. If a parent berates a child, telling him how bad he is, the child may feel horrible; but if the guilt feelings come from the parent's condemnation instead of from within the child's own conscience, no real repentance will be produced. Any teenager who is sorry only because he got caught has not really repented. A guilty conscience is the mother of invention—he may change his outward appearance in the same way he might try to avoid punishment. Remorse that is caused only by punishment or the fear of punishment will never change a person (see 2 Corinthians 7:9-10; 1 John 4:17-18). So be very careful not to lay a guilt trip on your teenagers in an attempt to control them.

As your children reach adolescence, you discover that punishment and guilt tactics become less effective, even to control outward behavior. After they've arrived in the teenage zone, your kids will probably have learned how to manipulate you, performing their disobedience in new and ever-more-creative ways outside your line of sight. While you are convinced that you are gaining the upper hand on them, they are busy using your rules to camouflage their real behavior. They just learn the magic words to keep Mom and Dad off their backs.

The Importance of Discipline

As stated above, discipline is done in the young person's best interests, to help him change his thinking and his heart, not just his outward behavior. There is a classic passage in the Bible about discipline located in Hebrews 12:4-11. The writer of Hebrews claims that if a Christian is without God's discipline he is spiritually "illegitimate," because God disciplines every son that belongs to him. That same principle certainly applies to the world of human fathers, from which the biblical illustration is drawn. If we do not discipline our sons and daughters, we are treating them as though they were illegitimate, as though we have no real love for them. The book of Proverbs emphasizes that parents who really love their children will discipline them.

As teenagers grow older and become more disobedient, parents can become weary of their job. It is easy to throw

up your hands and say, "I give up! If they are going to disobey me, let 'em live somewhere else!" Such a reaction is
often caused when parental punishment methods have lost
their effectiveness. Understanding that it was *never* really
effective should encourage you to move toward effective
discipline. God's advice to any parent who is attempting to
discipline his adolescent kids is: *Don't grow weary and
lose heart in doing what's right* (see Hebrews 12:3 and
Galatians 6:9). God promises to reward us if we keep on
keeping on in our striving against sin.

I like what Gordon MacDonald has to say about discipline. He writes, "To me, discipline is the deliberate creation of stress in a relationship with your children in order
to help them grow and learn."[1] Now that's the opposite of
our normal thinking, isn't it? We usually think of discipline
as what we do *after* our kids do something we don't like.
(That's the way punishment works). MacDonald hit on
something. Instead of reacting, a mature approach to discipline is to be willing, and even *plan,* for the deliberate creation of stress in our relationship by confronting our kids
with choices that come as a result of their actions. In other
words, we don't let things slide just because we know life
will be (temporarily) calmer if we do so. Instead, we take
what appears to be the hard road and confront our teenager about his behavior—and ultimately his character.

Hebrews 12:11 says, "All discipline for the moment
seems not to be joyful, but sorrowful; yet to those who
have been trained by it, afterwards it yields the peaceful
fruit of righteousness." The process of discipline trains
everyone—the one receiving and the one administering it.
Parents have to get tough, and kids have to suffer consequences, and that's never fun. I don't think this process is
ever truly enjoyable. Discipline is a lot like gargling with

....

[1]Jay Kesler, ed., *Parents and Teenagers* (Wheaton, Ill.: Victor Books, 1984), 411.

Listerine—it's the task you love to hate. Yet not to do it, or to do it inconsistently, is to seriously impact your kid's future.

As you discipline your kids, be prepared for your teenagers to verbalize that they don't like you. The day will probably come when one of your kids will announce he would like to go live at a friend's house, because "At least at Robert's house, they can do what they want to." (Well, is *that* so?) Our goal as parents is not to develop our own fan club; our goal is to raise godly kids who can make a way for themselves in this world. And sometimes in pursuing this goal, we'll be misunderstood by the very ones we're trying to protect and love. Expect it, because it goes with the territory.

When I think of discipline, I'm reminded of my first experience as a camp counselor. Fresh out of high school, Joe and I both took ten sixth graders for a week-long counseling adventure in Indian-style tepees. As I watched Joe develop a buddy relationship with his kids by going everywhere as a gang, I began to question if this "single-file, Indian-style" routine I had been advised to use (but disregarded) was really effective. But by the end of the week, Joe was pulling out his hair with discipline problems, while my kids and I had developed a closeness based on respect. If you try to be your teenager's best friend instead of his parent, you may end up losing his respect. And if you have to choose between respect and friendship, my suggestion is that you choose respect. Such esteem is a building block for any relationship, and without it your journey down the road of life will be difficult indeed.

Effective discipline produces a sense of security in your kids. When they see that you have their best interests at heart, and that you are willing to pay whatever price is necessary to help them achieve their own growth in independence, they will be much more likely to feel secure in your choices for them.

The Family Bureau of Investigation

Many teenagers resemble icebergs—only about one-eighth of their character is visible. With teenagers, what you don't know *can* hurt you. Information about what's going on in your family is extremely important. Proverbs says that a man should know the condition of his fields (i.e., he should know what's happening in his house).

It's wise to keep your eyes and ears open. You want to know what they're thinking, who their friends are, and what they're doing—especially in the early teen years, when they suddenly have lots of freedom and very little ability to discern their limitations. I can't tell you how many times I've been able to help my kids through a period of rebellion because I had learned about what they were thinking or doing from some outside source. Much of this information can be obtained simply through good communication with your kids, but don't ever assume that your kids are telling you everything that's going on in their lives. We all have secrets from one another; that's to be expected. But it is important for you to know their basic thinking, or you may wind up with egg all over your face—and worse, your kids may end up on the road to ruin.

If your teenagers haven't been taught that lying is unacceptable, now is the time to start. One of the things that has always been a major cause of disciplinary action in our home is lying. Nothing breaks down trust and communication faster than catching someone in a lie or half-truth. This is extremely important in determining if you are hearing everything from your kids.

Whenever we have the opportunity to quiz a school teacher, a youth worker, or another parent about our kids, we try to find out how they're seen and what they're doing that we are unaware of. This was especially important during the junior high years, and as our relations have improved, we have found it less important—but still a very good idea. Getting information is necessary, but this can certainly be a difficult subject. If your teenagers think that you are spying on them or going behind their backs, they may react to you. My answer to that would be, "Why are you so upset? Is there something that you're afraid I'm going to find out? Are you ashamed of anything you're doing?" Generally speaking, if you're subtle in your research, such encounters can be avoided. But sometimes a teenager needs to be reminded that parents are held legally responsible for the actions of their underage children. Also, just as they have a trust account with your name on it—you have a trust account with their name on it. And if they have done things to undermine your faith in their judgment, you will have to take a closer look at their activities.

On numerous occasions I've discovered things about my kids from indirect sources. That information has been invaluable in helping to put them back on the right track. But I have discovered that the best way to use this information is often just as a guide to ask probing questions. On some occasions I've had to say, "Is there anything you want to share with me before I discipline you for what you've done? If you admit and confess your behavior, I'll go much easier on you." Probably because of their own guilt, kids often assume you know more than you do and reveal everything.

I have a friend whose high-school son was implicated by the police in a series of daytime break-ins. The father immediately began to research his son's behavior, talking to authority figures about the crimes that had been committed and to school officials to figure out when his son had been truant, and he even checked (carefully) with some of his son's closest friends. He compiled a pretty detailed folder on what had no doubt been going on behind his back. Then the father sat down and confronted the boy. "Son, I've done extensive research on your afternoon escapades, and I must hear the truth. If you want my help and support in dealing with the authorities, you'll have to tell me everything. If you leave anything out, I'll know you're lying, and I won't support you."

Because the son knew he was in a fix and needed his father's protection and guidance, he revealed everything. The father was aghast at the extent of the crimes; the situation was far worse than what he had uncovered in his research. Together they were then able to work out a compromise with the authorities and a plan of restitution to the homes that had been vandalized.

As any good intelligence officer knows, you don't ever want to compromise your sources. In World War II the British allowed an English city to be leveled because they knew if they warned the people ahead of time, it would cost the life of a spy who was too valuable to lose. Never use the information you receive as a stick to beat them over the head. Use it to help your kids reveal themselves and their motives.

Motivations for Misbehavior

It has been claimed that there are only four basic motivations for misbehavior in children: 1) desiring attention, 2) grasping for power or control, 3) inflicting revenge on someone, and 4) attempting to avoid failure. Half the battle in dealing with teenage disobedience is to discover what motivates the behavior.

For instance, when a young girl gets involved sexually and becomes pregnant, what is her motivation? Pleasure? Not necessarily. The girl may desire from a boy approval that she is not receiving at home. Or she may be choosing to get even with her parents for the way they've treated her. Such action will certainly receive their attention. "Children in a family are like flowers in a bouquet," stated Marcelene Cox. "There's always one determined to face in an opposite direction from the way the arranger desires." It seems that every family is destined to have at least one defiant child to contend with, as if God is saying to us, *"Here!* This kid will show you how spiritual you are."

Wise parents obviously don't want to wait until their kids do something dramatic before determining what problems they have. You should be watching your kids, observing their character even more than their behavior, so you'll see potential problems before they surface in misbehavior.

When we talk about discipline, two other words come to mind. One is *control,* and the other is *influence.* In the earliest years of a child's life, the parents must maintain control, guiding him down the proper road. But as such, control can and should only last so long. As the youth grows older, control should slowly be replaced by our influence. When our kids move out, all we will have left with them is whatever influence we've achieved during their adolescent years.

To keep from attempting to control your teen's every action, you must maintain a certain amount of tolerance and flexibility. Sometimes the art of being wise is the art of knowing what to make an issue of and what to let go. In dealing with the excesses of your teenagers, you will find that there are times when it will be important to overlook things that you don't like, simply because they will sidetrack you from the real issues of their ultimate growth and development. To keep on track, never lose sight of your long-range goals.

The Preestablished Standard

For discipline to work effectively it must be based upon a preestablished standard. That standard becomes everyone's measuring rod by which we test all our behavior. Without it, a parent will end up punishing his children according to the whim of the moment. If he's had a bad day, the rules change, and the adolescent never knows where he stands.

One of the reasons the world is struggling with its concept of discipline is that there is no preestablished standard upon which everyone agrees. Our world reminds me so much of the message found in the book of Judges: "Everyone did what was right in his own eyes" (21:25). Our families have begun to break down because everyone is living by his own standard, independent of everyone else.

So what should our standard be? As Christians, our standard is the Word of God. The Bible gives us our measure of what is right and wrong; with Jesus Christ we see the perfect standard of God in human flesh. The Lord even told us that we are to be perfect, even as our Father in heaven is perfect (see Matthew 5:48). Now *that's* some standard!

Because everyone in the family has the same criteria for behavior, you won't end up with a double standard. Besides, no one really believes in two standards anyway. If I tell my children to do what I say instead of what I do— I'm declaring the real standard to them by my life-style. And I can be sure that they will learn how to obey that standard whenever my back is turned. Parents must hold themselves to the same yardstick to which they hold their kids, or discipline within their household will quickly become a sham. (Everyone will end up pretending that they are living by the same standard, when in reality they are all living by their own agenda.) A good place to start to implement the principles found in the Bible would be your family character blueprint (see chapter 5 and also appendix B).

Developing a Philosophy of Discipline

It always helps to know where you want to take your kids. In chapter 5 we discussed the need to have a parental mission statement, but I think it is important that both you and your spouse sit down and develop a new philosophy of discipline for your teenagers. This is an area where parents have a lot of arguments, so to avoid laboring at cross-purposes with one another, you need to come up with some form of working agreement that you both can live with.

In developing your philosophy, make certain that you both agree to use the language of respect whenever you deal with your kids. Plan to spend listening times when you will let them vent themselves. Call your own "situation meetings" whenever you sense that your family is starting to move in the wrong direction. (This is a meeting in which you explain to the family the current situation and let everyone talk out how it can be corrected.)

Commit yourself to understanding before you attempt to be understood. Focus on helping your children set and follow after their own long-range goals instead of looking for short-term fixes. Help your children plan ahead for their future, then work together to help them achieve their goals. If teenagers fully understand that you are working to help them develop their independence, they are much more likely to join your team than resist it. If you can communicate that discipline is part of the process for their independence, they'll be less likely to rebel against what you're attempting to do.

I have put together a sample philosophy of discipline in appendix C so that you can use it as a starting place for developing your own philosophy. Take what works for you, and eliminate what doesn't. As you continue along this hard road, I'm certain experience and the Word of God will provide many new insights for you.

SUMMARY OF KEY POINTS

1. If a child received good discipline at the elementary level, he'll be much easier to handle as a teenager.
2. The purpose of punishment is to inflict pain; it focuses upon past misdeeds, represents a hostile attitude, and produces fear and guilt in the one being punished.
3. The purpose of discipline is to train someone for correction and maturity; it focuses upon creating good behavior, represents a basic attitude of love and concern, and produces security.
4. Punishment is an ineffective tool in curbing undesirable conduct because its results are only temporary.
5. Making a teen feel guilty about his behavior will only temporarily change his behavior.
6. A parent shouldn't make a teen feel guilty by condemning him, but he should help him feel the pain that his sin causes others.
7. God doesn't want parents to grow weary of disciplining their teenagers; it is a necessary activity.
8. Discipline is the deliberate creation of stress in a relationship with your children in order to help them grow and learn.
9. A parent is wise to keep his eyes and ears open so that he knows what his teenagers are up to.
10. The four basic motivations for misbehavior are the desire for attention, power, and revenge, and the avoidance of failure.
11. A parent cannot control a teenager forever; eventually he will only have influence over him.

12. For discipline to work effectively, it must be based upon a preestablished standard; the Bible is the Christian standard.
13. A family is wise to establish their own philosophy of discipline.

12

TEENS AND RESPONSIBILITY

"Education is a process not of stuffing people, like sausage into a casing, but of eliciting from people the potentialities hidden even from themselves."
~Sydney Harris

....

One father complained that his teenagers really brightened up his home—that's right, they never turned off any lights. Another father couldn't understand why his teenagers always complained that there was nothing to do—then wanted to stay out all night doing it. Add to this the fact that most teenagers are usually quick to give their parents the full benefit of their inexperience, and you might think that the words *teenager* and *responsibility* are thoroughly incompatible terms. But contrary to the prevailing experience of many parents, it is possible to motivate teenagers toward responsibility. *No,* you may be thinking, *motivating my teenager would be nothing less than "the impossible dream." What little energy my kid expends at home is spent either sitting in front of the television set or listening to music on his bed!*

But I want to assure you—it can be done. After all, contemplate this thought for a moment: You were once a teenager, and somehow you became a responsible human being.

Do Your Kids No Favors

One of the ways you know that your children have finally become teenagers is that they start asking questions that can be answered. But the danger for you as parents is to begin to answer all their questions and make them dependent on you. So much of their later adult behavior will be determined by how well they learn the lessons of responsibility taught by their parents. If your teens never have to do anything around the house, the chances are good that they will expect their spouse to do everything for them (and we all know where *that* can lead).

My daughter has a friend whose parents have enrolled him in an expensive private school. Recently they gave him his own vehicle, several stereos, and multitudes of CDs. In addition to all this, he receives an allowance of *$500.00 per month*—all just for showing up! And out of that money he doesn't even have to pay for his own gas. My daughter questioned him about all this and his they-owe-it-to-me attitude. His reply: "What else would my parents spend their money on?" Poor kid. His parents are doing him no favor. I feel sorry for that young man when he leaves home and finds out what the real world is all about. But more than that, I *really* pity whoever marries him.

Don't do that to your kids! Even if you have lots of money, make your kids work for the things they get. Teach them responsibility, and in the end they will have enjoyed their lives far more than they would if everything was handed to them on a silver platter. It is interesting that people who are on welfare often produce offspring who also end up on welfare. Obviously, such parents train their kids in the fine art of depending on other people to provide their livelihood. No one gains any self-respect in receiving. Jesus said that it is better to give than to receive. Giving improves a person's character; receiving tends to destroy it. You won't be doing your kids any favors by pampering their every whim.

You can't hand responsibility to teenagers; they must achieve it by the sweat of their brow. Some character skills must be learned through training instead of teaching. To be taught is often to be told something; to be trained is to be given an opportunity to learn through experience.

Sports is a good example of this; a person can only learn so much through reading a book. To really develop skill at any sport, hands-on experience is an absolute necessity. That's also why they have two kinds of driver's ed classes in school: one helps the students learn the rules of the road and driving theory, and the other is for behind-the-wheel experience. Only one type of educational experience would create woefully inadequate drivers.

Because your kids each have their own bent toward sinning, you'll have to train them according to their individual needs. I like the way *The Amplified Bible* translates Proverbs 22:6. "Train up a child in the way he should go [and in keeping with his individual gift or bent], and when he is old he will not depart from it." Because every kid has a different personality, you must look for the proper motivation to keep him moving. Your plan for each child should be tailor-made to apply the Scriptures to his specific needs.

If we want our teenagers to grow with mature character, it is vitally important that we train them to be responsible. Responsibility is caught more than it is taught. Our adolescents must see that we act responsibly with our obligations and that we pay the price whenever we don't act responsibly. We have already emphasized in previous chapters how our character speaks volumes to our kids before we ever open our mouth. So when you attempt to impart the lesson of responsibility, you will need to constantly look at your own character to make certain you are indeed practicing what you preach.

Motivating Your Teen

Perhaps in the past you decided to delegate some responsibility to your teenager. Maybe you asked your daughter to cook the evening meal, hoping to get a mini-vacation. But she decided to concoct some exotic dish that was way over her head. So instead of kicking back, you found yourself hovering nearby, sniffing the odors rising from the stove and constantly making suggestions to avoid a culinary disaster. When it was all over, you thought to yourself, *It would have been a lot easier if I had just cooked dinner myself.* Or perhaps you want your teen to keep his room clean. You told him exactly what you want him to do, but then you had to stand over him to make certain he performed because you knew, instinctively, that if you turned your back nothing would be accomplished. Unfortunately, neither of these approaches will do much toward building responsibility in your teenagers. Delegation involves trusting the one to whom responsibility is given. So you're not really delegating if you have to supervise every move. In the room-cleaning example, you will not have accomplished much. The room may be clean today, but just stop prodding and everything will revert to its usual form.

You know what I'm talking about, unless you're one of those blessed parents who have naturally tidy kids. (I can't relate.) Almost every parent has encountered the difficulty of motivating a teenager toward responsibility at some time. He won't work, but, unfortunately, you can't fire him. Someone quipped that an allowance is what you pay your kids to live with you; it certainly couldn't be because they actually do anything around the house.

So how can you motivate your teenagers? If you want a clean teen bedroom, probably the most important thing you must accomplish is for your adolescent to *want* to see his room clean. Without expressing a judgmental attitude, you want to discuss the appearance of his room and get him to express that he really doesn't like living in a pigsty. (But be sure not to put those words in his mouth). Bedroom messes create all sorts of problems, from misplaced items, to ruined clothes, to cockroaches. A recent study revealed that teenagers judge their own peers on loyalty, dependability, and clothes, *but cleanliness was the most often noticed trait.*[1] This means that the vast majority of teens would like to live in a clean room—they just lack the desire to get it that way. Once he admits that he would like to live in a clean room, you're moving down the right road.

When my two daughters roomed together, they decided to get rid of their bunk beds and buy futons. But they hadn't counted on the extra floor space the new beds would require. Suddenly there was no room for dirty clothes to be dropped on the carpet because that no longer left any room to walk. So they found themselves becoming much more motivated to clean up their room and ask their parents for help (wonder of wonders!).

What are the desired results both you and your teen want to see? What do both of you want accomplished on a regular basis? In this case you want your adolescent's room to be clean, and your goal is to have it accomplished without your continued intervention. Is this actually possible? I believe it is—through trust. You want to be able to trust him to clean up his own room. And in the process, you also want to build within him the ability to trust himself to do this job. He needs to know that he can do this job and be happy with himself. As Stephen Covey put it: "Trust is the highest form of human motivation. It brings out the very best in people. But it takes time and patience, and it doesn't preclude the necessity to train and develop people so that their competency can rise to the level of that trust."[2]

Few things build responsibility better than being trusted to do something. But with our teenagers, this usually will

....

[1] *Psychosocial World of the Adolescent: Public and Private,* by Vivian C. Seltzer (New York: John Wiley & Sons, 1989), n.p.

[2] *Seven Habits,* p. 178.

not happen automatically. It takes a lot of work and a great deal of patience to bring their desire, skill, and self-control all to the place where they can accomplish such a task on a regular basis. The following is a strategy to develop responsibility in your teens.

1. Establish what is expected.

At this stage, you and your adolescent must determine exactly what a clean room is. The standard of performance to which he will be held accountable must be clear to both of you. The last thing you want to see him do is to attempt to pawn off a half-cleaned room as sufficient. The desired results must be obvious to both of you. In this case you want nothing left on the floor. Clean clothes should be put immediately away in his drawers (not left in clothes hampers). Dirty clothes must be in the proper hamper; trash must be in the wastebasket. School books should have their place, and there should be no clutter on the desktop or chest of drawers. And the bed should be made each morning. You might sum up your expectations with the words "neat and clean."

Stress any guidelines that will clarify the job to be performed. Ask him, "If you put everything out of sight in cluttered drawers, under your bed, or crammed inside the closet—is that neat and clean?" The answer, of course, is no. What you're both after is neat and clean, not the *appearance* of neat and clean.

Spend the necessary time to make certain that he understands the goal; help him visualize exactly how it should look. Remember, you must be patient; this is a learning process, and he really doesn't know how to clean his room. (Nor does he probably even understand what clean really means). Ask your teen to verbalize how his room is to look; make certain the goal is firmly implanted in his mind. If he begins this process of learning how to clean it up and keep it cleaned with a view to the ultimate goal, he will be much more likely to stay committed to the project.

2. Clarify any resources that are available for this task.

In the case of cleaning his room, he has access to any of the household appliances, such as the vacuum cleaner, brooms, dustpans, wastebasket liners, window cleaners, rags, etc. At least in the beginning, he also has your resources. He can ask you to help him if that's necessary, but your resources are limited.

Often teenagers will say: "This mess is impossible. I just don't know where to start. Would you help me?" You should expect this in the beginning if he has never learned how to clean up his room. He will need the motivation of someone else helping him to get over the hump. But stress the fact that this is his room and it will therefore be his job—not yours—to clean it. You don't want to have to tell him how to do the job (I know this is hard for the average parent). You want to trust him to figure out how to do this job on his own, although you can give him pointers if he wants them. You want to keep the responsibility for the results squarely upon his shoulders. He is the one who must take on the obligation, and it is his duty to perform it. Stress that you trust him to successfully complete this task.

I've just begun this procedure with my five-year-old son. It works well with him. He's "the boss" of his room, so he's the one who's responsible to make his room neat and clean. I let him tell me what to do and how I'm to help him. He usually assigns me to do the projects he can't do, like putting his hats up on the high shelf in the closet.

Remember, your teen is in charge of his room. If you come in and start cleaning everything up, you've just taken

204 THE TEENAGE ZONE

away his responsibility, and you don't want to do that. He is in charge, so he must tell you what he wants you to do. Let him give you an assignment, such as, "Would you help me organize my desk?" Also, if he stops working, you should stop working. You are a resource as long as he doesn't take advantage of you; you cease to be a resource if he starts to depend upon you to get the job done.

3. Establish and clarify his accountability.

You've already set up the standard of performance that is expected; now clarify how this accountability works. This is his room; therefore he must be accountable for it. He will have to judge how well he has fulfilled the standard of performance the two of you established together. You also want to determine when the evaluation will take place. In the case of his room, maybe twice a week.

At the evaluation time, say every Monday and every Friday night before dinner, you'll come into his room, and the two of you will go over your checklist to see if it is neat and clean. But you let him evaluate it; don't ridicule him and tell him what a slob he is. Remember, your assignment as a parent is to build responsibility, not tear it down. If you communicate that you don't trust him, he will obviously give up on himself. If you feel that your adolescent can never change, you can be certain that this project is destined to fail, if for no other reason because of *you*. It will be a rare day that you can motivate your teen to do something you don't believe he can do.

4. Set the consequences.

The consequences must be clearly set at the beginning so you will know how to respond. This is probably as much for you as it is for him because parents are prone to lose it when their kids fail to perform. But such a reaction will only confuse the issue. Your ultimate goal here is not just to see his room clean, but to train him to *know how to clean up after himself*. Knowing this should make it easier to keep from reacting in frustration when he doesn't rise to the standard the two of you have set. Instead, you will simply apply the natural consequences, whether good or bad.

I would suggest that both rewards and penalties be applied to a chore like this. If he cleans his room as agreed, he receives some specified allowance (my daughter wanted to be paid in long-distance telephone calls to her friends). On the other hand, if he does not clean it properly, he not only doesn't get his allowance, but perhaps he will have to give you something of value. A good consequence might be for him to turn over one of his treasures—perhaps a favorite shirt that's been heaped on the floor, or maybe a prized cassette or compact disc. He should also have a "buy-back clause" so that he can repurchase his items at a reasonable rate (perhaps from his allowance). But those treasures must stay in your possession until the next favorable evaluation report. Let the penalties be something he will actually feel, but make absolutely certain that he has agreed to them so his motivation to keep from failing will be real.

When the evaluation time comes, never put down his effort as being inadequate. Praise the obvious improvement. But then point to those little things he will no doubt miss on the floor, under the bed, or hidden behind closed closet doors and dresser drawers. "If this was my room, what kind of evaluation would you give me on this? Do you consider this neat and clean?" Let him come to the conclusion himself that the room really only *looks* neat and clean. The evaluation should be pass or fail, because if you are happy with the progress he seems to have made and say "that's close enough," you will have just lowered the standard for what is neat and clean. Either the room is up to par or it isn't. If you've established ahead of time what you're both looking for, he should be able to come to the right conclusion about the job he's done. So the penalties come if it does not achieve the proper standard; the rewards arrive if it does.

Learning through Success and Failure

Your kids need to know that this is the way life runs. If you don't get your work done in a neat and timely fashion, your boss will eventually fire you. And if you don't have a job, your landlord will eventually boot you out into the street. Living with parents is living in a rarefied atmosphere where many of the natural cause-and-effect relationships are often put on hold; most parents find it difficult to lay down the law consistently.

We are often so impatient to see our kids succeed that we try to insulate them from failure. But we must learn to let our teenagers fail from time to time. Failure teaches many lessons that can never be gained through success. Believe it or not, basketball superstar Michael Jordan was actually cut from his high-school team in his sophomore year. Because of that failure, he had to carry the team's uniforms just so he could ride the bus; that failure motivated him to practice harder so he could make the team the following year. The rest is history.

We need to give our children enough opportunities that they will have occasions to fail. Failure will drive them to find answers for life's problems. In fact, I would suggest if your teenagers succeed at everything they do they are not really being tested for life. Everyone needs a little failure to learn how to rise through adversity. Don't try to hide them from the pitfalls along the road of life. And don't try to insulate them from the consequences of their wrong actions (otherwise known as *sin*). Natural consequences are one of the best teachers God has given us. If we suffer for our indulgences, it is inevitable that we will rethink those sins. I heard a proverb about an employer who asked one of his employees to put together a bonus package for another worker from their warehouse. He was told, "Put in it what you would like to have if I was giving it to you." But the worker didn't really like the employee who was going to be the beneficiary, so he skimped and put together an inferior package that had only the appearance of quality. Imagine his mixed emotions when his employer gave the bonus package to him.

But there is another side to this coin; some teens fail too much and need opportunities to succeed. Accomplishment can bring needed confidence to someone who has been labeled as a failure for most of his life. This is as important to an underachiever as it is to a teen who has a low IQ. It might interest you to know that a person's intelligence score is not set in concrete. Studies have proven that scores go up and down based upon many factors, including what the student had for breakfast on testing day. Also, if a teacher thinks someone is gifted (when his IQ scores are actually low), that student will rise to the occasion. It is important for parents to believe in their teenagers no matter how unsuccessful they have been in the past. Tell them that you believe they can do great things, and they will.

Added to this, I would strongly recommend that you try to provide a home that will stimulate both creativity and the intellect. Encourage your kids to read (especially during summer vacations); go to museums and libraries and cultural events like classical music concerts, plays, and art exhibits. Because I was exposed to such things as a youth, I grew up with a great desire to participate in the creative arts.

Help Your Teenagers Develop Skills

Out in the so-called real world, your kids will need skills in order to survive, especially considering that the competition is often quite fierce. By skills I don't necessarily mean learning a trade; I'm talking about young people having the life-management skills that will help them survive the inevitable times of crisis they are going to face out on their own.

Remember that old proverb "Give a man a fish and you feed him for one day. Teach him to fish and you feed him for a lifetime." The principle stands true. We must train our adolescents how to survive in a dog-eat-dog world (without developing canine character). They must know how to respond to life's cruel realities in a way that will keep them off welfare roles, out of the poorhouse, and away from the divorce courts.

If you're not convinced that helping your teenagers learn to clean their rooms is really all that important, ask yourself how an adult will fare in this world if he cannot keep his things and his life comparatively organized. Most kids don't know how to keep their rooms clean because they've never really stopped to work it all out in their minds. Being neat has certainly not come easy for me. I was allowed to have a messy room growing up and never learned how to pick up after myself. So I've always had to struggle to keep the top of my desk from looking like the aftermath of World War III. For a couple of years I had a secretary who made certain that the top of my desk was cleared every night. Soon I began to cherish that amazing open expanse of work space—which I had seldom seen before—and came to realize how much more efficient I was working in a clean environment. Now I file away all that paperwork and have learned to depend upon my personal appointment calendar and my "do-list" to remind me of my obligations.

If you've learned similar lessons, there is no reason why you can't pass on the benefit of your experience to your children. This assumes, of course, that they are ready to hear it. You can't preach at them, but you can share insights you've picked up when life presents a few of its many teachable moments. But to do this you must have built up your trust account as well as the communication skills necessary for your teenagers to hear you. What a pleasant experience when your kids actually ask for your opinion.

Believe it or not, according to a national survey taken in 1992, by the time a typical teenager reaches upper-class status in high school, he will have a greater interest in having his parents involved in helping him with his homework and regulating the amount of his telephone and television time.[3] My experience has certainly borne this out. (Yes, things can actually get better!)

The Value of an Education

On the average, people who have a college education will earn considerably more than those who do not go on with their education. I like the way one teenager put it: "The amount of education you have determines your loot in life." It is wise to encourage our children to plan to go on to pursue some kind of higher education, whether it's college, technical school, or business school. But an irresponsible student who maintains a low grade-point average will have very few doors open to him after graduation. Once again, the best thing you can do for your teenager is to motivate him to acquire the necessary study skills to make the grade on his own.

....
[3]"Teens want more rules, attention," *San Francisco Chronicle,* May 12, 1992.

A friend of mine wanted his daughter to succeed, so he sat down with her and set up a plan where she could prepare herself for higher education. Together they selected an Ivy League college, and she dedicated herself to achieve the high academic marks it would require. Her father worked out a plan to help her wake up early each morning so she could study when there were no distractions. She worked hard and achieved all of her goals through junior and senior high and ended up graduating from college with honors.

If you want your teens to succeed in high school, you must start as early as possible to help them develop the study skills and the confidence to achieve success in the educational process. Confidence is important. Because most teens have never acquired any study skills, they often feel inadequate when compared to their peers, especially at grade time. To improve their grades, most teens need to learn how to study *smarter,* not necessarily *harder.* Adolescents who are enrolled in private schools usually do better, not just because the schools are better, but because parents who care enough and can afford to pay for private school usually take more of an interest in helping their teens develop and use their learning skills. So your involvement in your children's education is extremely important to their educational success.

Somewhere between the sixth and the ninth grades, most students go through what may be thought of as an academic valley of darkness. Some quit working altogether, others decrease their output, but very few are unaffected. The reason for this short-circuiting of adolescent intellectual achievement is the emergence of the happy hormones. When one's interest in sex takes center stage, who can think about school?

You can't supervise their homework on a regular basis. If you try, everyone will be frustrated. And you don't want to waste your life scolding, coaxing, or reminding them. You cannot hold their hands; remember, we're talking about building responsibility. You must train them to be responsible, and this can be done using the trust method previously outlined.

If they can't see the value in their going on in school (and most junior highers have a difficult time seeing the value of anything beyond the next fifteen minutes), they will have to be taught the value of education to their future. Your daughter may say, "I don't need to go to college because I'm going to get married anyway." Ask her what she'll do if she never gets married, or if her husband dies or divorces her. She must have something to fall back on.

SUMMARY OF KEY POINTS

1. It is possible to motivate teenagers to be responsible.
2. Responsibility is a character quality that can't be handed to teenagers; it can only be achieved it by the sweat of their brow.
3. Responsibility is caught, not taught. It is vitally important that we train our teenagers.
4. Few things build motivation better than being trusted to do something.
5. When building work habits, first establish what is expected.
6. Then clarify any resources that are available for the job.
7. Establish what the teenagers' accountability will be, but don't tell them. Let them say it.
8. Set consequences for the conclusion of the task.
9. Teenagers need to have experience in both success and failure to understand the way life works.
10. Help your teenagers develop life-management skills that will help them survive.

11. Share your insights about life during the teachable moments that come along in everyday living.
12. Help your teenagers learn the value of future education to success in life.

13
SEX CRAZY OR WHAT?

"Oh, what a tangled web do parents weave, when they think that their children are naive." ~Ogden Nash

....

Adolescence is the period of time in a boy's life when he first notices that a girl notices he is noticing her. You may wonder why it is that your daughter is so poor in history but so high on dates? When she brings home a boy with a body too big for his brain, you may be convinced that the only thing this kid could pass in school would be the football. If by some miracle your daughter actually asks whether kissing is dangerous, Mom can always answer, "Of course it is. That's how I got your father!" Although this period is an extremely crucial time for teenagers—a time that will no doubt establish much of their sexual behavior for life—most parents struggle to know what they are supposed to do.

A 1991 survey of two thousand junior high students in the inner-city schools in the San Francisco Bay area revealed that 20 percent of these young adolescents were sexually active. Sixty percent of those involved were between thirteen and fourteen. A third of them had their first intercourse by age twelve. An alarming nationwide survey conducted in 1990 by the Center for Disease Control reported that by ninth grade, 40 percent of those surveyed had already had sex. We live in a day when parents can never assume that their children know less about sex than they do.

The Awakening of Desire

At some curious moment in a young teenage boy's life, something strange happens. His interest in girls gets a complete overhaul. No longer does he think of them as weak and a waste of his time. Suddenly he becomes incredibly aware of the female body. He sees things that he has never really seen before. Erotic daydreams suddenly begin to consume much of his free time. He discovers the intense pleasure in his own genitals that comes from masturbation. He may begin to search for pornographic magazines. He may even begin peeping into bedroom windows after dark, his heart racing at the thought that he might actually see something. He becomes obsessed with sex, locked in his own private fantasy world he must keep hidden from adults—especially his parents—at all costs. In the locker room, he takes an interest in comparing his anatomy with the other boys'. He begins to grow hair between his legs and under his arms. As he discovers that other boys his age feel the same overpowering desires, the conversations begin about the best-looking girls or the sharing of sexy magazines. The more precocious boys begin to brag about their sexual exploits, and a boy's head often becomes filled with erotic fantasies.

At the same time, girls become aware of their new and blossoming bodies, and of the fact that boys are suddenly looking. The knowledge of these new powers fills a girl's heart with mixed emotions. She sees other girls snagging boyfriends and begins to dream about having one of her own. She starts to use makeup and dresses with the boys in mind; her conversations with girlfriends often focus upon talk about cute guys. At this age, a girl falls in love with love. She is not so much interested in a particular boy as she is in what the boy represents. Having a boyfriend is a rite of passage that proves she is attractive and popular.

Because of this, many boys are often going steady even before their voices are.

Adolescence is brought on by puberty, and the purpose of puberty is primarily sexual in nature. A child's body is being changed to prepare for procreation. It's important to recognize that the pressure toward sexual relations will ultimately prevail. The normal male teenager becomes biologically ready for intimacy, fantasizes about sex, desires sexual intercourse, and eventually will participate in that consummation—and all that leads up to it.

Why Are We So Unprepared?

Probably no other area troubles parents more than the subject of sex. When it suddenly dawns on a parent that his child is about to enter puberty, he tends to quake in his boots. For some reason, Americans have had a difficult time developing any sort of customs or tradition in which parents sit down with their children and explain the facts of life. Indeed, the standing joke for many Americans is that Dad is eventually supposed to have a conversation about the birds and bees with his sons. I think that euphemism for the big talk is a reminder of just how much this subject terrifies us.

Parents resist this subject as if talking about it might stunt a child's growth. The thought of bringing up the subject prematurely is like the fear of death—no other subject terrifies an adult more. *How am I going to talk about sex with my own kids? Suppose they ask me what we did when we were dating!* The thought seems horrid. You can probably picture everyone nervously staring at the floor while your kids say, "Ah ha, ah ha—can I go now?" Most parents hope desperately that the school or church youth group will take care of this delicate subject for them. But if that doesn't happen, they just hope that their kids will somehow figure it all out on their own.

As difficult as this subject is for you, do you really want to leave it to the "experts" in the public schools? Most of these experts teach that only a teenager can decide when it's the right time to have sex. They also preach that every teenager should be given free access to condoms. And young girls should have the right to have abortion counseling and even an actual abortion without their parents ever knowing. Some of these so-called experts are even saying that one young person in ten is a homosexual—but just doesn't know it yet. Of course, after they've performed their teaching duty, the kids will "come out of the closet" because they believe that homosexuality is natural and normal. Do you really want these experts teaching your adolescents about sex? Not if you want to instill Christian values. Whenever my wife and I heard that our kids were going to be talking about such subjects, we made certain that they were exempted from those meetings. I don't want anyone teaching my children about sex like it is just biological plumbing. To present sex on that level not only cheapens it, it also creates increased peer pressure to participate in it.

Well, you might be thinking, *can't we just leave this subject for our church youth group?* If the youth workers are older and married and have a close relationship with the parents, this can certainly be appropriate. But my experience is that most youth pastors are unprepared to teach on this subject, are too close to the age of their youth groups, and generally don't clear the program with the parents of their kids. So I wouldn't depend upon your church youth pastor.

A Plan for the Birds and Bees

I am absolutely convinced it is of prime importance for every family to make this subject a high priority. Sex must be put in its proper context. In many cultures (where there is absolutely no dating or sexual involvement until the wedding night), this discussion is done right before the marriage ceremony; in our society it would be extremely risky to wait until that day. But if your parents didn't discuss this subject with you, you probably don't have a clue about how to approach such a talk with your own teens. "I kept waiting for the right time," says a mother in Southern California about talking to her thirteen-year-old daughter, "but I am just too afraid to bring it up. I'm not sure what to say." One sex ed teacher estimates that three out of four parents never talk to their teenagers about sex.

Now before you get too nervous, let me assure you this really isn't as bad as it seems. The task will be much easier if you have taken the time to develop good relationships with your children. If you have applied the information in the earlier chapters in this book on love, trust, and communication, I think you'll find this task much easier.

Talking to your daughters about sex

Probably the best way to do this is for Mom to sit down with the daughters and Dad to work with the sons. This should probably be accomplished one kid at a time. To make this task easier for yourselves, I would suggest that you pick up a few good Christian books on the subject of sex and read up on it so you have all your facts right before talking with your kids. You might want to keep that book as a handy reference, especially for diagrams of the reproductive system. The tendency, of course, is to put off such meetings. But if you do, you can be certain that your kids will hear about sex from some other source before you get to them. Because you definitely don't want that to happen, make certain you don't put this off.

The logical time for the first talk with your daughters

would be right before menstruation. Certainly every girl needs information about what to expect and how to handle her flow. Many girls desperately want to hold this off, while others are anxious for it because they want to grow up quickly. Girls who begin earlier or later than their peers may struggle emotionally and need special encouragement. (My wife informed our daughters about the coming period when they were very young, so that when it arrived, it was not a big surprise).

When a girl is introduced to the meaning and purpose of menstruation, a mother would be wise to discuss the subject of sex. Although your daughter may initially be squeamish about the thought of sex, don't let this throw you. Although most girls are not necessarily interested in sex, they are interested in boys—and boys *are* interested in sex. Talk to her about the joys of marriage and how sex was created by God to be shared by two people within the context of marriage. I once heard sex compared to good, rich garden soil. It's great in the garden—where it belongs—but if you bring it in and throw it on the carpet, it loses its goodness. So does sex when it is taken out of the proper context of marriage.

Create a positive atmosphere for your daughters. Help them feel that you are on their side and that they can come to you at any time to get their questions answered. You want to become their confidant so they'll come to you later if they ever have questions about morality.

Talking to your sons about sex

I believe it is extremely important for a father to build a relationship with his sons so that it will be easier to talk to them about this subject when it's time. What you say in one meeting is probably not as important as how you behave daily and how you use those teachable moments from everyday life. For example, when you come into contact with a lurid magazine rack, don't just walk away; point the product out for what it is. But whatever you do, don't lie about it. Don't say something like, "Only unregenerate perverts look at trash like this." Instead, be truthful. "Son, this stuff can be addicting to any red-blooded guy; a wise man knows he should stay away from it because God tells us in Proverbs that it's like playing with fire—it will only burn you." The consistency of these teachable moments will help reinforce the major birds-and-bees talks you will have together.

Because upwards of 98 percent of teenage boys eventually become involved with masturbation, it is important that it be addressed and discussed. Don't worry about giving him ideas; it's important to create an open atmosphere for discussion of this common addiction. The so-called secular experts have attempted to make light of the harm that masturbation can cause, referring to repressive attempts in the past to make young people think that the behavior would bring on everything from warts to acne to insanity. Most Christians would agree that such guilt-laying attempts do more harm than good. Although the Bible does not specially mention masturbation and therefore doesn't directly condemn it, Jesus taught that if a man looks upon a woman to lust after her, he has committed adultery in his heart (Matthew 5:28). Because it is virtually impossible for the average young man to keep from thinking lustful thoughts when masturbating, we can assume that God is not happy with this activity.

Not only do erotic daydreams defy reality (the mind conjures up perfect women who always respond fully, begging for more), they also challenge our beliefs as Christians. We are to be wholly committed to one woman, and erotic daydreams are notorious for the variety of women they encompass. This self-pleasuring focuses only upon a man's sexual fantasies and ignores completely how women really feel, thus propagating the male myth that girls are things that can be used. A young man must keep his lust under control, because sin always begins in the heart before it finds its expression in our behavior.

When I was in high school there was a joke making the rounds. Someone would say, "Did you know that people who are hard of hearing . . . ," and then would mumble the rest of the sentence.

"What?" the victim would ask.

"I said," the practical joker would say, beginning to raise his voice, 'Did you know that people who are hard of hearing *have a sex problem!*'"

Let's face it, talking about sex to our kids is extremely difficult for most men because *we* still "have a sex problem." If red blood flows through your veins, you're probably still struggling with your own thought life. How can you preach against it if you find it so difficult to practice it? Simple: by being pledged to the same standard to which you want your sons to be committed—that of bringing every thought captive to the obedience of Christ.

One of the advantages of a father talking about sex with his teenage boy is that he knows the temptations that his son is going through and can encourage him to be strong in them. A father should train his son to respect girls and treat them with honor, not as things to be taken advantage of. A young man should be challenged to plan and build his life for that spouse God will one day send his way. Encourage your son to enter marriage with no regrets.

Fathers and Their Teenage Daughters

I think it is important to stress the need for a father to be vitally involved with his teenage daughters. Many studies of prostitutes have indicated that women often enter that

decadent profession because of the emotional wasteland
their fathers created in the home. I don't think it can be
overemphasized that a father's relationship with his daughters is *extremely* important to their spiritual and psychological well-being.

The Bible indicates that a father had charge over his
teenage daughters, even as to whether they would be
allowed to marry or not (see 1 Corinthians 7:36-38). If a
father endeavors to raise his daughters in the biblical way,
he will endeavor to build a strong relationship with them
with the idea of helping them in their selection of a spouse.
A father is the best judge of character of any incoming
boy; he can usually see through the average guy. That's
why it is extremely important for him to help his daughters in their dating selection process. I've told my daughters that I want to meet any guy who is interested in them.
I don't want any kid coming along who thinks that he can
date (and seduce) one of my daughters without having to
answer directly to me. My daughters are my spiritual
responsibility until the day that I give them in marriage to
their husbands.

About the time each of my daughters turned sixteen, I
sat them down and gave them a ring that was to symbolize
the commitment they made to me and to the Lord that
they would remain chaste until the day they got married. I
think it is so important to encourage a girl toward this
commitment. One of the best motivations for good behavior is the teens' knowledge of how their transgressions will
impact others—especially those that love them most.

Instilling Proper Sexual Values

Sex is not just another form of pleasure, like a participa-
tion sport or a ride on a roller coaster. It has serious and
important ramifications for your children's lives. They

need to have their values reinforced with solid beliefs taught from God's standard, the Bible. Here are some things that you need to know and teach your kids.

1. Avoid any situation where you can become emotionally involved with the opposite sex before it is the proper time. Dating is an American social custom that really didn't exist before we invented it. Back in the olden days, when a man "came courting," he inevitably spent his time with the girl right under her parents' noses. In most situations, two kids were never allowed to be together unless they were under the watchful eye of a chaperone.

One of the best things you can do for your teenagers is to discourage them from dating. The more I see what's happening to the other teenagers in our community, the more convinced I become that dating will only ruin our kids. It puts them into a position where they can become emotionally aroused. From there it is but a short step to physical intimacy. Such statements are always laughed at because they seem hopelessly old-fashioned. But virginity and abstinence are also considered hopelessly old-fashioned.

The fact that everyone else is dating means nothing to me. I see what's happening to other adolescents, and it makes me all the more determined to protect my kids from that. I'm not just talking about the non-Christian kids; I'm talking about the Christian teenagers who are allowing their hearts to become emotionally involved so they are willing to follow after what the Bible would call "strange flesh" (see Jude 7)—which is sex with someone other than your spouse. If we let our kids do everything that the world is doing, we can't really be surprised when they suddenly come to us in tears to tell us that "they couldn't stop themselves."

If you want your sons and daughters still to be chaste by the time they finish high school, begin while they're in junior high to emphasize the importance of keeping their hearts free of emotional attachment to someone before they are ready for that commitment.

2. God clearly tells us to avoid immorality. First Corinthians 6:15-20 makes a lucid presentation of the fact that being involved with someone outside of marriage violates the spiritual essence of our relationship with Christ. Premarital sex is a violation of physical and spiritual oneness by joining sexually with another person. Other sins are outside the body; joining yourself to a loose individual is a way of sinning against your own body (see also 1 Thessalonians 4:1-8).

To make this easier, a father should teach his daughter how to hold off boys who seek to touch her. This apparently innocent act, even if it is just a pat on the shoulder, is an attempt to build intimacy because touching reveals one person's "rights of possession" over another. I believe that touching, including hand-holding, should be held off and reserved for the guy to whom she is ready to become engaged. A girl (or guy) should become serious by developing a friend relationship, not by physical intimacy.

3. God tells us that sexual sins can destroy our conscience. In 1 Corinthians 6:9-10 Paul makes it plain that unrepented sin (including adultery) sends a man to hell. Our teenagers need to know the seriousness of sexual sin. In Proverbs the man who goes in to a prostitute is called a naive fool who may lose not only his life, but also his soul (see Proverbs 7:21-27). The problem is that when we partake of something that we know is wrong, we tend to sear our conscience, making it that much harder to respond to God's conviction (see Romans 1:18-27).

4. Premarital sex develops a great deal of guilt and shame. Remember there are two kinds of guilt: true guilt and guilty feelings. Premarital sex produces both types. This guilt will continue to haunt young people years after they have indulged, defiling their memories and forcing them to one day have to admit their behavior to a future spouse.

Let's talk for a moment now about shame. In Genesis Adam and Eve were both naked, but they were not ashamed—until they sinned. Suddenly, for the first time, shame rose to the surface of their emotions. Shame, like guilt, is a built-in mechanism that God put inside our brains to cause us to avoid sinful behavior. After we have succumbed to sin, shame causes us to be remorseful for our actions.

"Shame has a cruel, destructive side," says Sharon Sheehan in a recent *Newsweek* article, "but it also protects us. It prevents us from treating others despicably. And it protects what one author calls 'the sanctity of our unfinished or unready selves.'"[1]

Shame is a moral dipstick to help us measure whether we're on the right road. If adults try to cover up teenagers' feelings of shame, they'll only be sweeping the problems under the rug. And that only produces a lumpy rug. The solution to eliminating shame is for us to turn away from our sins, not to candy-coat them.

5. Sexual experimentation before marriage creates opportunities for comparison and later marital dissatisfaction. I know more than one man who has a videotape in his brain of sexual experiences he had before he got married. Unfortunately, the erotic mind has a tendency to conveniently forget the bad and savor all of the good sexual experiments, creating an erotic standard to which no wife could possibly measure up. Instead of appreciating his wife's attempts to be sexy for him, a man with such a memory may often feel unfulfilled because of all the many past "great nights" with which his wife must compete. A male

....

[1]"Another Kind of Sex Education" by Sharon Sheehan in *Newsweek*, July 13, 1992, pp. 10–11.

is wise if he never allows such memories to be created in his heart.

6. *Sex before marriage carries the tremendous risk of unwanted pregnancy.* Each year there are one million teenage pregnancies, indicating that teens are not using birth control methods properly. Teenagers are often urged to use condoms as protection, but sex often "just happens" when young people are not prepared for it. Unless young people have an inner moral restraint to say no, they will simply not be able to stop long enough to secure the limited protection of a condom. The teenage boy usually isn't worried about the girl getting pregnant (because he views that as *her* problem), and so you can bet that he will push her into intercourse even if he has no condom. Even if condoms worked 100 percent of the time, which they don't, they will never be truly effective for teenagers because of the spontaneous nature of sexual passion.

7. *Extramarital sex carries a tremendous risk of contracting sexually transmitted diseases.* There are approximately thirty-four sexually transmitted diseases on the rampage today. Kids have no idea what is out there and how easy those diseases are to catch. Many STDs can be caught *even with a condom* since condoms can break and are often used improperly. If they are not foolproof in stopping pregnancy, there is a definite risk of catching something like genital herpes, a lifelong disease, or AIDS, which seriously shortens one's life.

Most young people feel indestructible; because they probably don't know anyone with AIDS or an STD, they naturally assume that they can't get it through unprotected sex. The problem is that AIDS symptoms take so long to show up that a young person may have it and be transmitting it to others *for years* before he even realizes he's infected. Millions today are already infected and are passing on the deadly disease to others without even realizing it. As an example of what may happen in this country, point your teens toward Africa. As a result of sexual promiscuity, Africa has been decimated by AIDS. I've heard estimates that as much as *20 percent of the continent* will be infected by the year 2000.

But don't let young people be lulled into thinking that they must have sex to get AIDS. The disease is transmitted through body secretions, and research indicates that saliva is more infectious than even genital secretions. Dr. Helen Singer Kaplan states that "saliva is an ideal environment for the AIDS virus. In fact, the count is larger in saliva than in the blood of an HIV-positive person."[2] That means it is highly likely that a young person could contract the disease just through extensive kissing with a person who is infected. That's a scary thought, and all the more reason to encourage our kids to be abstinent, even platonic, until marriage.

8. Premarital sexual intercourse dramatically increases the odds of a person becoming promiscuous later during married life. Studies have shown that the younger a person has premarital sex, the more likely it is that he will have affairs after he gets married. Illicit sex is much more exciting simply because it is forbidden. If a young person gets addicted to it before marriage, it becomes hard for that person to stay committed to only one person after the wedding. The desire to repeat those feelings can be a strong temptation after matrimony.

9. Illicit sexual relationships create all sorts of character problems. When teenagers have premarital sex, they will usually have to hide that fact from the adults in their life. Nothing is worse than to have strong sexual desires that cannot be fulfilled in a righteous way. Teenagers know that

....

[2] "Producers need to know a French kiss may bring AIDS," *Redding Record Searchlight*, August 12, 1992.

they are violating their parents' trust to secure their own pleasure, and that knowledge creates a need to lie.

This problem is greatly exaggerated because it is easy to follow the same double standard later when the young people get married and cheat on their spouse. Adultery destroys a marriage because no one can be committed to two people at the same time. Duplicity and lying become a natural consequence as the guilty party hides what's going on. God says that hidden sin eats away at us from the inside. Such behavior will have deadly impact upon a person's character and spirituality.

10. Homosexual behavior is unnatural and is clearly condemned by God. In today's world, homosexuality is being touted as a normal, if alternate, life-style. But the Bible makes it very plain that this sin, like so many other sexual sins, is an offense to God (1 Corinthians 6:9-11). God calls the practice an abomination, and any young person who feels drawn toward the same sex must understand that it is as wrong as premarital sex or adultery.

Homosexuality is condemned by God both in the Old Testament (Leviticus 20:13) and in the New (Romans 1:24-27). If a young person is attracted sexually to the same sex, he must reject those feelings in the same way that he must reject attraction toward someone who is already married. He must flee from those thoughts, not leaving himself any opportunities to fall to such "evil imaginations."

This sin is probably as difficult for parents to accept as it is for teenagers to admit. Let's face it, if a son or daughter comes to you claiming that he or she is gay, you will probably have a difficult time accepting the fact (that you could have produced someone with this sin). On the other hand, there is growing tendency for today's Christian parents to be so open-minded that they accept such a confession without pointing the young person in the right direction.

If you really love your children, you won't condemn them, but you will expose them to what God's Word has to say about giving in to this lust. Turn them to the many passages in the Bible that condemn homosexuality. Show them also that to lust in your heart is to be guilty before God (Matthew 5:28). The attraction isn't sinful in itself (see James 1:14-15), but the lust can certainly lead to sin—and that will lead to their spiritual destruction.

If your children are attracted to the same sex, bring them back to God's standard and let him convict them of the error of pursuing such a sinful life-style.

SUMMARY OF KEY POINTS

1. After puberty boys become extremely sex-conscious; girls discover that boys are interested in them.
2. Probably no other area troubles parents more than how to tell their teenagers about sex.
3. Parents should avoid letting the public school educate their teenagers about sex.
4. Every family should discuss with their teens the subject of sex and put it in its proper context.
5. Mothers should sit down with their daughters to discuss sex near the onset of menstruation.
6. Fathers should talk to their sons about sex and deal with subjects such as masturbation.
7. Fathers need to nurture their daughters, as a healthy relationship between them is important to the girls' future.
8. God clearly tells us to avoid immorality.
9. Premarital sex causes a great deal of guilt and shame.
10. Sexual experimentation creates comparison and later marital dissatisfaction.
11. Sex before marriage carries the tremendous risks of

unwanted pregnancy and contracting a sexually transmitted disease.

12. Premarital sex increases the odds that a person will be
promiscuous even after marriage.

13. Homosexual behavior should be discouraged because
God clearly condemns it.

INFECTING YOUR KIDS
WITH CHRISTIANITY

"Let us not fool ourselves—without Christianity, without Christian education, without the principles of Christ inculcated into young life, we are simply rearing pagans." ~Peter Marshall

....

As a college student, I often went down to one of Southern California's beaches during summer vacation to take religious surveys designed to open up a conversation about Christ. One Sunday afternoon, I approached a guy sunning himself on the sand near the Huntington Beach pier.

"What is this?" he asked when he saw my clipboard. "Do I look like a horrible sinner or something? You're the second person to come up to me on this beach trying to talk to me about God."

As I witnessed to him, he kept making quips. "Hey," he said, "have you ever thought that this Christianity stuff might not be true? And if it turns out that it isn't, think of all the fun you will have missed out on."

"Yes, but if *I'm* right and you're wrong, think of where you'll end up—in hell."

"You've got a point there," he said with a chuckle. But the man continued to quip through our entire conversation, apparently in an attempt to keep God's message from becoming too personal.

Life's Most Important Decision

That man didn't become a Christian, because he had no sense that he had transgressed the laws of a holy God. At the time, I had no idea how to bring a person under conviction of sin. Many teenagers from Christian families never become believers because no one ever tells them that they have offended God by disobeying his commandments. They don't realize that their self-centered life-style is an abomination to him, because their Christianized home makes nominal belief acceptable. Whether or not your teenagers see their sin and respond to the Lord will be, in the final analysis, the most important decision that they ever make. Every parent should make absolutely certain that his children have had a real opportunity to see their lost condition and then be exposed to the gospel.

Unfortunately, many parents assume their church will lead their children to the Lord. *After all, isn't that why we pay the pastor and the youth pastor? Isn't it their responsibility to make certain our kids follow after God?* I'm sorry, but it is not. God has called us to be responsible for the spiritual lives of our children. *We* brought these kids into the world, and God says they are *our* spiritual responsibility. Believe me, the so-called paid professionals will find it very difficult to do the job for us if we fail to minister at home.

Years ago, I heard a statistic that said it took the typical pastor—on the average—365 days to reach one person with the gospel. I don't know how true that is, but I wouldn't doubt it. Perhaps you attend a church where little evangelism takes place. One pastor felt certain his church would be the first one up at the Rapture because he read the Bible verse that said, "The *dead in Christ* shall rise first." From personal experience I can tell you that the church is just not prepared to lead all its young people to the Lord. No church has the resources to do the job God has called parents to do. And besides, the hardest kids to reach are those whose parents are surface-level Christians who rarely show any spiritual vital signs.

Spiritual Inoculation

As a youth pastor I quickly discovered that my most fruitful ministry took place with the kids whose parents were not Christians. We had far more of them come to Christ than any other group. But the most difficult kids were almost always from the families of the church pillars who demonstrated little Christianity in a practical way at home.

I'm afraid most youth groups are not much better; youth pastors often attempt to reach kids by presenting a fun-and-games program into which they try to slip the gospel after they have convinced the kids that being a Christian really isn't so bad. "You've tried drugs; now try Christ," we say. "Come to Jesus because he loves you and has a wonderful plan for your life. He'll give you love and joy and peace." The problem with this message is that it does not produce any conviction of sin. The so-called believers created by such a message have no understanding that they have displeased a holy God. They don't come broken, and thus they don't really come to Christ.

Picture a crowded commercial airplane. The pilot's voice suddenly squawks on the intercom: "This is your captain speaking. You've probably noticed that two of our engines have just fallen off the wing. We are now descending rapidly, and we will soon be making a sudden, unscheduled stop directly into the ground. Please take the parachute from under your seat and prepare to jump."

Although most of the passengers are too busy laughing, listening to music, and watching the in-flight movie to listen to the captain or to take any action, one man hears the announcement and immediately pulls out his parachute and straps it on. He is grateful that the airline has provided him a parachute and holds onto it for dear life. But because he knows the airplane will soon crash, he becomes concerned that most of the other passengers have failed to heed the pilot's warning. He turns to the man next to him and, not wanting to offend him, says: "I'd really encourage you to put on that parachute. You know, it will greatly improve your flight. Not only that, I'm sure it will give you a sense of love, joy, and peace."

"Really? Love, joy, and peace?"

"That's right."

So his seatmate slips on the parachute. But soon he notices how bulky and uncomfortable it feels. And worse, he sees that the other passengers are laughing at him for wearing it. Eventually he takes if off and throws it down on the floor, feeling that he's been lied to. Why? Because he has not heard that the airplane is about to crash. He has no idea about the real reason he needs that parachute.

That's what many of our churches are teaching today. By touting the benefits of being a Christian, we are missing the most important first step in presenting the salvation message: that God is about to judge mankind. And because our converts have no conviction of sin, they easily backslide when the going gets tough.

When the doctor gives a shot to inoculate someone, he is actually injecting a live (but weakened) germ or virus. The body's natural mechanism fights off this weakened strain and in the process builds up antibodies that can be used later to fight off the full-strength virus if it ever attacks us. Unfortunately, we parents do the same thing to our kids; we inoculate them against Christianity. When we parents *talk* Christianity, but don't really *live out* our relationship with Christ, we make it harder for our kids to ever want to come to the Lord. They don't see in us the fire that comes from someone who knows that the world's plane is soon going to crash. They don't see in us an abhorrence of sin and a consciousness of the holiness of God. Therefore, they see no real reason to strap on their parachute, because they recognize that we don't see the world's plight as any big deal.

Kids who have been exposed to this kind of Christianity are very difficult to reach. Because they resent being in church, they become a headache for any serious youth worker and make it more difficult for the other kids in the youth group to really learn how to follow the Lord. If your kids are hardened toward the gospel, you can be pretty certain what has caused this lethargy.

Your Plan of Action

No one should care more about the salvation of your children than you do. And if your teenagers don't know Jesus by the time they graduate from high school, the chances will diminish each passing year that they will ever respond to the Lord. So you've got to make certain they don't escape while they're still in their sins.

I won't attempt to give you some pat plan of salvation with all the well-known Bible verses so you can lay it on your teenagers. If your adolescents are resistant to the Lord, you will need to understand more than just a set of basic salvation verses to reach their hearts.

1. *First, recognize that you must earn the right to minister the Lord to your teenagers.* Now you might be thinking, *I'm their parent. Doesn't that give me the right to minister to them?* Yes and no. If they perceive your Christianity as being shallow, without any real brokenness before the Lord, they will probably reject it as being superficial. The thing you must therefore do is prove to them that your Christianity is the genuine article.

Of course, that means that the Lord must actually be real to you. Perhaps it's been a while since you became a Christian, and you've grown stale in your walk. This certainly becomes a motivation to examine yourself to see if you've lost your first love for the Lord (see Revelation 2:4-5; 3:15-21). If you are lukewarm, you need to get the flame of your Christianity burning brightly once again.

When was the last time you repented? Not only must repentance take place when we become Christians; it must also happen in our lives on a daily basis. A fact of the Christian life is that we continue to sin after becoming believers. We must therefore continue to repent of those sins. God hates the sins of Christians just as much as he does those of unbelievers. Sin is sin. We can never allow ourselves to embrace sin just because we've been forgiven. That's not the grace of God—that's license. God wants us to be constantly willing to face the reality of our transgressions by continually repenting of the deeds of darkness into which we often fall. If we fail to do that, our kids will sense that all we have is churchianity.

It is always more difficult to minister to those who know us best because they know our inconsistencies. They will have seen our temper flare. They will have heard us criticize others behind their backs. And the only way to counteract such excesses on our part is to repent whenever we fall short. Sure we'll fail, but if we are willing to take the blame for our sinful inconsistencies and ask for forgiveness from our kids when it is necessary, our Christianity will be much more palatable to them. Most kids aren't asking for their parents to be perfect—they just want them to be honest.

2. *Pray for their salvation.* We discussed this in several other chapters, but it is important to emphasize that real victories in the spiritual world are almost always won first through prayer. Don't leave this important part of your arsenal unused. You don't know what's going on inside their heads, but God does. Therefore, you need God's supernatural intervention if they will ever come under con-

viction and turn to the Lord. Prayer is also the only way
you can really prepare your heart to minister effectively.

3. *Expose them to the teaching of God's law.* This is one
of the most important things you can do to bring your
teenagers to repentance. They have to know that they have
transgressed the law of God. They have violated God's
wishes, and thus they will have to pay the consequences.
The only effective way of doing this is to share God's Old
Testament law with them, especially the Ten Commandments.

The Need for Conviction

Ray Comfort's classic book, *Hell's Best Kept Secret* (Whittaker House, 1989), calls the church back to the full message of biblical salvation. In his book, which I highly
recommend, Ray points out that around the turn of the
century much of Western civilization turned away from
preaching and teaching God's law and began to present the
"Good News" to men who were not under conviction of
sin. Because of this, we have produced a generation of
Christians who have very little concept of what true conversion is all about. In fact, about 90 to 95 percent of all
modern-day converts fall away. The reason for this is that
they were never really believers in the first place. They did
not understand their lost condition, and their Christianity
was not a living relationship but a dead religion.

It was Charles Finney who said, "If you have an uncon-
verted sinner, convict him. If you have a convicted sinner,
convert him." So how do you bring a young person to conviction over his sin? You expose him to God's law. It is a
good idea for every Christian family to continually expose
their children to the Ten Commandments. Let them read
them. Have them memorize those commandments. Let
them understand that God's standard for sin has not

changed. Show them Matthew 5 and other New Testament passages where the Lord interprets the meaning of the Law and makes it clear that if we lust or hate in our heart, we have broken the commandments and deserve the fires of hell. James 2:10 goes so far as to say that if we break one commandment, we've broken them all. If we have not repented, we are still under the curse of the law (and the penalty that goes with it). Listen to the powerful words of Charles Spurgeon:

> There is war between thee and God's Law. The Ten Commandments are against thee. The first comes forward and says, "Let him be cursed, for he denies Me. He has another god besides Me, his god is his belly, he yieldeth homage to his lust." All the Ten Commandments, like ten great cannons, are pointed at thee today, for you have broken all God's statues, and lived in daily neglect of all His commands.
>
> Soul! thou wilt find it a hard thing to go to war with the Law. . . . What will ye do when the Law comes in terror, when the trumpet of the archangel shall tear you from your grave, when the eyes of God shall burn their way into your guilty soul, when the great books shall be opened, and all your sin and shall be punished?[1]

If a young person realizes how God sees his transgression, if he realizes that the law and its punishment apply to him if he does not turn from his disobedience, he will do one of two things: Either he will harden his heart, showing its real condition, or he will break down before God. This must be your goal for your teenager—that he will come to

-----

[1] Quoted in Comfort, *Hell's Best Kept Secret,* pp. 23–24.

the knowledge of his own iniquity. For a teenager to come to true repentance, he must first possess the same opinion about himself that God holds.

A thorough study of the New Testament reveals that salvation always comes strongly packaged with our need to understand our transgression against God. We are told the purpose of the Law was to act like a tutor to show us of our need for Christ (Galatians 3:24). The Law was never written for righteous people (that is, those who are trusting in Christ for their righteousness); it was written for the unrighteous (see 1 Timothy 1:9ff). It is a mirror by which we can see how great our offenses are toward God (see Romans 3:20; 4:15; 7:7-9; James 1:25). By exposing your teenager to that standard, you can enable him to see his need. Christ's death on the cross means nothing to someone who does not fully realize that it was he who is responsible for the Lord's death. Once his need for a Savior hits him, he has come under conviction.

But conviction or sorrow over sin is not salvation (2 Corinthians 7:10). A teenager may know that what he has done is wrong. He may know that God dislikes his behavior and attitude; he may even feel emotional about his sin. But unless he is willing to yield the control over his sinful heart to the Lord, he will not truly be coming to Christ. His conviction must lead him to forsaking the pleasures of sin. A teenager who truly repents will not be ashamed of his conversion; he won't care who knows that he is a believer. And even if he falls away from the Lord for a season, he will still feel the weight of conviction upon his heart.

Finney has some insight on this:

> The real Christian is filled with peace at the very time his tears are flowing from conviction of sin. And each repeated season of conviction makes him more and more watchful, tender, and care-

ful, until his conscience becomes so sensitive that the very appearance of evil will offend it. But the other kind of sorrow, which does not lead to true renunciation of sin, leaves the heart harder than before and soon sears the conscience like a hot iron. (*Crystal Christianity,* pp. 29–30)

You'll know what I'm talking about if you have ever fought with a teenager about going to church. Perhaps he wanted to go when he was younger; now he may only go kicking and screaming. Chances are good that such behavior reveals a teen who has never truly been converted. He must therefore be brought under conviction so that he will not harden his heart further.

Last year when I asked one of my daughters to do something for our church, she became upset with me because she felt I was not giving her enough opportunities to do things with her friends. I pointed out that it appeared that her friends had become more important to her than the Lord (see the first commandment). She went into her room, but after only a few minutes she came back with tears streaming down her face.

"It's true!" she sobbed. "I can see that my friends have become more important than the Lord. How can I change? I don't want anyone or anything to be more important than the Lord!"

I encouraged her to repent of her attitudes, and she was quick to do so. I share this incident with you to contrast the kind of conviction a true conversion produces in a teenager's life on an ongoing basis.

Helping Your Teenager Take the Final Step

Whenever I share Christ with someone, I try to be sensitive to what's happening in the spiritual realm. I learned a number of years ago to ask a question like, "While we've been talking about the Lord and your need to confess and forsake your sins, has something been saying in your heart, 'This is true; I need the Lord's forgiveness'?"

I base this question on John 6:44, 65, where Jesus says that no one can come to him unless the Father draws him. I've found that when I ask this question, the answers I receive are black or white. Some have no idea what I'm talking about because they are only mildly convicted of their sins. The others say *yes* because conviction grips their hearts. This means that they are ready to respond to the cross of Christ.

At this point it's probably good to draw a circle, labeling one side as being hot and the other as being cold. Ask your teenager where he is in his relationship with the Lord. If he's the typical nominal Christian (who is really a nonbeliever), he'll probably put his mark somewhere in the center because it will probably seem like the safest place to be. (At least that way he won't have to admit that he's really cold).

Turn to Revelation 3:15-21 (Christ's message to the church at Laodicea). The passage talks about how God would prefer that we be either hot or cold, instead of lukewarm. It's easy to understand why the Lord wants us hot, but for years I didn't understand why the Lord would rather have us be cold than lukewarm. Then one day it dawned on me. A lukewarm Christian thinks everything is OK, and, therefore, *he will never come to the Lord because he thinks he already has.* At least a young person who is cold knows that he is not a believer. He therefore becomes much more likely to repent than the tepid Christian.

The Lord continues in this passage to encourage the readers to see their sin for what it is. They must repent and then invite him into their hearts. Verse 20 is the classic verse believers so often use to help someone "reccive Christ," but too often we skip the Lord's challenge to repentance found in verse 19. Without repentance, you really don't have salvation.

"Son," you might say to him, "can you think of any reason why you wouldn't want to repent of your sin and ask Jesus to come into your heart and dwell with you?"

Most people usually can't think up any reasons for not becoming a Christian—so I suggest some. (I'd much rather that he not make a decision than make it without fully comprehending what he's doing).

"What if your friends at school will give you a hard time about being a Christian—would that keep you from following the Lord?" Or, "What if your girlfriend thinks being a Christian is silly—would that stop you from becoming a believer?" You know him; you know the things that could stand in the way of a true conversion. Don't try to make it easy for him; easy decisions don't stick. Show the cost of commitment clearly and honestly. Jesus indicated that many people would not come to him because they would decide the cost was too high. Whatever you do, don't talk him into making a decision, because then it will be *your* decision, not his. (And we parents are too good at doing that, aren't we!)

If he wants to repent, suggest that the two of you pray together. I usually ask the teen to pray first, saying that I will pray after he does. And when he prays, I listen to see that he is using words that indicate that he is repenting of his sin and turning to Christ. If he misses the essence of what the sinner's prayer should be, I'll stop him and say, "Hey, you didn't repent. Why don't you pray again, and this time you can . . ." Also, when you pray, support and encourage his commitment. Ask the Lord to confirm what he has promised and seal the decision.

After the Decision

After a person receives the Lord, I like to turn to 1 John 5:11-13. Have him read the passage aloud. Point out that eternal life is in God's Son, Jesus Christ. If he has the Son, he therefore has life. But if he doesn't have the Son, he doesn't have life. Does he have the Son in his life now? If yes, then what does he have? Eternal life. But don't tell him—let the Holy Spirit do that.

Verse 13 says that these things are written that you might *know* that you have eternal life. This Greek word for *know* used here means to know intellectually by observation (in contrast to experiencing something through the senses). The Word of God is given so that we can know that we have eternal life. Later, he'll know experientially, but right now he needs to know that eternal life is promised to those who have the Son.

One of the most important things you should explain to your teenager is what his relationship should be with the world. The world is condemned and judged before God; the world lies in the control of the evil one; the world crucified the Lord and is the enemy of God. We are not to love the world or to be conformed to it; if we do, we make ourselves out to be the enemy of God (see Romans 12:2; James 1:27; 4:4; 1 John 2:15-17).

The Bible tells us that we must hate the world and all that it stands for. If we don't, we will inevitably fall back into its snare. However lovely the world may appear, it must be forsaken. If you study the Scriptures, you'll see that salvation often refers to our position before God as it relates to the world. Salvation is to be saved out of the world, not just out of hell, for the world is under the judgment of God.

It is important for a new Christian to be baptized, but it is also important for him to know why we baptize. Baptism is a public announcement in which he will declare, "I have come out of this world." According to the Bible, salvation is more a matter of coming out of the world than just escaping hell. Watchman Nee expands upon this concept in his book *A Living Sacrifice:* "If one becomes a Christian secretly without being baptized, the world will still consider him one of its own. The believer may say he is saved, but the world will not accept his statement. Not until he is baptized does he compel the world to see his salvation" (p. 10).

Your teenager needs to know that he died with Christ. Of course, death is the prerequisite for burial. New believers should be instructed that on the basis of their death with Christ at his crucifixion, they should be requesting to be "buried" in water. When he steps into the water, he should understand that baptism is a picture of his death to the world (Romans 6:3-5).

I can't overemphasize the importance of the believer dying to the world. This will be his greatest battle, especially with all the temptations at school. If he doesn't come right out in the beginning and declare that he is a Christian (by words and deeds), his decision will wither, like the plant that dries up under the scorching sun (Mark 4:16-17), because his roots will not have gone down deep enough.

SUMMARY OF KEY POINTS

1. Parents should see leading their children to the Lord as one of their major spiritual priorities.
2. Parents can inoculate their kids against Christianity if they are inconsistent in their walk with the Lord.
3. Parents must earn the right to minister the Lord to their teens.
4. Parents should pray for the salvation of their kids.

5. Teenagers should be encouraged to be involved in programs that will stretch their relationship with the Lord.
6. It is important to know what the plan of salvation is all about.
7. When someone truly comes to the Lord, sin will be seen as "exceedingly sinful."
8. Conviction prepares a teenager for repentance by showing him just how far short he falls of God's standard.
9. For a teenager to come to repentance, he must have godly sorrow for his sin.
10. As a parent witnesses to his teenager, it is important to determine if God is drawing the teenager to the Lord.
11. If an adolescent is under conviction, a parent should pray with him so that he repents of his sins and asks Christ to take over his life.
12. Follow-up should help a teen see the importance of being saved from this world.
13. Baptism is how the new believer proclaims that he has died to the world.

15

HELP FOR BROKEN AND BLENDED FAMILIES

"We all agree that forgiveness is a beautiful idea until we have to practice it." ~C. S. Lewis

....

In November 1992, Dr. Louis Sullivan, secretary of health and welfare in the Bush administration, identified "the greatest family challenge of our era" as fatherlessness. Recent statistics seem to indicate that 60 percent of two-year-old children will end up in single-parent households by the age of eighteen. And half of those children will be part of a "blended" family, as every year half a million new stepfamilies are created.

In our day divorce is so popular, I'm hoping that husbands and wives will decide to stay together just to be different. If you feel like rebelling against the world, work together toward celebrating your fiftieth wedding anniversary someday. Unfortunately, as the statistics demonstrate, the phenomenon of the blended family (also called the stepfamily or the remarried family) has become an entrenched part of the social landscape of North America and is bound to become an even greater factor in the future.

In chapter 2 we talked extensively about the nature of the family according to God. You might want to review some of those points before you launch into this section. It is important, once again, to remember that the Lord is the one who invented the family. His standard is the biological family: a husband and wife (of different sexes) committed

in a covenant where they can raise their biological offspring under the nurture and instruction of the Lord. The
husband is the head, the wife is in submission to him, and
the children obey. Now this is not to say, of course, that
modern biological families are perfect. But this is the
model or norm that the Lord set up for us to measure ourselves against. As far as is possible, pattern your family on
this scriptural ideal and commit yourself to all the biblical
directions that God left us in his Word.

The best solution to problems that single-parent and
blended families face with their teenagers is to work at
solving root problems. Blended families inevitably come
out of the intense pain of shattered relationships and broken marriages. Until the sources of that pain are dealt
with, the problems will no doubt continue to simmer
under the surface. Believing this, I have aimed this chapter
more at solving the adult problems than at the more symp-
tomatic difficulties teenagers suffer as a result of the conflicts in their parents' lives.

The Trauma of Divorce

God hates divorce, and there is a good reason for that:
Divorce causes great violence to all members of the family
(see Malachi 2:16). Marriage is not like a dance party
where we flippantly swap partners on a whim. It is a
moral, spiritual, and social framework that binds people
together in a truly meaningful lifetime way. That bond was
designed never to break, but when it does, everyone suffers
immeasurably.

Some couples have sought to avoid the trauma of
divorce by not bothering to get married at all. Such thinking certainly eliminates the divorce papers, but it won't
eliminate any of the other emotional trauma that comes
with the breakup and will provide less protection for the

women and children (who almost always receive the greatest financial setbacks from a breakup).

God says that a man who divorces his wife (especially for no good reason other than wanting to trade her in on a "new model") will find that his spirit and his relationship with God will be dramatically impacted (see Malachi 2:13, 17). God jealously guards the spirit he has put in us, and such callousness toward the wife of our youth will unquestionably be punished.

If you've been through one or more divorces or major relationship breakups, I don't have to inform you about the pain and suffering you have already been through. But I mention it because this will obviously impact your relationship with your teenagers. It is always difficult to put forth your best effort toward raising your children when you are being consumed by the agony of a marriage that has come or is coming apart at the seams.

Whenever a marriage fails, especially if you are not the initiator of the breakup, there will usually be a crisis in your self-confidence level. "Why did this happen?" "How did I fail?" "What could I have done differently?" And worst of all, "God, are you punishing me for some sin in my past?" The emotions that come from the breakup are painful and may even be debilitating to the point where you may just not be able to cope with much.

Traumatized Children and Adults

All of this, obviously, impacts your children. If they were standing on the sidelines while Mom and Dad argued behind closed doors, they might have seen the results without having heard the sound of the explosions; this would certainly have been unnerving for them. On the other hand, many parental confrontations take place in front of the children, so the kids may be all the more traumatized by the intensity of anger, the bitterness, and even the violence that may have entered their home.

Because my wife and I are foster parents, we have seen firsthand that the children who have entered the system because of the breakdown of their families are often severely retarded in their ability to socialize with others. Broken families produce broken children. And most of those kids will spend the rest of their lives compensating for their own perceived failure in the breakup of their biological family.

So if you now find yourself in a traumatized family or one that is now blended, how do you deal with the emotional debris of past problems? Certainly guilt is a major problem for parents who have come through such troubled waters, and it must be dealt with if you are to be able to minister adequately to your teens. In chapter 11 there is a section explaining the nature of guilt that might be worth rereading at this time. Also, remember that in chapter 8 there is a discussion about the power of forgiveness. Both are subjects that can and should be applied to the guilt that comes from the breakup of a marriage. I can't think of any time when it is more of a necessity for a parent to deal with his guilt than after a divorce. If you've gone through these bitter waters, even if it's been years since it happened, you must still deal with your own sin and the ongoing ramifications of it.

Often people refer to the innocent party in a divorce suit, usually meaning the one who is jilted. But because I know human nature, I know that there rarely is a truly innocent party in a breakup. Because we're all sinners, everyone has some fault and contributes something toward the problems that lead to divorce. It is precisely those feelings of guilt that cause many to struggle deep within their souls in the aftermath of a breakup.

The best thing you can do to eliminate your sense of

guilt is to ask God for forgiveness for your part (however little you might feel it was) in the breakup. Freely confess to him what your actions were and also what you are feeling now in the matter of wounds and bitterness toward your ex. Don't hold anything back. And don't blame your former spouse before God, no matter what he might have done. (Remember, God knows exactly what happened, and we know he hates divorce.)

What God wants you to do is accept the blame for your part in the breakup and ask God to forgive you. Remember the key to forgiveness is being truly convicted of your transgressions, then repenting of that behavior. Above all else, you must now desire God's direction and peace in your life. If you are truly repentant, those sins are under the blood of Jesus Christ (see 1 John 1:7). Making certain that you have obtained your own peace with God is incredibly important to the way you will deal with your teenagers.

The Single-Parent Trap

Certainly a parent who has been through a divorce will deal differently with his teenagers. Because your relationship with your spouse has changed, you will undoubtedly find yourself facing a different home environment with new pressures that are unfamiliar and challenging. Teens will often add to your heartache by trying to dump the guilt they feel (for the breakup of your marriage) back on you in a futile attempt to lash out at someone to relieve their own pain. Even though they might be having tremendous guilt feelings, for both of your sakes you should not let them unload on you. You might want to say something like, "I know you are hurting because Dad isn't here anymore. Believe me, I am too. I wish things had turned out differently. But blaming either one of us won't take away the loss you're feeling. We've got to depend upon the Lord. We've got to pull together as a family and continue with our lives."

Things are always harder financially after a divorce. And those money problems inevitably will cause single parents to have to work harder to make ends meet. Of course, this puts added strain on relationships with your teens. Not only is the other spouse no longer around, but the kids see less of you. Certainly this is a time for greater effort in prayer to help the children cope with all these strains without turning to drugs, premarital sex, or gangs. As well as you are able, keep your kids involved with church and Christians who can help them handle the losses they are experiencing.

Unless your marriage was extremely abusive, your teenagers might put pressure on you and your former spouse to get back together. Now it's highly likely (in many situations) that the Lord would want that if both parents can repent of their rift-causing behavior, but your teens may put their desires over your feelings by trying to lay a guilt trip on you to encourage you to get back together. They may say things like: "I sure miss Dad, don't you?" Or, "I sure wish we could see Dad more. Do you think . . ."

Now such statements may be completely honest, but they certainly imply to a parent that it's in their power to change the situation and allow Dad (or Mom) to come back. But, of course, it may not be in one parent's power to let another come back. You don't want to react if you feel that your kids are trying to manipulate the two of you back together. "I'm sorry you feel that way," you may have to say. "It certainly hurts when we can't see someone we love. Maybe we can pray together that God will make things better." Don't focus on what they are trying to get you to do; focus instead on them and their feelings. Offer them your love and support, but make it plain that you cannot give them something that is out of your control.

Teens will often have a difficult time trusting God through a family breakup, especially if they've prayed against it and the divorce still goes through. It's important to use these real-life experiences to emphasize that God doesn't always give us everything we want, even things we want very badly. But he shouldn't be blamed as a cosmic killjoy who loves to inflict pain on his children. Remind them that sometimes even his hands are tied by the sin and unbelief of human beings. He certainly won't force us to do what's right; he always allows us to make our own choices.

Compensation Prizes

Whenever marriages break up, there is a tendency for the parents who do not receive custody to attempt to compensate for what they cannot do for their kids. They may give too many presents, offer excessive fun-filled trips to amusement parks, and in general smother their kids with love and attention. They may feel they have to cram all sorts of activities into what little time they have with their offspring. Beware of such "guilt offerings."

Teenagers from broken families don't need whirlwind vacations and sophisticated toys as much as they need consistent guidance. They need to know and see that you'll be there. Give them your time by doing things that will build your relationship. Offer them the opportunities to communicate and receive your advice in a relaxed atmosphere. When you go out to have fun, look for the kind of outings that can build relationships (like backpacking, fishing trips, or a Christian retreat). A good rule of thumb: spend half as much money and twice as much time.

Reread chapter 8 on building up your trust account. If

ever someone needs to keep those principles clearly in mind, it is the absentee parent dealing with a broken home. Follow the suggestions given there, knowing that your teenager will have a much more difficult time trusting and loving you if he doesn't understand why "you allowed" this horrendous thing to happen in his life. So concentrate on building trust and a deeper love, not a fantasy world in which you subconsciously teach your child that the world wants him to be entertained all the time.

The Rotten-Rat Trap

Another mistake to avoid is the rotten-rat trap. If you've gone through a particularly messy and bitter divorce, it becomes very easy to blast your ex in front of your kids. This can lead you into manipulating the kids into punishing the former spouse. You may justify your bitterness by telling yourself that you don't want them to experience any more pain, or you may feel that they deserve to know how much you've been hurt.

Because your children love both parents, bitter words will only cause them tremendous difficulty in sorting out their feelings. Face it, this kind of behavior on your part is very counterproductive. It places your focus on the hurts and keeps all those afflictions vividly alive—no matter what changes take place in your ex's heart. Not only will this slow up the healing process, but such behavior is clearly condemned in the Scriptures (Hebrews 12:15). It will defile you and those you love.

The secret to eliminating such words is to eliminate the bad thoughts that cause them. Most of us would be quick to forgive anyone who fell down on their knees and begged for it. But it is unrealistic to wait for that kind of behavior. One of the best examples in the Bible of how to forgive is found with Joseph in the book of Genesis.

Remember how he was sold into slavery and then went to prison? Later, when God had raised him up to become the prime minister of Egypt, his brothers found themselves under his power. But he never punished them for what they had done to him, and later, when their father died, the brothers became worried that he would wreak his vengeance upon them. So they claimed that old dad had commanded Joseph from his deathbed to forgive his brothers.

How did Joseph respond? Did he forgive them? No. He didn't have to. He said, "Do not be afraid, for am I in God's place? And as for you, you meant evil against me, but God meant it for good" (Genesis 50:19-20). Joseph didn't need to forgive them because *he had already forgiven them*. Although he recognized that they had, indeed, tried to hurt him, God used their evil and turned it around to serve his purposes.

There probably isn't any evil that God can't turn into something good. If you can forgive your ex, no matter how cruelly you have been treated, it is highly likely that God will raise you up as a result of your faith in him. But you need to forgive before he is repentant; forgive before she asks for it. Why? Because God has forgiven you.

A few years ago, a couple from my church came to me for advice. Stacey had two daughters by a previous marriage. Whenever the girls went to visit Jack, her ex-husband, he allowed his new wife's older teenage son to sexually harass them. Stacey and her new husband were considering legal action against Jack because of the situation. Once again, this is the kind of problem that is best solved by looking under the surface. As I began to question Stacey, looking for answers, she revealed that her ex-husband was doing all sorts of spiteful things to her, like putting all his assets in his new wife's name to avoid having to pay her any child support. It immediately became obvious that Stacey must have deeply wounded Jack in the past, probably when the divorce took place. I asked her how she left that first marriage, and her answer revealed the real problem. Stacey had run off with her present husband while still married to Jack. In fact, she revealed that Jack had no idea they were even having marital problems until she served him with the divorce papers. In so doing she had become the rotten rat.

"It sounds to me like you've greatly offended your ex-husband. He probably feels that you are at fault for the breakup of your marriage because he was the last one to know about the problems you had with him. I get the distinct impression Jack is trying to get even with you by using the kids to hurt you."

"You're right," she said, nodding. "Even though he's remarried, I know he's still upset. But what can I do about it now? The past is the past."

I suggested that Stacey and her husband should sit down with Jack and his wife. She and her new husband did this and explained that they had both recently become Christians. Then she admitted that it was her fault that her marriage to Jack had ended so abruptly. She then asked for his forgiveness for the way she had left him. Her new husband also asked for forgiveness because he had wooed a married woman. Stacey and her present husband took full responsibility for the past problems; they told me later it was like the sky opened up. Jack not only forgave them, he responded by immediately clamping down on the aggressive behavior of his teenage stepson, and, amazingly, he agreed to catch up on all his back child support.

The best way to deal with family problems like this is to look for causes. Obviously, not all solutions will work out this easily. Forgiveness will definitely not always come so quickly. But my guess is the rule for step- and blended families is that some unresolved sin will quite often be lurking under the surface. If you can find and address this sin, your chances of resolving the behavior problem will be greatly increased.

Yours, Mine, Ours, and Theirs

When a new marriage includes children from previous relationships, the new blended union will often face intense rivalry as teens may be coming from many different "sources" (i.e., yours, mine, ours, and theirs). Plan for problems. When you have kids with different parents thrown together, you will inevitably have problems (no matter how nicely the television sitcoms present such arrangements).

The Scriptures give us many illustrations to confirm what happens in families composed of half brothers and half sisters. Think of Jacob's twelve sons by his two wives and two concubines, and the conflicts that developed among them, such as trying to kill Joseph, their father's favorite; firstborn Reuben even slept with one of his father's concubines. And think of the conflict between Isaac and Ishmael, who had the same father but different mothers; that difference led to the long-standing conflict between Arab and Jew.

There are typically many conflicts that develop between stepsiblings. In any new marriage there is an adjustment period in which you and your spouse will be trying to figure out exactly what your relationship is going to be. First-time newlyweds without children often find this period difficult as they attempt to understand each other; how much more formidable will this process be in a marriage combining two ready-made families with preset ideals about how things should be?

At the end of chapter 5 we talked about establishing a family character blueprint. Although this is an excellent idea for most families, you might want to start with something similar but more basic for your new family. I would suggest that you meet with the kids and get their help in writing down a list of house rules for everyone in your family to abide by. Things like, "Don't borrow anything without first asking the owner." "If you borrow something, put it back." "If you make a mess, clean it up." "If you ask somebody to do you a favor, say please." "If someone does you a favor, say thank you." (See appendix D.)

Now all of these house rules may seem unnecessary because we assume that everybody knows such things. Or do they? Giving kids a clear idea of what's expected in your house can go a long way toward solving problems later on. And when you have two families merging together with different ways of doing things, this becomes all the more important. Kids coming under "new leadership" should quickly be given guidelines so they know where they stand in the family and with their new parent. After you have finished, you can all sign the house list of rules indicating that you agree to them and will obey them.

Children in blended families need to have order and routine put back into their lives as quickly as possible. They should know what chores are expected of them and what privileges will belong to them. Families are always run differently, and teens will be used to a set pattern of behavior. After the merger takes place, they need to understand if the rules have changed. The more input you can give them in establishing these guidelines, the better things will probably be. You should probably assume that the kids who have to change the most will react the most.

Remember that your teenagers will be going through the same getting-acquainted process you are, only they are not in love with their new blended family. Without some guidance, they may feel they've lost the attention of their recently single parent to the new parent and all his or her kids. The teens may struggle with resentment of this disruption of their lives. Tension may develop between the adolescent and the parents.

If major problems develop, ask yourself what the root is. If you married against your children's wishes (by the way, teenagers often oppose their parent's remarriage), you will inevitably have issues to deal with. You certainly don't want to allow disrespect to come into the new family relationship, toward either you or your new spouse. If it festers, you can expect it to explode later in open rebellion. Get to the root of it and be willing to admit it if you were not sensitive when you wed your new spouse.

Remember, every choice we make affects our kids (and vice versa). If you didn't listen to their counsel, you may have a difficult time now getting them to listen to yours. Your offenses, whether imagined or real, must be dealt with. Clear the air and take responsibility where it needs to be taken; this is important to rebuilding their trust. You may also have to point out your teenagers' lack of responsiveness to your wishes and deal with their rebelliousness.

The Potential for Incest

Don't blind yourself to the potential for incest just because you are in love with your new spouse. You simply can't throw a bunch of unrelated (or semi-related) teens together in a new family and expect them to act like biological siblings. Keep in mind that although you are now related by marriage to your new spouse, the kids had different parents. Incest becomes a grave possibility, especially if the teenagers convince themselves that "she's really not my sister," and "he's really not my brother."

If there is a spark of attraction between two stepsiblings, and they are allowed to come home to the same empty house, you're setting them up for trouble. To put any two teenagers together in a house alone for one or two hours is like putting them in a bedroom and pulling down the shades. (Even among biological siblings this can be a problem.) The Bible gives an example of a similar type of incest. King David fathered many children through his seven wives. Although each wife's family had its own housing, one of David's sons, named Amnon, lured his beautiful half sister, Tamar, into his apartment, where he then raped her. For this sin, Amnon was murdered by Tamar's full brother Absalom. It is also not uncommon for a man to be attracted to his new wife's daughter. Don't consider it unthinkable; it can and will happen if you turn your back and ignore the possibility.

How can you avoid such problems? Keep your eyes peeled for signs of emotional and physical attraction. Remember that just because two kids have violent arguments does not mean that they are not strongly attracted to each other. In fact, such arguments may feel like safe behavior to them as they test whether the attraction is mutual. It is important to eliminate the kind of teasing common to those who have an attraction for one another. Tell them it is simply not appropriate to roughhouse or wrestle.

Let everyone in the family know that the rules for acceptable behavior within the house have changed. No longer can they come out of their bedrooms in their underwear or in other skimpy attire. This should apply to both sexes. No longer can the boys go into the girls' rooms (and vice versa). Because the rooms are being shared, even biological siblings must now stay out of one another's rooms. You and your family must treat your home like you would if it was full of unrelated boarders; they must be cautious and careful never to tempt anyone toward evil. And do your best to keep the teenagers from being left alone in the house when you are not home.

These same rules should also apply to foster children

and stepfather/stepdaughter relationships. A mother should avoid allowing her new spouse to spend large amounts of time with her daughter, especially when she is not present. This may also be a problem with mothers and sons. Just last night I read the shocking front-page headline story about a foster mother who became involved sexually with her foster son. The woman was a Christian, so don't ever think that such things can't happen in your house. Whenever two unrelated people come together, there will always be the potential for sexual fireworks. A wise family will take every precaution to guard against any improprieties that might end up creating great trauma.

SUMMARY OF KEY POINTS

1. God established the biological family as the ideal family unit.
2. God hates divorce because of the violence it brings into the family.
3. Parents who have come through divorces should make certain that they have adequately dealt with guilt and forgiveness.
4. The best thing people can do to eliminate their sense of guilt is to ask God for forgiveness for their part in a divorce.
5. Because single parents have tremendous pressures upon them, they have a great need for the Lord's guidance.
6. Absentee parents must concentrate on building love and trust with their children instead of showering them with compensation presents.
7. To deal with harsh words toward an ex-spouse, eliminate the bad feelings by dealing with bitterness.
8. Whenever major conflicts surface, it is important to seek the root cause of the emotional reaction.

9. A good tool to help blended families is to have everyone help create a list of family house rules.
10. Teenagers in blended families need order and routine to help put their lives back together.
11. Whenever two families merge, parents must anticipate the potential for incest and take appropriate steps to prevent it.

16

YOU GOTTA LAUGH

"With the fearful strain that is on me night and day, if I did not laugh I should die." ~Abraham Lincoln

....

I'm convinced that the only way to actually enjoy having your kids in the teenage zone is to develop your sense of humor. If you can't laugh at yourself and have a little fun with your kids *it's gonna be a long seven years.* When things are going badly, we certainly need to be able to laugh at ourselves.

What's your sense of humor like? Can you laugh in the middle of serious situations so other members of your family can relax? Or does this skill come hard to you?

I've only met one man in my entire lifetime who claimed he had no sense of humor. He and his wife (who had a very well-developed sense of humor), came over to our house for dinner one evening. After he admitted that he found virtually nothing humorous he kept saying, "I don't find that funny" to things the rest of us were laughing at.

My response to him was, "Now that really doesn't mean anything, does it? Because you don't find *anything* funny. The problem has to be with you—not the joke."

Fortunately, that man never had any kids. If you don't find life with a bunch of teenagers to be funny—at least some of the time—the problem is with you. Anyone who can't laugh at a situation is taking himself too seriously.

We parents so often get uptight with our kids. I think part of the reason is that we have neatly planned out our lives, and then they do something stupid to upset our nice little world—so we explode. Half of the emotional battles we face with our teenagers involve learning how to deal with those unexpected emergencies. What do you do when your daughter runs the car into a ditch (as mine did three weeks ago)? What do you do if your son breaks his leg playing football—and you don't have insurance? What do you do if you find drugs in your kid's bedroom? Here are some possible ways you can use humor with your teenagers to neutralize the intensity of these situations:

1. *Whenever anything bad happens, focus on the things that really matter—especially the people.* If there is an accident, most fathers immediately ask the question, "How's the car?" instead of "Are you all right?" And they may be thinking, *How will my friends view this?* Believe me, cars come and go, churches come and go—but your kids last a lifetime. Make them more important in your heart than what anything costs or what anyone else might think.

The same night our daughter ran our car into a ditch, our assistant pastor's son hit black ice and totaled his father's truck. Fortunately, none of the kids in either accident were hurt, but I asked the assistant pastor if he'd heard that it takes some kids about three-and-a-half cars to learn how to drive. "Just think, you only have two-and-a-half cars to go!"

2. *Find opportunities to laugh at yourself.*

Question: If you put three teenagers side by side with their ears together, what do you have?

Answer: A wind tunnel.

Question: What do you call a teenager with half a brain?

Answer: Gifted.

Actually these were originally blonde jokes my daughters shared with me. I live in a household full of blondes, but all of them delight in hearing a good joke about blondes.

I think it's great that my family enjoys laughing at jokes aimed at their particular group. If you can't laugh at yourself, you won't really be able to enjoy much else. Learning to laugh at yourself and use humor in your relationship with your teens is a great way of keeping your sanity when things seem to be getting out of control.

When you become the focus of jokes, you may realize that you're doing something right. In several positions as a youth pastor, I could tell when I was beginning to reach the teens in my youth group when they started to kid me. Now certainly, this can go too far, where someone is making fun of you instead of playfully kidding. But humor is a sign of a connection between people. I've learned in my communication through books, public speaking, and in films that humor is an excellent means of communication. If someone can laugh with you, it's likely that they will also cry with you.

I can't think of anything more fun than to watch someone try to do an imitation of you; at least that proves that they are paying attention to you (even if all they remember are your idiosyncrasies). When President Bush was leaving office, he invited comedian Dana Carvey into the White House to entertain the outgoing staff with his imitations of the president. Bush eventually got up on the stage and went through his typical gestures side-by-side with Carvey. What great fun that a president doesn't take himself too seriously to do that.

Writer Joyce Landorf once told a story on herself. When she came through customs in an airport, the female inspector saw her Bible with her name on it.

"I read your book," said the woman, looking up with a smile.

For a moment, Landorf didn't know if the inspector was referring to one of the books she had written or to the Bible. But rather than make a mistake by assuming the woman was talking about one of her books, she decided to talk about the Bible.

"Oh," she gushed, "isn't it *wonderful!*"

But the customs officer grimaced and turned away, revealing that she had been talking about one of Landorf's books. Oops!

Telling a story like that about yourself certainly makes people more comfortable, because we've all had things like that happen to us; we've all stuck our foot in our mouth at some time. How good it would be if parents felt free enough about their own identity to tell an occasional story on themselves. Don't worry about looking bad. Believe me, your kids will definitely appreciate your willingness to let down your hair.

3. Avoid hurtful put-down humor. No one likes to be made fun of, and unless you have an extremely delicate touch, you probably won't "win a son" or "influence a daughter" with such an approach. Years ago a youth pastor friend of mine would have "put-down parties" to see who could verbally slam-dunk the best. What a bad idea. Teenagers, by their very nature, are all-too-quick to put down their peers. The last thing we need to do is encourage that type of humor.

Adults often argue over which parent is responsible for a teenager's conduct, as if only one person's genes are to be blamed for marginal or aberrant behavior. Certainly parents can be playful about who's at fault for a kid's behavior in such a way that no one is offended and it's done in good taste. But an accusative line like, "There you go again, you're just like your mother" can be a major put-down to both mother and daughter and certainly won't build up the family.

Avoid any kind of humor that is destructive to relationships. It's certainly an easy trap to fall into. Always keep in mind how you would like to feel at the other end of a remark. And if you inadvertently say something that you shouldn't, be quick to ask for forgiveness. I've discovered that people often try to camouflage their true intentions by putting their real feelings in the form of a comical put-down. Whenever someone addresses some cutting remark toward me, veiled as a joke, I immediately try to listen with serious ears.

"Is that really how you see me?" I may ask.

"Oh, I was just joking," he may say. But I've learned that too often humor at someone's expense is disguised criticism. Wise Solomon points this out in Proverbs 26:18-19, "Like a madman who throws firebrands, arrows and death, so is the man who deceives his neighbor, and says, 'Was I not joking?' " We are also commanded to avoid "coarse jesting" in Ephesians 5:4.

A second form of humor to be careful with is teasing. Playful teasing has its place in human relationships, but the key is playfulness. The moment it moves from being good-natured to being criticism masquerading as humor, it will lead to offenses.

Parents often tease their children in areas where they want to see their children improve. When I was about eight years old, we received a Christmas demo record in the mail. Because nobody seemed to want it, I decided to break it in half (having never seen a broken record before). But then my father asked for the record, and I had to confess what I'd done. Not too long after that he introduced me to some of his friends as his "record-breaking son." I'm certain they thought his remark was a compliment, but I knew better, and it stung me.

Don't underestimate how destructive such humor can be to a relationship. The key will often be your intent. If you are trying to hurt, and if your goal is to put someone down, or if you are so intent on being funny that you don't care who is hurt—you need to rethink how you are using your tongue, because God condemns this.

Sarcasm is another form of humor that should normally be avoided. Sarcastic remarks tend to leave a bad taste in other people's mouths; they can also defile us, because inherent in sarcasm is a sense of self-righteousness or superiority on the part of the speaker. We may see the incongruent things of life and make our pithy statements against them as if we alone have a sense of the truth. But as a general rule, such humor is negative in its outlook and therefore counterproductive. But I have seen some splendid exceptions.

The senior pastor in our church has one of the rarest gifts of humor that I've seen in a long time. He uses sarcasm to make the medicine go down a little easier whenever he has to lay down a "heavy" on the congregation. He makes these announcements with such a great sense of humor that you laugh and are not offended—but you also get the point. One night after a concert, the solo musician went on and on advertising about all of the CDs and tapes he would have for sale after the service, to the point where everyone was fidgeting. When the pastor was finally given the microphone back, he quipped, "And if you would like a copy of those announcements, we'll be selling them for $3.95." Everyone roared. His message was clear, but he hadn't been offensive to the musician in the way he did it. Believe me, that is a rare gift.

If you can do that with your teenager, go for it. But most people lose their sense of proportion and slam-dunk with their sarcasm.

4. Use humor to defuse difficult situations. Often it seems that many of the major crises of growing up would not seem so horrible if parents could look at things with a bigger sense of humor.

A good example of how to use humor to defuse some-

one happened a few years ago when heavyweight boxing
champion Muhammad Ali stepped aboard an airplane.
The flight attendant reminded the well-known boxer to fas-
ten his seat belt.

"Superman don't need no seat belt," he replied with his
typical braggadocio.

"Superman don't need no airplane," retorted the flight
attendant.

Ali buckled up.

We can't all be so quick on our feet, but we can learn to
approach life from a lighter side by looking for something
to say that will take the bite out of the situation.

When one parent looked at his son's horrendous report
card, he said, "Well, one thing is definitely in your favor
here—at least I know you're not cheating!" This kind of
response lightens the load of a difficult situation (for both
the teen and the parent). Humor at tense moments makes
it easier for all of us to get past the upset feelings to the
real problem. A parent's natural response (in the flesh) is
to hit the roof, raking the teen for his failure. But let's face
the facts: if report-card time is the first time you found out
that there was a problem, you haven't been doing *your*
homework! Staying on top of what's happening at school
is our responsibility. To overemphasize a student's failure is
only to make matters worse. Everyone probably needs to
spend a whole lot more time working together. That
means you, your kids, and their teachers. Reacting only
makes the matter worse, not better. A better approach is to
identify with him using a little humor. "When I was your
age," (remember those are the words every teenager
cringes over), "I once got grades like these." (Now you've
got his attention). "But let me ask you, how would you
feel if you discovered that the surgeon who was going to
operate on you had received grades like these in medical
school?"

5. Look for ways to teach your children with humor.
Probably the best thing that "The Cosby Show" contributed to parent-teenager relationships was the value of a
sense of humor in communication and problem solving.
Because Dr. Huxtable did not react to the problems he
encountered, but skillfully played with humor to cause his
television children to think, they were able to see truth a little more clearly.

I'm not saying I agree with the bumbling TV persona of
the Dr. Huxtable character, or even Bill Cosby's personal
philosophy on raising children, but I am saying that his
approach of using humor with adolescents to make them
think through both their problems and their reactions was
unparalleled in the history of . . . well, television anyway.
Some of his encounters with his television offspring are
absolute classics.

Another television personality that I have enjoyed over
the years is Lieutenant Columbo. For some reason—in my
silly mind—I can picture what the lieutenant would be like
as a father. Perhaps his dialogue with his teenage son
might go something like this:

The son comes into the living room and asks his father
for the keys to his family car.

"Ah, excuse me, Son," says Columbo as he wanders off
down the hallway towards his son's messy, messy room.
"Ah, Son, you'll excuse me for looking in here, but I . . . I
was just noticing that I didn't see your schoolbooks anywhere."

"That's because they're still at school, Dad," replies the
teen.

"Oh, I see, they're still at school because you don't have
any homework tonight, how silly of me. I guess you
always get your homework done before you come home."

The kid looks down at the ground. "Yeah, I guess so."

"Mmm. You know, I was just wondering, then, why I

got this in the mail today." Dad Columbo pulls out a crum-
pled piece of paper from the pocket of his trench coat.
"This here is a progress report from your history teacher,
Son," he says, looking up. "You know what this is for?"

The boy shakes his head.

"But I guess I shouldn't bother you with this. . . . I
mean, you were about to go out and have a good time."

"What does it say, Dad?"

"Oh, yeah, this Mr. Gab-out-ski . . . is that how you say
that, Son? He says that you haven't turned in any history
homework this semester. Now I know that he probably
made a mistake. After all, you said you always get it done
at school. . . ." Busted!

The beauty of "Columbo" is that we know exactly what
is coming, exactly how the character is going to act in each
episode. And precisely because we know that, and the
killer does not, we delight in Columbo's bumbling way of
ensnaring the culprit. Perhaps, as parents, we could take a
little tip from Columbo. Maybe we need to approach our
kids with more simple logic and less know-it-all self-righteousness to cause our kids to think things through.

When I was substituting in an English class last week,
one of the students looked at the test paper I placed in
front of him and said, "This is ridiculous! You don't
expect me to have to fill this out, do you?"

"Don't be silly," I shot back. "Of course you don't have
to fill it out. Why should you have to fill it out? Just write
a big *F* on the top of it and put in the box over there for
your teacher." He filled out the test.

*6. Learn how to get your teenagers to think about posi-
tive things."* In Philippians 4:6-7 we are told not to let ourselves be anxious about anything, but to let our requests
be known to God, and he will guard our hearts with his
peace. Verse 8 then tells us to let our minds dwell on whatever is true, honorable, right, pure, lovely, the things of

good repute, the excellent things, and those worthy of praise.

I'm convinced that life's problems are generally not as bad as we perceive them to be. If we can learn to smile in the face of adversity, we can make our problems work for us instead of against us. I don't think this passage is talking about positive thinking, which is often just a way of attempting to deny or manipulate reality. It's telling us that to eliminate much of the anxiety in our lives, our focus should first be on the Lord. Then, we need to keep our eyes on those things that are going to build us up, instead of concentrating on all those things that will tear us down.

We need to help our teenagers make life worth living. Their world is full of constant put-downs. Everyone in junior and senior high school seems to be locked in a never-ending slam-dunk contest that they mistakenly think will make them feel superior to their peers. But such a focus only makes school a jungle in which everyone tries to get others before they themselves get "got." Instead, encourage them to focus on the good things.

Now when things are truly serious, I am certainly not recommending that we make light of the situation. But because most of us have a tendency to overreact to life's crises, making everything more difficult than it really should be, we'll be much better off looking at the bright side of things. A little humor could certainly make those problem situations more palatable.

I heard of a Christian woman who had a reputation for finding something good in everyone. When someone asked her what she thought about Satan, she had to pause and think for a few moments before responding, "Well, at least you have to admire his perseverance!"

Usually all bad character traits have a good side to them. For instance, someone who is always late generally has a corresponding strength—that of being *flexible*. Now

I know if you try hard enough, you can probably come up with some good characteristics that are revealed by each of your son or daughter's weaknesses or bad traits. Let's work on this together:

> Keeps room messy ~ shows a relaxed attitude.
> Has a temper ~ shows a flair for the dramatic.
> Doesn't do homework ~ reveals a confident kid.
> Won't eat certain foods ~ a choosy eater.
> Girl crazy ~ he's devoted.
> Boy crazy ~ she's trusting.
> Fearful about fitting in ~ a conscientious side.
> Gets poor grades ~ he's a future laborer.
> Clothes never look nice ~ he isn't pretentious.
> Always has something bad to say ~ thinks hard.

I'm sure you get the drift.

If you can force yourself to find a light side to silly or stupid behavior, the chances are better that you won't over-react to the problem. Also, you want to help your teenagers see the bright side to life when they're down on themselves or their situation. When they fret that they just have "nothing to wear," you can remind them that they're lucky because with no clothes to wear, they won't have to worry about loving their possessions. Keep it light and bright, perhaps by intentionally misunderstanding their comments.

"I'll just die if I have to wear that," your daughter may say.

"Oh, I see that this situation is serious. I didn't realize how horrible those clothes were that the store sold you. Perhaps we should just sue the store. After all, you're in danger of dying because of these hideous clothes they sold you."

Teenagers are so prone to exaggeration—just do them one better.

SUMMARY OF KEY POINTS

1. The only way to enjoy being parents of teenagers is to develop your sense of humor.
2. Humor has a tremendously positive impact on most people.
3. Whenever bad things happen, focus on what really matters—the people.
4. Parents should find ways to laugh at themselves.
5. Avoid hurtful put-down humor.
6. Use humor to disarm difficult situations.
7. Look for ways to teach teenagers through humor.
8. Always try to focus on the bright side of things, putting things in their proper perspective.

17
THE WONDER YEARS

> *"Slow down, parents! Your children will be gone so quickly, and you will have nothing but blurred memories of those years when they needed you."*
> ~James Dobson

It was Clarence Darrow who quipped, "The first half of our lives is ruined by our parents and the second half by our children." I'm sure a lot of the parents of teenagers—especially junior-high teenagers—have had similar thoughts. It seems when you're young that your parents are always telling you what to do; then you grow up and your kids end up making your life so difficult.

Many parents probably do feel that their teenagers have made their lives miserable. But let's face the truth—no one makes us miserable. Unhappiness is a choice. If we blame our kids for our troubles, we're really not seeing reality very clearly. I like the way Ed Howe put it: "If you can't learn to laugh at trouble, you won't have anything to laugh at when you're old." Nothing is worse than to see a person grow old ungracefully, where everything in life just seems like a problem to them.

Keep That Sense of Wonder

I remember when my first child was born and how incredible it all seemed. To think that I could actually help bring into the world a living child, one who was a very part of me, yet totally independent with a will of her own (*and what a will of her own!*). It seemed too wonderful for words that God would allow us to perform such a mysterious feat.

If you've ever worked in a nursery, you can always tell the firstborn from the lastborn simply by the way the parents react. Most new parents have such a difficult time leaving their first babies in the care of others. *After all, he might cry if I leave; or worse, he might even not miss me at all.* One of the biggest problems our church nursery workers have is when the parents stick their faces back in the room just to see how junior is doing and whether he's stopped crying yet. Inevitably, junior had stopped crying the moment after they finally left the room, but when they pop their faces back in, he explodes all over with those glass-breaking wails. Such parents don't realize that the kid's crying just for them because they're wrapped around his chubby little finger.

But then there is the parent of the lastborn child. One mother in particular stands out in my mind. She was new to our church, bringing her child and depositing him in the nursery with the efficiency of a German-run airline. No sooner had she handed the young boy over than she headed for the door with an attitude that said: *Here's the kid; good-bye.*

"Any special instructions?" asked the nursery worker as the lady fled.

"It's on the bag," she replied.

"His bottle?"

"In the bag," she said again, her hand on the door.

"His name?"

"The bag."

And then she was gone. No sentimental, goo-goo-eyed good-byes for this woman. It was obvious she'd been through this many times before. She knew her kid would survive nicely without her, thank you.

Now if you've had a lot of teenagers, there comes a

point where you may become like that woman. The wonder has long since wandered away. You've seen it all, heard it all, and probably now think you know it all. So why make a big deal out of anything to do with the crazy teenagers you've got? *Let's just get this show on the road,* you think. Somehow the "wonder years" sounds much more like reruns of a canceled TV show than a description of the quality of life in your house.

To be happy and purposeful parents, we need to keep our perspective on life. Understand that there are millions of people who would love to have kids—and can't. If they had the choice, there are probably millions who would love to have *your* kids. ("Are you *kidding?* Tell me who they are!") You no doubt need to regain that sense of wonder that makes life so much more enjoyable. That sense of excitement is so easy to lose, yet so important to maintain.

The Good Old Days

You've probably never thought about the fact—especially when your teenagers are giving you fits—that you're living in the *good old days*. That's right. *These* are the good old days. Years from now, you'll look back and say, "Remember how great it was when . . ." As time passes, life tends to play games with our perception of reality. Our brains filter out many of the painful and unpleasant experiences and leave us with only the memories that really matter. That's why we look back and remember how great things were, when at the time things didn't seem so great at all.

But our brains aren't really lying to us about the truth of our experiences; over time they sort out what is really important (if we are not consumed by bitterness) and choose to accept only what's worth remembering. Wouldn't it be better for everyone if we could learn to do that while we're in the midst of those memory-making days? How nice it would be if we didn't let our problems get to us because we looked at our day-to-day lives from the perspective of eternity. In other words, I believe that we can and should choose to let the good old days be good while we're experiencing them. Why not? So much of life is based on how we perceive it anyway. And if we want to choose to enjoy these years, that's certainly up to us.

I remember when my first child was born. Because I was able to go into the delivery room and coach my wife in natural childbirth, I had excitedly prepared myself to see Rebecca's first appearance into the world of light. So I had my camera up and ready and got some great pictures. Later I brought my camera out at the birthday parties and during vacations and other special events. Why? Because I knew that someday I would look back and want to remember those special days.

But then life just seems to happen. Sometimes it seems that it has been years since I pulled out my camera to record some momentous family event that should have been recorded for posterity. The memories slip by, and I miss the changes in my children's lives because I got too busy with my mundane concerns to think about the need for momentarily arresting the passage of time. And suddenly all I have left are mental images with nothing to refresh my memory.

A few years ago a beautiful young woman, the wife of one of our deacons and the mother of two little sons, contracted cancer. Valerie was a vibrant Christian, but her body wasted away in just a matter of months. "I don't mind dying," she told me, "because I know that I'll go to be with the Lord. But it makes me cry to think that I won't be there to see my boys celebrate all their many birthdays." They were so young that it was difficult for them to comprehend why Mommy was abandoning them. I made a suggestion that seemed to help. She could record several taped messages on ten or twelve different cassettes for each of her sons' coming birthdays. That way she could allow her voice, her love, and her thoughts to remain alive for them as they passed from childhood and through adolescence. She could communicate her joy for them from heaven as they became more mature and better able to understand why she had left them behind. Be thankful, my friend, that God has not yet called you home in the midst of your labors. You still have time to complete the parenting task the Lord has called you to.

When you're slaving through those difficult hours, remember that someday soon you'll look back and wonder, *How did my kids grow up so fast?* Know too that in a few years you'll experience what is commonly called the empty nest syndrome. Waves of melancholy will crash over you because there are no more teenage problems to solve. I think G. K. Chesterton summed up what I'm trying to say: "The way to love anything is to realize that it might be lost."

God's Gift to You

As long as you see your kids as a gift from God, soon to be moving on, you'll be able to keep your parental perspective. Your teens will not always remain teens. Someday they'll be responsible adults. Really. I know you may find it hard to believe, but it's true. Look at them as a temporary gift that God is entrusting to you for a season. Because the day will surely soon come when they'll leave, and then all you'll have left are the memories.

Something else to think about is that someday the roles will be reversed. Erma Bombeck talked about this in one of her columns. She remembered that when her kids had been young and she hit the brakes while driving, she would instinctively place her right hand in front of the child sitting in the front seat to keep her head from hitting the dashboard. Later, she performed that same protective action with her mother. But what really upset her was one afternoon when her daughter was driving her someplace, and reached out *her hand to keep Erma from hitting the dashboard.* Suddenly it occurred to her that life had come full circle.

Longfellow stated that "youth comes but once in a lifetime." Although we can never regain our youth, most of us will be children twice. Not too long ago when my father was being crotchety, I reminded him that we are not too many years away from the reversal of roles. None of us remain the parent forever. We soon become the child all over again, and our children will, in essence, become parents to us, hopefully seeing to it that everything goes well for us in the sunset of our life. While that day may be a long time off in the future, it is wise for us to remember what's coming, if for no other reason than to sow good seeds with them and to enjoy their youth.

So appreciate your teenagers *with* their youthful inexperience and zeal. Don't squander the precious moments you could be having right now by longing for that day off in the future when your task of raising them will be over. That day comes all too quickly. Savor those young buds that God has entrusted to you. Their lives are like the back of a tapestry; it doesn't look too good from that point of view, but in a few years when you turn the tapestry over, you'll see what God has performed though all your hard work.

What's Your Legacy?

A legacy is something that is passed down from one generation to the next. Some families leave money in the form of trusts; others hand down a good (or bad) name. Usually families pass down their political and spiritual beliefs. Often a family heritage is bestowed in the form of character traits that show up in generation after generation.

Most of us don't think too much about building a legacy or passing anything down to our children because we're too busy just scratching out a living. When one man's will was read, it said: "I, being of sound mind and understanding, *spent it all.*" We may not have much to leave in the way of financial riches, but we have much to pass down in the way of spiritual blessings. The Lord has called us to build a godly family legacy that will stand forever.

As Christian parents, we want to see our offspring walking with the Lord for all eternity. We want their marriages to be successful and to produce grandchildren that will also come to know Christ. We desire to bestow virtuous character upon our children so that they can pass it to our descendants from generation to generation. It is wise to give prayerful consideration to this legacy because, whether we have ever thought about it or not, we do have one. We're passing something on to our kids. The question is, *what?*

Someday your kids will all be grown. What will they look back on? What kind of teenage years will they feel they've had? Will they have good memories or bad? Will they know that they are part of a larger, greater family (hopefully one that is becoming more strongly Christian over the years)? Will they be part of a family that will be an example to all the pagan homes in your community?

A few years ago I was asked to do a funeral for a lady, a grandmother whom I had only known for a few weeks. She was a sweet Christian woman, but I knew very little about her. As the family slowly arrived from various places across the country, I began to quiz them about her in an attempt to write a eulogy. Now as a general rule, I dislike the typical eulogy that a minister reads at a funeral that is designed to placate the living and convince them that the departed loved one really wasn't such a bad person after all.

In this case, it became increasingly clear that this woman had been a strong Christian who had lived out her beliefs in a tireless display of selflessness for her children. As I put together the eulogy, I told each of her three sons and one daughter that I always like to provide a time during the service for people to share how the deceased impacted their lives. I know from experience that few people want to hear some preacher drone on about someone he barely knew. But it is extremely moving when those who were intimately acquainted with the person share those little incidents that sum up what the person meant to them.

Without exception, all of this woman's kids told me that they would be too broken up to say anything at the service. The family didn't seem particularly close, but I decided to go ahead and open the service up, hoping that some of the friends might share. To my surprise, one of the sons stood up. "I'm Paul, the baby," said the forty-year-old man, "and I just want to say that Mama led me to Jesus Christ. If it hadn't been for her godly life, I wouldn't be a Christian today." He was followed by his sister and then another brother with similar statements of love and appreciation for a woman who had obviously left a great impression upon all of them.

I looked over at the oldest son, a quiet man in his early fifties. He had strongly assured me that he would never be able to speak in front of that crowd. But slowly he stood up. "I'm George, the firstborn son. I wasn't going to say anything. But I'm the firstborn, and I can't sit here and be quiet any longer. My mother was a saint. And I'll never forget all that she did for me. She kept the family together through the bad times. I'll . . . I'll miss her." And then he sat down.

Seeing that man defy his own quiet nature because he

knew that he had to provide leadership for his siblings and all their kids still brings tears to my eyes. As I closed the service a word came to my mind, and that was the word *legacy*. I encouraged the family to embrace the legacy that this woman had helped create for their family.

After the funeral, the oldest son came up to me and firmly shook my hand. "Thank you," he said with emotion, "for helping us pull our family together."

"Your mother pulled your family together," I replied. "I just reminded you of it."

Never forget that you're leaving your own legacy. Someday your family will remember what you meant to them. And someday you'll all be together in heaven (if you've done your job). Let me cheer you on. Let me encourage you that it is worth all of the time you're putting in. The planning, the prayer, and the development of your own personal character will all be worth the results. Someday you'll look out onto life's playing field and say, "That's my son! That's my daughter! Look at what they're doing! I couldn't be prouder!"

Can I stand on the sidelines and cheer for you? Someday, perhaps in eternity, I would love to hear that you were inspired to build a great spiritual legacy with your family that will produce generations of godly offspring. Don't ever underestimate what you have to say to future generations that will be coming from your loins. If you develop your plan of attack today and pray for tomorrow, you can produce a great dynasty of godly posterity. Leave behind something in your life that is truly worthwhile: a spiritual legacy. You can leave nothing greater.

SUMMARY OF KEY POINTS

1. Parents should regain that sense of wonder and excitement about having kids—especially teenagers.

2. Parents should choose to see the joy in the midst of the everyday hassles of life.
3. Realize that the way to love teenagers is to realize that all too soon they will be moving on.
4. Remember that someday teenagers usually end up taking care of their parents.
5. Every family has its own legacy; parents should strive to create a legacy that everyone will be proud of.

STATEMENT OF
PERSONAL MISSION

1. My primary goal in life is to glorify God.

   - I am committed to living a godly life.

   - I am committed to an ongoing program of personal prayer and Bible study.

   - I will impact other lives for Christ through my life-style and my ministry.

2. My secondary goal is to love and nurture my wife (or husband).

3. My children will receive thorough love, consistent direction and discipline, and adequate time from me.

Family Character Blueprint

I am committed to:

1. Loving the Lord my God with all my heart, soul, mind, and strength (Mark 12:30).

2. Loving my neighbor as much as I love myself (Mark 12:31).

3. Treating other people as I would like to be treated (Matthew 7:12).

4. Worshipping no one but God (Exodus 20:3).

5. Having no idols in my life (Exodus 20:4-5).

6. Keeping my speech free from swearing or using God's name in a curse; I will not make rash vows, but let my speech be simple and honest (Exodus 20:7; Matthew 5:33-37).

7. Setting apart and committing every day to the Lord (Exodus 20:8-11; Psalm 118:24; Ephesians 5:16).

8. Honoring my parents and obeying them (Exodus 20:12; Ephesians 6:2).

9. Turning the other cheek. I will not let myself hate anyone or allow myself to become violent toward others (Exodus 20:13; Matthew 5:21-25).

10. Saving myself sexually for only my spouse (whether or not I'm married) and avoiding any sexual sins—including looking at another person with lust in my heart (Exodus 20:14; Matthew 5:27-28).

11. Not stealing from anyone in any way (Exodus 20:15; Ephesians 4:28).

12. Not lying about anyone or anything (Exodus 20:16; Ephesians 4:25).

13. Not lusting after anyone else's body, talent, or possessions (Exodus 20:17).

14. Obeying the laws of the land (Romans 13:1-2).

Appendix C

Philosophy of Discipline

1. We are committed to being God's "hands and feet" with our children and recognize that they are on loan to us from God. We will endeavor to keep all of our discipline in line with his Word and his will for our children.

2. We will pray over our children on a regular basis, knowing that not only do they need God's help, but we parents need to have our perception toward them constantly controlled and balanced by the Lord.

3. We commit ourselves to loving each other with a strong, consistent love, knowing that this will ultimately be a great encouragement and tonic for our children's behavior and growth.

4. We are committed to disciplining our children as a team. Whatever situation comes up, neither of us will violate the authority of the other spouse. We will always support one another in front of our children, and if we have any differences about how to discipline them, we will attempt to solve them in private.

5. As a father, I will make a special effort to avoid provoking my children to wrath through the display of a harsh spirit. If my wife points out that I have been harsh toward my children, I will stop and pray about the problem and endeavor, through God's power, to be open to her counsel and willing to correct the problem with my teenagers.

6. As a mother, I will work on being firm with my children. Although I want to be loving at all times, I will strive not to let any merciful feelings I have towards my kids influence me to take their side against my husband. I will endeavor, by God's power, never to step between them and my husband in an attempt to protect them.

7. We will seek, not to punish behavior, but to discipline character. We will endeavor to determine what character qualities need to be improved and work at putting together disciplinary action that is appropriate to each need. Our goal will be to help our teenagers see life from God's larger frame of reference, and we will therefore endeavor not to let ourselves get bogged down by attempting to press the kids into our own mold.

8. We will work at being patient with our teenagers, avoiding rash statements and actions. We commit ourselves to first understanding our kids and how they feel before attempting to communicate what is on our mind.

9. We will focus on helping our children set and follow after their own long-range goals instead of looking for short-term fixes. We will help them plan ahead for their future, then work together with them to achieve their goals. We understand that we are ultimately working toward our teenagers' independence.

Appendix D

House Rules

1. Don't borrow anything without first asking the owner.

2. If you borrow something, put it back.

3. If you make a mess, clean it up.

4. If you ruin something, replace it.

5. If you ask somebody to do you a favor, say please.

6. If somebody does something for you, say thank you.

Appendix E

Hints for Leaders of Support Groups

We parents of teenagers need all the help and encouragement we can get. A support group that is committed to assisting us with our teens will fill a timely need. If you or your church desires to form a support group, the following section is designed to assist you.

Focus of the Group

The focus of your support group should be firmly established in the leader's mind before any meetings take place. While you're still in the planning stages, it would be a good idea to survey the parents to determine their most pressing needs and how best to meet them. Most will want to talk about the problems they are facing with their teenagers and will be open to learning from other parents' experience.

The support group should probably be organized to follow the chapters given in the book. Because there are seventeen chapters, this might present a problem to groups that meet during a thirteen-week quarter. As a general rule, I would encourage groups to meet all seventeen weeks. Some chapters will provide a great deal of discussion and will be difficult to finish in one meeting. You don't want to rush this process by trying to put two chapters together in one session. If you are tied to a thirteen-week quarter, I would suggest that you expand the material to include two quarters. This way you can extend a chapter's subject for a second week if you don't get through everything.

As a leader, I would encourage your program to be organized as follows:

1. Opening Presentation Time (15–20 minutes)

Here you will summarize the material contained in that week's chapter. Emphasize the biblical concepts taught in the book, as they are certainly more important than anything I have contributed. Make certain in your preparation time that you reread the chapter and reacquaint yourself with those points you feel will be important to the parents in your group. At the end of each chapter you'll find the summary of its contents. Refresh yourself with those points so that you have a good understanding of the material. As you review what was taught in the chapter, you might want to share some of your own personal illustrations that tie into that week's topic.

The opening chapters in your text deal with basic information designed to cause parents to look more carefully at their personal character and their relationship with God and with their spouse. To some, this material may seem to have little to do with raising teenagers, but such things are *extremely important* to a balanced approach in raising teenagers and should not be skipped over.

When you discuss the material in this text, don't "canonize" what has been written. There may be points that you or members of the class disagree with, and certainly many will have information to add. Allow your heart to be open to fresh ideas from God and his Word. The Lord likes to stimulate us through the mutual interchange of ideas (see Hebrews 10:24). I'm sure most support groups will formulate many new ideas beyond what has been presented in this book. Unless someone's suggestions contradict the Scriptures, I would encourage you to welcome them.

2. Discussion Time (20–25 minutes)

If every family has a copy of this textbook, everyone can be reading the chapters along with you. This will cause your discussion times to be much more productive because the material will stimulate them to come up with questions and/or answers about concepts that will help the entire group.

To facilitate your discussion, I have provided several Discussion Starter questions you can use to stimulate your group's interaction. *The free communication of ideas is the ultimate foundation of this group, and that is essential to your success.* Parents want and need answers to their specific problems in dealing with their teenagers, and the discussion time will greatly help them get the answers to their questions.

Avoid letting the meeting degenerate into a "group counseling session" in which everyone tries to help one parent or family to solve a particular problem. This can put a strain on the group. Some may go away feeling cheated because their problems were ignored. It can also lead to embarrassment for the family who received all the attention. Group counseling sessions can also cause a feeling that the meeting has gotten out of balance and may repel some of the participants.

Encourage the individual members of your group by saying that you want to give everyone an opportunity to express themselves. If one or two people tend to dominate the discussion, you might want to encourage the group to let some of those who don't speak have an opportunity to communicate. Sometimes I've told groups, "As we begin you all have the same number of chips. If you use your chips up too quickly, I may not be able to call on you later so some of the more quiet group members can get an equal opportunity to speak."

If you can avoid it, never tell anyone their answer is wrong in front of the group. I've found that anyone can be devastated by being embarrassed in front of a group. If members share something that is a little off-base, try not to put their answer down, but merely contrast it with what the Scriptures say. You can say something like, "That's an answer" (You haven't said that it is a *good* answer).

The discussion questions are not designed to provide right or wrong answers. Their purpose is to stimulate free discussion and to get people's problems and feelings out in the open. As much as is possible, avoid black-and-white concepts that might communicate that only the answers presented in this book are correct. That material is a starting point; certainly it is not the last word on the subject.

3. Project Assignments (10–15 minutes)

At this time you will want to check on the projects that were done the previous week and ask the participants what they got out of the assignments. It is very important that *you* do these projects so you can speak from personal experience. By doing your own homework, you will help your group see that it is worth putting in the effort.

The goal of these assignments is to stimulate parents to try new approaches with their kids and to find out what works more effectively. Individuals need to hear what other people have experienced, both good and bad, so they can be challenged to apply the biblical principles of parenting that they are learning. If no one applies the material to his own family, everyone will get much less out of the class. Getting parents to remember to do their homework can be a real chore. Adults just get so busy they will tend to forget about their assignments. It might be good to encourage wives (who will usually remember) to remind their husbands so they can both perform the projects.

At the close of every discussion time, talk over the suggested projects for the coming week. If you can, type up the projects on a piece of paper and photocopy them so that everyone (both spouses) has a copy. Even though the projects are already listed in their personal copy of this book, putting the list of projects in their hand will make it easier to remember them. Ask each parent to commit to one or more projects that they will attempt to accomplish in the following week. Don't expect anyone to do them all.

Chapter 1 / The Teenage Zone

Discussion Starters

1. How much of a negative impact do you notice from the media upon your kids? This includes such things as TV, movies, teen magazines, radio, CDs, and videos.

2. Does long-term exposure make the changes in your kids less obvious?

3. What moral changes have you noticed taking place in America over the last few years?

4. How does having teenagers in the house make you feel like you've entered a war zone?

5. In what ways have your kids become more hostile since becoming teenagers?

6. Do your teenagers seem to be moving along with the trends of this world? If so, how?

7. What are the biggest changes that have happened in your household since your children reached adolescence?

Project Assignments

1. Over a one-week time span, keep a diary of how many television programs present a message that is inconsistent with biblical Christianity. Note violence, swearing, sexual content, visually stimulating content (skimpy clothes, etc.), or pro-abortion, anti-Christian, pro-evolution, or antiauthority bias, and so on.

2. Develop a plan to determine how and when your family should turn off an offensive television program.

3. Plan to discuss the message of any television program that contradicts your Christian beliefs.

4. Listen to the music your kids are listening to, and discuss it with them.

Chapter 2 / Is There a Family in the House?

Discussion Starters

1. Would you say that your family is close? Why?

2. Do you feel that your teenagers have emotionally checked out of your family? Do they consider this your family or theirs? Why?

3. Have your kids ever said they don't think you really care about them?

4. Do you feel that you have ever adequately communicated to your teenagers your family's goals? How did they respond?

5. Would you say that Christ is the center of your house?

6. Do you feel that all family members are fulfilling their own personal roles (husband, wife, child) as they were intended?

7. In what ways do you and your spouse work as a team in bringing up the kids?

Project Assignments

1. Discuss with your children how they feel about their family. Do they like it? Do they wish that they were in another family? If so, why? Do they feel that they have any say in what happens in the family?

2. Sit down with your children and make plans for your next vacation. Get their input on what they would like to do and where they would like to go. Begin now to build up their interest in that vacation, and plan how you can make it a spiritual success.

3. Begin a prayer list for your children. Write down the things you will pray for on a regular basis.

Chapter 3 / Follow the Leader

This chapter is geared primarily for men. One suggestion for facilitating a better meeting would be to have this week's meeting attended only by the men. If both husbands and wives come, let the women know that this meeting is primarily for the men, so much of the discussion will be focused on them.

Discussion Starters

1. Do you find being a father easy or hard? Explain.

2. Would your wife feel that you abdicate your parental responsibilities?

3. What kind of a parent was your father?

4. How much are you like your father (honestly)? How much have your kids turned out like you?

5. What kind of feedback have you gotten from your wife and kids?

6. Do you have any difficulty being the spiritual leader in your home? In what ways?

7. How important do you see loving your children's mother to be for the emotional maturity of your kids?

8. Do you find it easy to provoke your teens to anger?

Project Assignments

1. Keep track of how many times you lose your temper at home this next week (or let your wife keep track for you).

2. Make a list of all your father's traits that you don't like. Then ask your wife how many of them she feels you have. How many of them do you see in your children?

3. Let your teenagers choose a family game you can all play together. Plan ahead of time that this will be a spiritual experience. Make certain your goal is not just to win, but to build up your family. Rate how well the game went and how much everyone enjoyed himself or herself.

Chapter 4 / Any "Characters" Here?

Discussion Starters

1. How important do you feel your character is to raising your teenagers?

2. Do you feel responsible for your family's condition today, or is someone else to blame for its strengths and failures?

3. How often do you find yourself saying "if only" about your family?

4. Men, have you made any personal sacrifices in your life-style in the interests of bringing your teenagers up right? (No, we're *not* talking about going to work.)

5. How much unsupervised time do your teenagers have on their hands?

6. What is the one thing in your life that consumes most of your emotional energy?

7. Does that thing often come between you and your children?

Project Assignments

1. Get away by yourself and write out what each member of your family would say about you at the judgment seat of Christ.

2. Take one thing that your family would be better without and, after discussing it with your spouse, remove it from your house this week.

3. Ask God to reveal one major negative character quality that impacts your family and that he wants you to improve on.

Chapter 5 / Where Are You Going?

Discussion Starters

1. Does your family seem to have lost its way?

2. What are the most important values in your life by which you live?

3. How difficult is it for you to plan ahead?

4. How often do you pray for your family? How much time do you spend?

5. When was the last time you had a family hour meeting? What was it like?

6. Is there any character blueprint or standard that you consistently live by? If so, what is it?

7. How consistent are you in practicing what you preach?

8. How difficult is it for you to depend completely upon the Lord?

Project Assignments

1. Sit down and write at least the rudiments of your own personal mission statement.

2. Sit down with your family and begin to work on your family character blueprint. Discuss its meaning with your teenagers.

3. Plan and have a family hour with your kids. Make certain that you do things that they want to do. Afterwards, with your spouse, evaluate how well it went.

Chapter 6 / Temporary Insanity

Discussion Starters

1. Do you ever feel that your teenagers are driving you mad?

2. What changes in your teenagers have been most disturbing and mystifying to you?

3. Could you see some of these changes coming in the preadolescent stage?

4. How have all these puberty changes impacted your children's personality?

5. How important has the opposite sex become to your teenagers?

6. Are your teenagers struggling with depression?

7. How have you been able to provide a safe environment for your teenagers?

Project Assignments

1. List your teenagers' character traits that drive you crazy.

2. Discuss with your spouse the differences you see in your kids since they passed into the teenage zone.

3. During your family hour, try to do something with your kids that shows you accept them and the physical changes they are experiencing. Also, put in some more work on your family character blueprint.

4. Dad should take out a teenager for a special shopping and fast-food night.

Chapter 7 / Do You Really Love Your Kids?

Discussion Starters

1. Do you struggle in your love toward your adolescents?

2. Would you say that you have created a loving family environment in your home?

3. Which of your deeds best communicates your love toward your teenagers?

4. Do you currently have a difficult time loving God?

5. What is your experience with *agape* love?

6. How difficult is patience for you?

7. Name two kind acts you've done for your teenagers lately.

8. Which word best describes your relationship with your teenagers: *reaction* or *response?* Explain.

Project Assignments

1. At your family hour, ask each of your children to evaluate your love for them on a scale of one to

ten. (*Important:* If they give you a low score, you must not jump all over them. Remember, this is an exercise to evaluate *your love,* not an opportunity to straighten them out.)

2. Make a list of all the parts of God's love as expressed in 1 Corinthians 13, and determine which parts you struggle with the most.

3. In what tangible ways can you show your kids that you love them this week? (Will you tell them of your love? Will you buy them some special little treat?)

Chapter 8 / Building Your "Trust Account"

Discussion Starters

1. How important do you consider trust in your personal relationships?

2. Do you find it easy to trust your teenagers? Why?

3. Do your teenagers have a difficult time trusting you? Why?

4. Is your "trust account" overdrawn with your teenagers? If so, why?

5. What are some ways you've been able to build up your teenagers' trust accounts lately?

6. How hard is it for you to perform those little kindnesses for your teenager?

7. Do you find it easy or hard to keep your commitments with your teens?

8. How hard is it for you to acknowledge your own inconsistencies?

Project Assignments

1. Evaluate what your balance is in your teenagers' trust accounts. Have your spouse evaluate your account balance from his or her perspective.

2. At the end of each day, keep a tally of all your contacts with your teenagers, and evaluate whether you made deposits to or withdrawals from your trust accounts.

3. Have a family hour in which you discuss ways to build trust in one another.

Chapter 9 / "Why Can't He Hear Me?"

Discussion Starters

1. How do you (and your spouse) rate your communication level with your teenagers?

2. Is it true that your communication level mirrors the health of your relationship with your teens? Explain why or why not.

3. What is your personal credibility with your teenagers? How do you think they see your character? Do they see you as one who says what he means and means what he says?

4. How often do you only half-listen to your teens?

5. Do you listen to your teenagers with the intention of giving them advice?

6. Do you find it difficult to concentrate on listening to what they're really saying to you?

7. What kind of body language have you seen your teens exhibit?

8. How often do you find yourself using negative or disrespectful words with your teenagers?

Project Assignments

1. In your next conversations with your teens, try repeating the essence of what they are saying to improve your listening skills and stimulate the conversation.

2. Try rephrasing the meaning of your teenagers' words.

3. Try watching your teens carefully for body language, being careful to observe their emotions to help you discern what they're really trying to say. Attempt to repeat back to them what you think they're feeling and see if they confirm your understanding.

4. Try to have a conversation in which you make no judgment of your teenagers' thoughts, feelings, or deeds.

5. At your family time, give your teens the opportunity to address the entire family on the subject of their choice.

Chapter 10 / Fear the Peer Dependence

Discussion Starters

1. How do your teens' close friends and other peers influence their behavior?

2. Have your teens ever been singled out by their peers as different?

3. What distinctive teenager jargon do your adolescents use?

4. What clothes are in, and what clothes are now out?

5. Have your teenagers had problems fitting in because of a change in schools or neighborhoods?

6. Do home-schooling parents in your group notice the same peer pressure that the other parents have noticed?

7. Are your teens struggling with peer dependence? If yes, what are the signs?

Project Assignments

1. Which of your teens' friends impact your adolescents the most? Come up with a game plan to develop a better adult-teen relationship with those friends.

2. Go out of your way to meet the parents of your teenagers' friends.

3. If you have a particular difficult situation, sit down with your spouse and discuss the pros and cons of home schooling.

4. Have a family hour in which you talk about how peer pressure and peer dependence can negatively impact your teens and family.

Chapter 11 / Getting the Situation under Control

Discussion Starters

1. Which have you used most with your kids: punishment or discipline?

2. How effective have your methods of punishment been?

3. How effective have your past methods of discipline been?

4. Do you see the need for new methods of discipline now that your children have reached the teenage zone?

5. Do you ever attempt to make your teens feel guilty? Why or why not?

6. Do you feel a need to control your teenagers' every move? Why or why not?

7. Can you think of ways you have deliberately caused stress to come into your teenagers' lives in order to help them grow?

8. Which of the four basic motivations for misbehavior do you see most often in your kids?

Project Assignments

1. Write down all of the verses in the Bible that you can find that give you insight into the disciplinary process.

2. Make it a point to obtain feedback from your teenagers' teachers and youth workers to see what their behavior is like when they are out of your sight.

3. At your family hour, ask your teens what they think are their most common motives for misbehavior: the desire for attention, power, or revenge, or the avoidance of failure.

4. With your spouse, go over appendix C and develop your own philosophy of discipline.

Chapter 12 / Teens and Responsibility

Discussion Starters

1. On a scale of one to ten (ten being the best), rate the responsibility level of your teenagers.

2. Do your teenagers enjoy working at anything? Why or why not?

3. In what ways have you trained your teenagers to be responsible?

4. Do you feel that you can trust your teenagers to do something when you ask them to, or do you have to check up on them constantly?

5. Share any successes you've had in teaching your teens responsibility.

6. Have your teens developed any life-management skills that will aid them when they are out on their own?

7. What teachable moments have you had with your teens lately?

8. Have your teenagers learned the value of going on to college?

Project Assignments

1. Select one major area of your teens' lives in which you would like to see an improvement in their level of responsibility. Follow the procedure listed in this chapter: establishing what is expected, clarifying available resources, listing accountability, and setting consequences for the conclusion of the task. For a set period of time, work with your teens to follow through on this project.

2. Rate yourself on your ability to be able to trust your teens to get a project done.

3. At your family hour, sit down with your teens and plan their educational goals after high school. (What matters here is that they understand the importance of getting good grades and taking the proper classes so that they will be accepted into college if and when they choose to go).

4. Have your teenagers write to and obtain college brochures from several prospective Christian and secular colleges and universities.

Chapter 13 / Sex Crazy or What?

Discussion Starters

1. How much interest do your teenagers have in the opposite sex?

2. Have your teenagers developed any steady relationships?

3. When your teens hit puberty, did you sit down and talk to them about the facts of life? Why or why not?

4. Did Mom explain about menstruation?

5. Have you let your teens participate in school sex-education programs? Why or why not?

6. Have you been able to communicate your values about premarital sex?

7. What kind of a relationship does Dad have with his sons and daughters?

8. Have you had any problems with the kids getting into pornography?

9. Have your teens ever talked about being gay?

Project Assignments

1. If you have never had a facts-of-life conversation with your teens, follow the guidelines in the text and plan out how and when you will share this information with your adolescents.

2. Fathers should plan to take each daughter out for a date night (to show them how they should be treated, etc.).

3. Plan now to secure a commitment from both sons and daughters that each one will remain a virgin until he or she is married. Purchase a ring for each teen that will signify this commitment.

4. At your family hour, using a good Christian textbook about sex, sit down with the entire family and talk about your kids' attitudes about what's going on sexually with them and their teenage friends.

Chapter 14 / Infecting Your Kids with Christianity

Discussion Starters

1. Are your teenagers Christians? How do you know?

2. Do your teens exhibit a lack of interest in church and the Bible?

3. Do you think your teenagers have been inoculated against Christianity?

4. Have you been praying for your teenagers' salvation?

5. Have your teens ever come under the conviction of their sins? If so, when was the last time you saw that conviction? (It should be ongoing.)

6. Have you ever exposed your teenagers to the Ten Commandments and the standard of God's law?

7. Have they ever repented of their sins? If so, do they continue to repent?

8. If your teens have become believers, have they asked to be baptized?

9. Have your teens turned away from the world, or does it still have a strong influence over them?

Project Assignments

1. Look up and study the salvation verses given in the text about conviction and repentance so you'll have a better idea what salvation is all about. Use cross-references to find similar verses that support the concepts given in the text.

2. Pray specifically that your kids will come under conviction for their trespasses against God's law.

3. Expose your teenagers to God's law, showing them the importance of measuring up to God's perfect standard. Show them the verses in both the Old and New Testaments that interpret what God's law means to us.

4. Obtain a copy of Ray Comfort's book and/or tape entitled *Hell's Best Kept Secret* (available from Ray Comfort, P.O. Box 1172, Bellflower, CA 90706).

5. Sit down with your teenagers, one at a time, and go over God's plan of salvation.

Chapter 15 / Help for Broken and Blended Families

Discussion Starters

1. Has anyone in your family been through one or more divorces?

2. Did that divorce bring violence into your family—especially emotional violence?

3. Have you asked God to forgive you for the guilt that has come into your life as a result of the marital difficulties?

4. If you are a single parent, what types of pressures are upon you in raising your teenagers?

5. If you are an absentee parent to your teenagers, how do you handle what time you do get with them? Are you able to give them any instruction in the Lord?

6. How have you dealt with past bitterness?

7. If you have a blended family, what basic rules have you established to keep everyone free from temptation?

Project Assignments

1. If you have never sat down with your teenagers to ask their forgiveness for the breakup of a past marriage, plan now to do so.

2. At your family time, begin to work out a set of "house rules" so everyone has guidelines for acceptable behavior in your house.

3. With your spouse, work out some basic rules (like males staying out of females' rooms) so that the temptation toward incest will be kept in check.

Chapter 16 / You Gotta Laugh

Discussion Starters

1. Would you say that you have a good sense of humor?

2. Is laughter often heard in your family?

3. When bad things happen (like car accidents), is it hard for you to focus on what really matters (the people)? How do you react when your kids ruin something?

4. How hard is it for you to laugh at yourself?

5. Is there a lot of put-down humor in your house?

6. How easy is it for you to use humor to disarm difficult situations?

7. Can you think of ways that you have used humor to teach your teenagers valuable lessons?

8. Do you focus on the bright side of things?

Project Assignments

1. During your family hour, ask your kids what kinds of things they find funny.

2. Rent a funny movie and watch it with your family.

3. Buy a good joke book full of one-liners and take turns reading it aloud during your family hour.

4. Keep track of how many times you lose your temper versus how many times you are able to laugh at difficult situations over the next week.

Chapter 17 / The Wonder Years

Discussion Starters

1. What word best describes how you feel as the parent of a teenager: *excited, tired,* or *bored?*

2. How often are you able to see the joy in the midst of everyday hassles?

3. Are you able to love your teenagers with the thought that someday soon you will lose them?

4. What legacy are you building for your children?

5. What have you been doing to encourage a legacy of godliness and respectability?

6. How much of a sense of legacy do you feel from each of your parents?

Project Assignments

1. Sit down with your spouse and discuss what you want your legacy to be to your kids.

2. At your family hour, ask your teens if they were suddenly grown up, what they would remember most about their family.

3. Ask your teens what it means to be a _____ (fill in your family name).

4. Plan a family hour that incorporates one or both sets of grandparents. Let them tell your kids the way it was "in the good old days."

....

SUGGESTED READING

Adams, Jay E., *Christian Living in the Home.* Presbyterian and Reformed, Phillipsburg, N.J., 1972.

Comfort, Ray, *Hell's Best Kept Secret.* Whittaker House, Springdale, Penn., 1989.

Dobson, James C., *Parenting Isn't For Cowards.* Word Books, Waco, Tex., 1987.

Dobson, James C., *Preparing for Adolescence.* Bantam Books, New York, 1978.

Dobson, James C., *The New Dare to Discipline.* Tyndale House, Wheaton, Ill., 1992.

Johnson, Greg and Mike Yorkey, *"Daddy's Home."* Tyndale House, Wheaton, Ill., 1992.

Ziglar, Zig, *Raising Positive Kids in a Negative World.* Oliver Nelson, Nashville, Tenn., 1985.

BIBLIOGRAPHY

Comfort, Ray. *Hell's Best Kept Secret.* Springdale, Penn.: Whittaker House, 1989.

Covey, Stephen R. *The Seven Habits of Highly Effective People.* New York: Simon and Schuster, 1989.

Finney, Charles. *Crystal Christianity.* Springdale, Penn.: Whittaker House, 1985.

Nee, Watchman. *A Living Sacrifice.* Manassas, Virg.: Christian Fellowship Publishers, 1972.

Other Books by John C. Souter

CHOICE ADVENTURES
#7 The Abandoned Gold Mine   0-8423-5031-4
A story of adventure and faith that lets young readers choose the plot.

Timely Resources for Today's Parenting Issues

40 WAYS TO TEACH YOUR CHILD VALUES
Paul Lewis 0-8423-0910-1
Creative ideas to teach kids about important skills and attitudes.

50 PRACTICAL WAYS TO TAKE OUR KIDS BACK FROM THE WORLD
Michael J. McManus 0-8423-1242-0
Practical examples to help teens deal with serious issues.

FAITHFUL PARENTS, FAITHFUL KIDS
Greg Johnson and Mike Yorkey 0-8423-1248-X
Successful Christian parents share methods for instilling faith in today's kids.

GETTING YOUR KIDS TO TALK *(Coming Spring 1994!)*
0-8423-1326-5
100+ ideas to get conversations going with your children.

HELPING TEENS IN CRISIS
Miriam Neff 0-8423-6823-X
A counselor presents facts about and preventive measures for pressures teens face.

HOW TO HAVE KIDS WITH CHARACTER (EVEN IF YOUR KIDS ARE CHARACTERS)
Nadine M. Brown 0-8423-1607-8
A handbook of character traits and methods for developing character.

PARENTING TEENS
Dr. Bruce Narramore and Dr. Vern C. Lewis 0-8423-5012-8
Guide teens through the dependent-interdependent struggles of growing up.